BRITISH BATTLES OF THE NAPOLEONIC WARS 1807–1815

DESPATCHES FROM THE FRONT

The Commanding Officers' Reports From the Field and At Sea.

BRITISH BATTLES OF THE NAPOLEONIC WARS 1807–1815

Compiled by John Grehan and Martin Mace
With Additional Research by
Sara Mitchell and Robert Cager

Pen & Sword
MILITARY

First published in Great Britain in 2013 by
Pen & Sword Military
an imprint of
Pen & Sword Books Ltd
47 Church Street
Barnsley
South Yorkshire
S70 2AS

ISBN 978 1 78159 334 9

Printed and bound in India by Replika Press Pvt. Ltd.

Pen & Sword Books Ltd incorporates the Imprints of Pen & Sword
Aviation, Pen & Sword Maritime, Pen & Sword Military, Wharncliffe Local
History, Pen and Sword Select, Pen and Sword Military Classics and Leo
Cooper.

For a complete list of Pen & Sword titles please contact:
PEN & SWORD BOOKS LIMITED
47 Church Street, Barnsley, South Yorkshire, S70 2AS, England
E-mail: enquiries@pen-and-sword.co.uk
Website: www.pen-and-sword.co.uk

CONTENTS

INTRODUCTION

Britain's involvement in the latter years of the Napoleonic Wars was dominated by the remarkable campaigns of the Duke of Wellington. Consequently his despatches form a considerable part of this collection.

These despatches were edited by Lieutenant Colonel John Gurwood and published from 1834 onwards. Though frequently referred to by historians, these published versions are not entirely authentic. Not only has the text been altered in many parts but also complete sentences, even whole paragraphs, have been inserted or deleted that were not in the original despatch. The names of some individuals as well as many Iberian place names in the original despatches will be unfamiliar to students of the Peninsular War accustomed to more modern spellings. Just to add to the confusion, there are occasions where the same place is spelt differently in the same despatch. An example of this is in the report on the Battle of the Pyrenees where both the Hispanic spelling of Pamplona and the archaic Pampeluna were written within just a few paragraphs of each other. Such names were changed in Gurwood's edition, and those altered names are the ones now in common usage, but what is reproduced here is what was in those first despatches sent back to London.

Equally, the designation of the various British divisions can be written in both words and numbers in the same despatch, (i.e. seventh division or 7th division) switching from one to the other and back again throughout the text.

The seemingly arbitrary use of capital letters has been retained as has the very individualistic style of writing displayed by some officers. It would seem that all nouns, not just proper nouns, began with a capital, as did numbers when they were written in words. It must be stressed, however, that there is little consistency and these observations should not be regarded at standard rules and towards the end of this period this use of such capital letter fell out of practice. This caveat includes the use of hyphens in military ranks. Even in the same despatch, Major Generals, Brigadier-Generals, etc. can be both hyphenated and non-hyphenated. Some names also, it will be noticed, are occasionally spelt differently in the same despatch.

Anyone that chances to read the original printed documents of this era will note the apparent use of the letter 'f' in place of the letter 's'. This letter is in fact not an 'f' but an elongated 's' which has its origin in the days before the printing press when hand-written script was highly elaborate. When the printing press came into being the printers of the day adopted the most popular scripts of the day, which included the elongated 's'. Once again, this was dropped in favour of the conventional style towards the end of the period.

Finally, we must acknowledge that transcribing such a large amount of text from documents that are 200 years or more old can sometimes be challenging. Whilst every effort has been directed towards complete accuracy, it is not impossible that, in the reading of faded print, errors have been made.

Most of these reports included a list of the casualties incurred in the battle. These, and most references to them, have not been included in the despatches in this book. This is because they would make for very uninspiring reading and would make the book unacceptably unwieldy. For the same reason where articles of capitulation and details of stores seized during successful assaults are listed, these also have been omitted.

This book makes no attempt at providing a comprehensive history of the British military involvement in the final years of the Napoleonic Wars. Its sole object is to present the despatches of the commanding officers. We have not attempted to include every action involving Britain's armed forces during this era. The remit of the book is to provide the reports of large-scale engagements from senior officers exercising independent commands. In some instances, where the engagements were combined operations involving both the Army and the Navy, separate reports were submitted by both the naval and military commanders. Where these are available or appropriate they have been included.

John Grehan and Martin Mace
Storrington, 2013

IMAGES

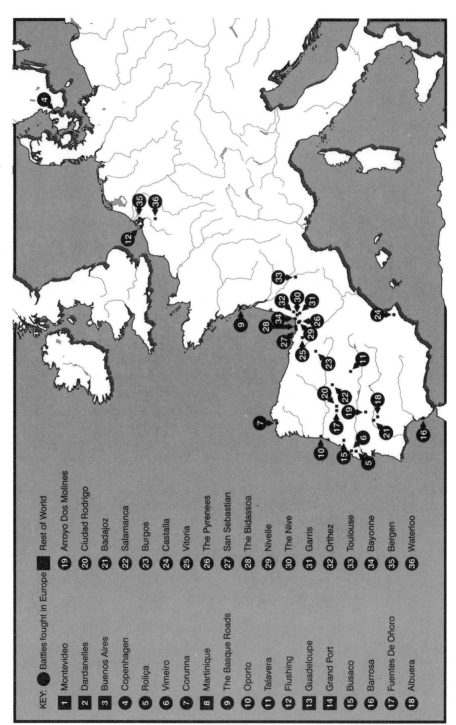

KEY:
⬤ Battles fought in Europe
⬛ Rest of World

1 Montevideo
2 Dardanelles
3 Buenos Aires
4 Copenhagen
5 Roliça
6 Vimeiro
7 Corunna
8 Martinique
9 The Basque Roads
10 Oporto
11 Talavera
12 Flushing
13 Guadeloupe
14 Grand Port
15 Busaco
16 Barrosa
17 Fuentes De Oñoro
18 Albuera
19 Arroyo Dos Molines
20 Ciudad Rodrigo
21 Badajoz
22 Salamanca
23 Burgos
24 Castalla
25 Vitoria
26 The Pyrenees
27 San Sebastian
28 The Bidassoa
29 Nivelle
30 The Nive
31 Garris
32 Orthez
33 Toulouse
34 Bayonne
35 Bergen
36 Waterloo

Battle locations in Europe

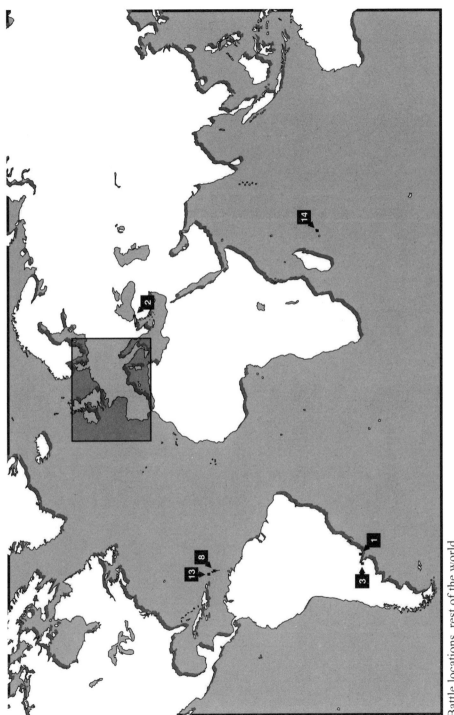

Battle locations, rest of the world

BRITISH BATTLES OF THE NAPOLEONIC WARS 1807 TO 1815

Britain's so-called 'blue water strategy' during the early years of the Napoleonic Wars had seen her make considerable gains in the East and West Indies and, in 1806, in South Africa with the capture of Cape Colony from the Dutch. Following this success, the Admiral that had led the invasion of the Cape, Home Popham, looked to further glory in South America by attacking the Spanish colonies of the Río De La Plata.

A small force commanded by Major General William Beresford took Buenos Aires, on 27 June 1806, and then seized Montevideo. When the Spanish colonists managed to bring their regular soldiers and some militia together, Beresford's corps of men was far too small to resist. Beresford surrendered on 14 August.

Matters did not end there, and a much larger force was sent to South America under General Auchmuty and a naval squadron under Admiral Sir Charles Stirling. This force assaulted and captured **MONTEVIDEO** on 3 February 1807. On 27 June Lieutenant General John Whitelock arrived in Montevideo to take overall command of the British forces on the Río de la Plata. Whitelock advanced against **BUENOS AIRES** on 1 July. The Spaniards under Santiago de Liniers fought stubbornly and after suffering over 2,500 casualties, Whitelock sought an armistice. He abandoned the expedition and upon his return to the United Kingdom Whitelock was court-martialed and cashiered from the Army.

With British forces still in Egypt, which had formerly been under the control of the Ottoman Turks, France tried to bring the Ottoman Empire onto its side against Britain and her coalition partners. French diplomatic moves proved successful and Sultan Selim III began to prepare for war. Britain moved to pre-empt Turkish aggression by despatching a squadron of eight ships-of-the-line, frigates and a bomb ship, to Constantinople. Russia, which felt threatened by Turkish mobilisation, agreed to support the Royal Navy with a further four capital ships, though these failed to arrive until after the operation.

On 19 February 1807, Admiral Duckworth led his squadron up the **DARDANELLES**. He attacked Turkish ships and landed marines who captured the shore batteries. Duckworth then sailed up to Constantinople. He remained off

Constantinople for two weeks hoping that the Turkish fleet would come out and fight. With no sign of the Turkish warships leaving harbour, Duckworth withdrew without even bombarding Constantinople.

Although Nelson had destroyed a large proportion of the Danish fleet in 1801, the Danes still possessed a considerable naval force. Denmark was officially a neutral country but after Napoleon had defeated Prussia in 1806, Danish independence looked to be in jeopardy. It was thought that Napoleon might try to seize the Danish ships by invading Denmark and the British Government decided to pre-empt such a move. A total of more than fifty ships carrying some 25,000 men sailed for **COPENHAGEN**. A British diplomat was despatched to offer the Danes an alliance but with the proviso that their fleet should be put under the command of the Royal Navy. The ships would be returned to the Danes at the end of the war. At the same time Napoleon sent his representative, Tallyrand, to tell the Danes to prepare to declare war on Britain or face invasion. The Danes therefore decided to reject the British offer.

British troops under General Wellesley were landed and, on 29 August 1807, defeated the Danes at the Battle of Køge. Still the Danes refused to surrender which compelled Sir James Gambier to bombard Copenhagen into submission. For three days Gambier's warships bombarded the city until, on 5 September, the Danes sued for peace. The ships of the Danish fleet which were still usable – including fourteen ships-of-the-line – were all seized and put onto the strength of the Royal Navy. The Battle of Copenhagen resulted in Demark allying herself with France.

Napoleon was also able to bring Russia onto his side against Britain. His intention was to deprive Britain of any opportunity to trade with Europe. In the so-called Continental System, Napoleon sought to close European ports to British ships. The main gateways into Europe for British goods still outside French and Russian control were Sweden and Portugal. The Russians attacked Sweden, and in November 1807, a combined French and Spanish force occupied Portugal. Under the pretext of reinforcing the French army in Portugal, Napoleon sent more troops into Spain, but instead of continuing to Lisbon they marched upon Madrid, taking control of the city.

In response to the removal of the Spanish royal family, riots broke out in Madrid against the French occupiers which soon spread across the country. The French tried to crush the rebellion whilst the Spaniards turned to their old enemy Britain for help.

Major General Wellesley was sent with a small body of troops to assist the Spaniards and the Portuguese (who had also risen up against the French), landing at Mondego Bay about 100 miles from Lisbon on 1 August 1808. He joined with a Portuguese force and advanced upon Lisbon. The French commander in Portugal sent a delaying force which was defeated by Wellesley at the Battle of **ROLIÇA**. Reinforcements were shipped to Portugal and Wellesley took up a defensive position to cover the disembarkation. Junot attacked Wellesley's positions on 21 August near the village of **VIMEIRO** but was defeated.

With the reinforcements came a more senior officer who superseded Wellesley. When Junot asked for a suspension of hostilities, the new British commander, Lieutenant General Sir Hew Dalrymple agreed. Under the terms of the infamous

Convention of Cintra, the French troops were allowed to sail back to France, taking with them much of the booty they had plundered from the Portuguese. Dalrymple and Wellesley were recalled to London to explain their conduct.

The troops in Portugal were then placed under the command of Lieutenant General Sir John Moore. Moore learned that Napoleon personally had marched into Spain at the head of a huge army to quell the Spanish uprising and, despite having a comparatively small force, he decided to attack Napoleon's line of communications with France.

When Napoleon became aware of the British army on his rear, he turned his army rapidly round in an attempt to crush Moore's force. A desperate race to the coast then took place, with the main part of Moore's force reaching the port of **CORUNNA** in northern Spain just ahead of the pursuing French. The French attacked before the British could join the ships that had been sent to rescue them, but they were driven off and the British were able to embark without further interference. Moore, however, was mortally wounded in the battle.

At the same time that British troops were withdrawing from Spain the Royal Navy was neutralising the threat from French warships in the Caribbean. Though the French navy was unable to meet the Royal Navy at sea, her bases in the West Indies were being used to attack British shipping. One of the main French-held islands was **MARTINIQUE**. On 30 January 1809, Vice-Admiral Cockrane with twenty-nine ships and 10,000 soldiers under Lieutenant General George Beckwith, reached Martinique and landed troops at various points on the island.

It took three days of fierce fighting before the invaders forced their way to the main French stronghold of Fort Desaix. Beckwith then undertook siege operations and on 19 February the bombardment of the fortress began. The French resisted until 24 February before capitulating.

The French warships also posed a threat to ships taking reinforcements and supplies to the British army in Portugal which was being re-formed after the Battle of Corunna. A force of eleven ships-of-the-line and four frigates had accumulated in the **BASQUE ROADS** of the Biscayan coast of France. Rather than wait for the French ships to realize the threat, it was decided to attack them at anchor in the Roads using fireships. On the evening of 11 April 1809 Vice-Admiral Cochrane led the attack into Basque Roads with two ships packed with explosives. Behind them came an assortment of deadly fireships. The French were aware that the Royal Navy intended to attack and had placed a boom across the entrance to their anchorage and the ships were flanked by gun batteries on the Ile d'Aix and the Ilôt Boyard. Nevertheless after the explosion ships had blown their way through the barrage the French abandoned their anchorage believing that the rest of Gambier's ships were also explosion ships. Many drifted ashore and ran aground and when Admiral Gambier sailed into Basque Roads the following day to attack the French ships they were virtually helpless. By the end of the battle four French men-of-war had been destroyed and one frigate.

The British Government had decided to persist with its efforts in the Iberian Peninsula and every readily available soldier was sent to Lisbon including Sir Arthur

Wellesley who, after being exonerated at the Inquiry over the Convention of Cintra, took over command of the forces in Portugal. A French army under Marshal Nicolas Soult had invaded northern Portugal and occupied the city of **OPORTO**. On 12 May 1809, Wellesley took Soult by surprise when his troops crossed the River Douro, despite the French believing they had secured every boat in the area. Wellesley pursued the French who were driven back over the border into Spain.

Wellesley's next offensive move was undertaken in conjunction with the Spanish army of General Cuesta. Together they advanced towards French-occupied Madrid but were halted by a French army under Marshal Claude Victor at **TALAVERA DE LA REINA**. After Cuesta had refused to attack the French, Victor withdrew only to be pursued by the Spaniards. Victor then turned on the Spaniards who withdrew back to Talavera. Over the course of 27 and 28 July 1809 the French attacked the Anglo-Spanish positions but were defeated. However, other French forces were marching to cut Wellesley's line of retreat upon Lisbon and the British were compelled to withdraw hastily back over the border. For this victory over the French, Wellesley was elevated to the peerage, becoming Viscount Wellington of Talavera.

The continuation of the conflict in Spain tying down large numbers of Napoleon's troops encouraged the Austrians to attack France. The Fifth Coalition was formed in April 1809 with Britain agreeing to support the Austrians financially as well as opening a second front in northern Europe.

This took the form of an expedition, in July 1809, to seize the key port and dockyards of Antwerp and the French warships that were in the Schedlt. Though this was the largest expedition that had been mounted from the UK, with some 40,000 troops and more than 200 ships, it was undertaken too late to help the Austrians. The British forces under Lord Chatham and Admiral Sir Richard Strachan, landed on Walcheren Island and captured the fortified town of **FLUSHING**. Delays caused by bad weather and difficult conditions allowed the French and Dutch forces to concentrate and the French ships to sail up to Antwerp where they moored under the safety of the port's heavy batteries. With no hope of achieving the expedition's main objective, and many men having become unfit for duty with what became known as 'Walcheren fever', the operation was called off in September, though British troops remained at Flushing until December.

In the Caribbean, **GUADELOUPE** was the last remaining island still in French hands and Cockrane and Beckwith put together a body of around 6,700 men to secure its capture, the first of which were landed on the evening of 27 January 1810. By 30 January the French forces under General Ernuf had been driven into the capital Basse-Terre. With Basse-Terre coming under bombardment from Cockrane's ships, Ernuf decided to face the British invaders on the battlefield. Though outnumbered, Ernuf attacked the British on the plain at Matabar on 3 February. Though initially successful, the weight of numbers finally told on the French. During the latter stages of the battle, Marines were landed at the undefended Basse-Terre and in so doing cut off Ernuf's retreat. He had no choice but to surrender. When the garrison capitulated, the Imperial Eagle of the 66me Regiment was seized and sent to London. It was the first Eagle taken in the Napoleonic Wars.

On the other side of the world, French frigates operating out of the Île de France (now Mauritius) still posed a threat to British shipping in the Indian Ocean. After capturing Île Bonaparte (Réunion) in July1810, the British had a base close enough for them to be able to mount an expedition against Île de France and the French naval base at **GRAND PORT**.

On the night of 13 August the fortified Île de Passe, which helped protect the approaches to Grand Port was seized, and Admiral Sir Samuel Pym's warships were able to blockade the harbour. On 29 August a squadron of five French warships were spotted approaching Grand Port and Captain Willoughby, whom Pym had placed in charge of the blockading ships, concealed his ships until the French squadron sailed beyond the Île de Passe. Through a series of mishaps, the French were able to force their way past Wiloughby's ships and into Grand Port. On 22 August Pym attacked Grand Port with four frigates and by evening the entire French fleet was grounded, though one ship was still able to fire. The attack though was a disaster and by the end of the battle on 24 August all four frigates had either been sunk or captured. The Battle of Grand Port is considered to be the Royal Navy's worst defeat of the war.

*

After his experiences in co-operation with the Spanish during the Talavera campaign, Wellington decided that he would remain in Portugal and hope to defend it against any moves by the French to re-invade the country. In anticipation of a French attack Wellington began preparing the vast defensive network of the Lines of Torres Vedras. Work on these fortifications was still being conducted when the French invasion of Portugal started in August 1810 after the French *L'Armée de Portugal* under Marshal Masséna captured the border fortresses of Ciudad Rodrigo and Almeida.

Wellington's Anglo-Portuguese army withdrew towards the Lines of Torres Vedras, ordering the Portuguese to abandon their homes and take or destroy all their food and livestock. The French found themselves marching through a wasteland and then encountered Wellington's army posted on the heights of **BUSACO**. On 27 September Masséna attacked but was driven back with over 4,000 casualties. Wellington continued his withdrawal to the Lines of Torres Vedras which, after his experience at Busaco, Masséna refused to assault. The French settled down in the deserted Portuguese countryside and Masséna appealed to Napoleon for reinforcements.

As well as defending Portugal, a small British army under Lieutenant General Thomas Graham was helping garrison the fortress-port of Cadiz where the Spanish Regency had established itself when the province of Andalusia had been overrun by the forces led by Joseph Bonaparte, the new King of Spain. The French laid siege to Cadiz and the army in Andalusia was entrusted to Marshal Soult.

When it was known in Paris that Masséna was in trouble in Portugal, Napoleon ordered Soult to make a diversion into southern Portugal to help draw some of Wellington's troops away from the Lines of Torres Vedras. In January 1811, Soult marched into Estremadura with the intention of capturing the border fortress of Badajoz. This left the forces outside Cadiz dangerously weakened and a combined

Anglo-Portuguese corps sailed along the coast to land behind the French lines. At the ensuing battle on the heights of **BARROSA** on 5 March 1811, General Graham's British contingent found itself unsupported by its Spanish comrades and faced Marshal Victor's larger force alone. Graham, however, achieved a remarkable victory. Without the aid of the Spaniards, Graham had to retire to Cadiz and the French siege was re-installed.

Marshal Soult's capture of Badajoz had failed to significantly help Marshal Masséna who was eventually starved into abandoning his expedition into Portugal. He retreated back to Spain, with Wellington in pursuit.

Wellington then blockaded the French-held border fortress of Almeida, hoping to force its surrender. On 3 May 1811, Masséna attempted to relieve the fortress, attacking Wellington's army at **FUENTES DE OÑORO**. The battle lasted for three days, with the French finally being forced to withdraw. The garrison of Almeida was able to escape in the aftermath of the battle. Masséna was recalled to Paris, his place being taken by Marshal Marmont.

Whilst Wellington was defeating the French in northern Portugal, a detached portion of his army under Major General Beresford, had been detailed to re-take Badajoz. Marshal Soult marched to the fortress's relief. Beresford raised the siege and placed his Anglo-Portuguese and Spanish force in Soult's path around the village of **ALBUERA**. On 16 May 1811, the two forces clashed in what was the bloodiest encounter of the Peninsular War. The French were defeated and Soult returned to Andalusia.

After the Battle of Albuera, Major General Rowland Hill took over Beresford's independent command and in October 1811, he received intelligence that a lone French division was operating close to the Spanish/Portuguese border. Hill received permission from Wellington to attack. After a series of forced marches, Hill fell upon General Girard's division at **ARROYO DOS MOLINES** on 28 October. Taken by surprise, Girard lost more than a third of his division before he was able to make his escape.

Wellington now wanted to re-take the border fortresses of Ciudad Rodrigo and Badajoz. **CIUDAD RODRIGO** was taken by storm on 19 January 1812 and **BADAJOZ** on 6 April, both assaults resulted in heavy casualties.

With the capture of these two fortresses Wellington could carry the war into Spain confident that his line of retreat, and his lines of communications, was secure. Wellington's first target was Marmont's 48,000 men posted around **SALAMANCA**. On 13 June 1812, Wellington crossed the River Agueda and made contact with Marmont's now inappropriately titled *l'Armee de Portugal*, two days later. The opposing armies were numerically evenly matched and neither Marmont nor Wellington was prepared to risk an action unless presented with an extremely favourable situation.

For over four weeks the two armies marched and counter-marched in an attempt to out-manoeuvre their opponents, but neither side had been able to gain the upper hand. The decisive breakthrough came on 22 July. Marmont, whilst trying to race around Wellington's flank, over-extended his line. Wellington immediately took advantage of his opponent's error and attacked.

Wellington's timing was perfect and Marmont's army was cut in two. Marmont himself was wounded in the ensuing battle and his army was routed. General Clausel, Marmont's senior divisional officer, assumed command of *l'Armee de Portugal* and withdrew northwards towards Burgos. Wellington was tempted to pursue Clausel but this would have exposed his line of communication to an attack from Soult in the south. He chose instead to march on Madrid, entering the city on 12 August, forcing King Joseph to abandon his capital.

Wellington's occupation of central Spain and his symbolic entry into Madrid meant that Soult's army in Andalusia was in danger of being cut off from all the other French forces in the Peninsular and eventually he was compelled to abandon the siege of Cadiz and retreat to the north of Spain to join the other French armies.

Wellington hoped to prevent the French armies concentrating. To this end he turned on Clausel's army which was driven further north. As he withdrew, the French general left some 2,000 men in the fortress of **BURGOS**, a place of strategic importance along the main road to France. Wellington's 35,000-strong Anglo-Portuguese-Spanish army laid siege to the castle of Burgos on 19 September 1812. Expecting an easy victory, Wellington attempted to storm the castle before his siege guns had been brought into action. They were driven off. Unsuccessful attempts were then made to bring down the walls of the castle with mines. As the days passed by, the French armies gathered and Wellington was soon in danger of being overwhelmed. On 21 October he raised the siege of Burgos and retreated all the way back to the Portuguese border. Joseph Bonaparte re-entered Madrid on 2 November.

It was not until June 1813 that Wellington felt he could resume operations. The French forces in Spain still considerably outnumbered his own and before he could risk moving onto the offensive he wanted to distract the French Army under Marshal Suchet based in Valencia. For this, he asked the Anglo-Sicilian and Spanish force which had been operating against the east coast of Spain to attack Suchet.

Under the command of Lieutenant General John Murray, the 18,000-strong Allied force manoeuvred threateningly towards the north of Alicante which prompted Suchet to attack. On 13 April 1813, Suchet fell upon part of Murray's Spanish contingent, which was routed, compelling Murray to concentrate the rest of his troops at **CASTALLA.** Again Suchet attacked but this time he was beaten and forced to withdraw.

Murray's activities on the east coast ensured that Suchet would not be able to help the other French forces in Spain, when Wellington launched his next offensive in the summer of 1813. This time his target was the 68,000-strong army of Marshal Jourdan which was strung out between the River Douro and the River Tagus. Wellington divided his army into two columns. He personally led the smaller of the two columns, marching directly upon Jourdan who retreated northwards. Lieutenant General Hill led the larger column round the French right flank to cut off their line of retreat.

The opposing forces met at **VITORIA** on 21 June. The result was a crushing victory for the Anglo-Portuguese-Spanish army. The shattered French army retreated towards the Pyrenees, and Napoleonic rule in Spain was effectively ended. Only the fortresses of Pamplona and San Sebastian that guarded the main passes of the **PYRENEES** remained in French hands.

Napoleon placed Marshal Soult in command of all the French armies in Spain and southern France, totaling some 80,000 men. Soult sought to relieve the garrisons of Pamplons and San Sebastian and on 25 July 1813 he attacked through the mountain passes in two columns. The first of these encountered a British and Spanish force under Lieutenant General Hill at Roncesvalles whilst the second met the British 2nd Division at Maya pass. Though both French attacks were held throughout the day, the Allied forces withdrew under the weight of the French assault that night. Wellington concentrated his strength in front of Pamplona, defeating the two French columns at the battle of Sorauen on 28 July. Soult retreated back over the Pyrenees into France.

Lieutenant General Graham, whose corps had responsibility for capturing **SAN SEBASTIAN,** had been instructed by Wellington to attack the fortress on 25 July. The attacking troops had been repulsed, suffering around 1,000 casualties. After the Battle of Sorauren, Wellington was able to concentrate on San Sebastian and on 31 August Graham's men assaulted the fortress a second time. The British broke through the fortress walls and into the town but the garrison retreated into a fort on a hill of Urgull overlooking the town. The garrison surrendered on 8 September.

With the garrison of Pamplona being the only French force left in Spain, Wellington decided to advance into France. On 7 October 1813, Wellington attacked Marshal Soult's positions on the River **BIDASSOA**. The French felt that their front was secure but Wellington had discovered that the river was shallow enough to be forded by infantry at low tides. The French were pushed back and Wellington's troops became the first Allied forces to become established on French soil. The French garrison of Pamplona surrendered to the Spanish on 30 October.

After the Battle of the Bidassoa, Soult intended to fall back on strong defensive positions that had been built in front of the River **NIVELLE**. But Soult was unable to settle his troops in position before the Allies attacked on 10 November. The French were badly beaten and withdrew deeper into France, stopping at a defensive line south of the town of Bayonne along the Adour and **NIVE** rivers. Dividing his army into two wings, Wellington attacked these positions on 9 December, forcing the passage of the Nive. The following day Soult launched a counter-attack against the Allied western wing which managed to hold off the French assaults.

Soult renewed his attack on the 13th against the corps led by Hill. When Wellington brought up reinforcements, the French soldiers refused to continue to fight. Faced with a virtual mutiny, Soult abandoned his operation and he withdrew back to Bayonne.

Poor weather over the winter months prevented Wellington from continuing his offensive until the middle of February. Soult had positioned his divisions in a line running from the fortress of Bayonne to the fortress of Saint-Jean-Pied-de-Port to the south-east and on14 February Wellington struck against the western end of the French line at **GARRIS**. Once again the demoralized French were beaten and Soult pulled back to a ridge near **ORTHEZ** that stood a little distance back from the Gave de Pau river. As before, the French line was penetrated and they were compelled to retreat.

With the French on the defensive on all fronts following Napoleon's disastrous Russian campaign, a British force was despatched to the Low Countries to help support an insurrection against French rule. Lieutenant General Graham was taken from Wellington's Peninsula army and given command of 7,000 men with the object of seizing Antwerp and, just as in 1809, the French fleet based there. In conjunction with a Prussian corps under General Bülow, Graham, with the local rank of General, advanced on Antwerp after pushing aside limited French resistance. The Allied force began bombarding the French fleet on 3 February. However, Bülow's corps was withdrawn and Graham was obliged to fall back. As an alternative to abandoning the expedition, Graham decided to attack the fortress of **BERGEN-OP-ZOOM**. The place proved too strong and an attack on 8 March was repulsed with many of the attackers being cut off inside the fortress and taken prisoner.

In southern France, Soult had disengaged his army from the Allies but the next problem he faced was deciding where he should make his next stand. He could either defend Bordeaux to the northwest or **TOULOUSE** to the east, but not both. He chose Toulouse

With Bordeaux undefended, a column under Beresford occupied the place on 12 March without opposition. A corps under Lieutenant-General John Hope also besieged Bayonne. Wellington attacked Soult's force in front of Toulouse on 10 April. Both sides claimed victory but it was Wellington that held the battlefield at the end of the day, with Soult withdrawing into Toulouse. Two days later Soult marched out of Toulouse, the city then surrendering to Wellington. That same afternoon, 12 April, news was received that Napoleon had abdicated and that the war was over.

Although Napoleon had abdicated, the governor of **BAYONNE,** General Thouvenot, attacked Hope's corps surrounding the city. This pointless battle cost the French over 900 men, the British also suffering heavy losses.

Peace in Europe lasted for less than a year. Though Napoleon had been exiled to the Mediterranean island of Elba, in February 1815 he escaped and sailed back to France. With very little opposition he resumed his place as Emperor but the Allied nations declared Napoleon to be an international outcast and they resolved to attack him as soon as their armies could be brought back into the field.

Rather than wait to be attacked, Napoleon launched pre-emptive strikes against the Prussian army and the Anglo-Hanoverian-Belgium-Dutch army in southern Belgium under Wellington.

The two Allied armies were driven back at the battles of Ligny and Quatre-Bras, with Wellington falling back to a position on the low ridge of Mont-Saint-Jean near the village of **WATERLOO**. Here Napoleon attacked Wellington on 18 June. During the course of the fighting Wellington was joined by the Prussians, their intervention tipping the balance of the battle in favour of the Allies. Badly beaten, the French army disintegrated and, relentlessly pursued by the Prussians, it was unable to reform.

Napoleon abdicated for a second and final time on 22 June 1815, bringing to an end the wars that will forever bear his name.

THE DESPATCHES

1

BATTLE OF MONTEVIDEO

Downing-Street, April 12, 1807.

A DISPATCH, of which the following is a Copy, was received this Morning at the Office of Viscount Castlereagh, one of His Majesty's Principal Secretaries of state, from Brigadier-General Auchmuty, to the Right Honourable William Windham:

Monte Video, February 6, 1807.

SIR,

I have the Honour to inform you, that His Majesty's Troops under my Command have taken by Assault, and after a most determined Resistance, the important Fortress and City of Monte Video.

The Ardent, with her Convoy, arrived at Maldonado on the 5th of January; and I immediately took under my Orders the Troops from the Cape, commanded by Lieutenant-Colonel Backhouse. On the 13th, I evacuated that Place without Opposition, leaving a small Garrison on the Island of Gorriti.

On consulting with Rear-Admiral Stirling, it was determined to attack Monte Video; and I landed on the Morning of the 18th, to the Westward of the Caretas Rocks, in a small Bay, about Nine Miles from the Town. The Enemy were in great Force, with Guns on the Heights, when we disembarked; but they did not advance to oppose us, and suffered me to take a strong Position, about a Mile from the Shore. A trifling Cannonade, and some firing at the Outposts, commenced in the Afternoon, and Continued occasionally during our Stay on that Ground.

On the 19th we moved towards Monte Video. The Right Column, under the Honourable Brigadier-General Lumley, was early opposed. About Four Thousand of the Enemy's Horse occupied Two Heights to his Front and Right. As we advanced, a heavy Fire of Round and Grape opened upon us; but a spirited Charge in Front, from the Light Battalion under Lieutenant-Colonel Brownrigg, dispersed the Corps opposed to him, with the Loss of a Gun. The Enemy on the Flank did not wait a similar Movement, but retreated. They continued retiring before us, and permitted us, without any further Opposition, except a distant Cannonade, to take up a Position about Two Miles from the Citadel. Our advanced Posts occupied the Suburbs, and some small Parties were posted close to the Works; but in the Evening the principal Part of the Suburbs was evacuated.

The next Morning the Enemy came out of the Town, and attacked us with their whole Force, about Six Thousand Men, and a Number of Guns. They advanced in Two Columns; the Right, consisting of Cavalry, to turn our Left Flank, while the other, of Infantry, attacked the Left of our Line; this Column pushed in our Advanced Posts, and pressed so hard on our Out-Picquet, of Four Hundred Men, that Colonel Browne, who commanded on the Left, ordered Three Companies of the 40th, under Major Campbell, to their Support: these Companies fell in with the Head of the Column, and very bravely charged it; the Charge was as gallantly received, and great Numbers fell on both Sides; at length the Column began to give way, when it was suddenly and impetuously attacked in Flank by the Rifle Corps, and Light Battalion, which I had ordered up, and directed to the particular Point. The Column now gave way on all Sides, and was pursued, with Slaughter and the Loss of a Gun, to the Town. The Right Column, observing the Fate of their Companions, rapidly retired, without coming into Action.

The Loss of the Enemy was considerable, and has been estimated at Fifteen Hundred Men; their killed might amount to between Two and Three Hundred; we have taken the same Number of Prisoners, but the principal Part of the wounded got back into the Town; I am happy to add, that ours was comparatively trifling.

The Consequences of this Affair were greater than the Action itself. Instead of finding ourselves surrounded with Horse, and a petty Warfare at our Posts, many of the Inhabitants of the Country separated, and retired to their several Villages, and we were allowed quietly to set down before the Town.

From the best Information I could obtain, I was led to believe that the Defences of Monte Video were weak, and the Garrison by no Means disposed to make an obstinate Resistance; but I found the Works truly respectable, with One hundred and sixty Pieces of Cannon; and they were ably defended.

The Enemy, being in Possession of the Island of Ratones, commanded the Harbour; and I was aware that their Gun Boats would annoy us, as we apprehended. A Two Gun Battery was constructed on the 23d to keep them in Check, and our Posts were extended to the Harbour, and completely shut in the Garrison on the Land Side. Their Communication was still, however, open by Water, and their Boats conveyed to them Troops and Provisions: Even Water for the Garrison was obtained by these Means; for the Wells that supply the Town were in our Possession.

On the 25th we opened Batteries of Four Twenty-four Pounders and Two Mortars, and all the Frigates and smaller Vessels came in, as close as they could with Safety, and cannonaded the Town. But finding that the Garrison was not intimidated into a Surrender, I constructed, on the 28th, a Battery of Six Twenty-four Pounders, within a Thousand Yards of the South East Bastion of the Citadel, which I was informed was in so weak a State that it might be easily breached. The Parapet was soon in

Ruins, but the Rampart received little Injury, and I was soon convinced that my Means were unequal to a regular Siege; the only Prospect of Success that presented itself was, to erect a Battery as near as possible to a Wall by the South Gate, that joins the Works to the Sea, and endeavour to breach it. This was effected by a Six Gun Battery within Six hundred Yards, and though it was exposed to a very superior Fire from the Enemy, which had been incessant during the whole of the Siege, a Breach was reported practicable on the 2d instant. Many Reasons induced me not to delay the Assault, though I was aware the Troops would be exposed to a very heavy Fire in approaching and mounting the Breach. Orders were issued for the Attack an Hour before Day break the ensuing Morning, and a Summons was sent to the Governor in the Evening to surrender the Town. To this Message no Answer was returned.

The Troops destined for the assault consisted of the Rifle Corps under Major Gardner, the Light Infantry under Lieutenant-Colonel Brownrigg and Major Trotter, the Grenadiers under Majors Campbell and Tucker, and the 38th Regiment under Lieutenant Colonel Vassal and Major Nugent.

They were supported by the 40th Regiment under Major Dalrymple, and the 87th under Lieutenant-Colonel Butler and Major Miller. The whole were commanded by Colonel Browne, The Remainder of my Force, consisting of the 17th Light Dragoons, Detachments of the 20th and 21st Light Dragoons, the 47th Regiment, a Company of the 71st, and a Corps of 700 Marines and Seamen, were encamped under Brigadier-General Lumley, to protect our Rear.

At the appointed Hour the Troops marched to the Assault. They approached near the Breach before they were discovered, when a destructive Fire from every Gun that could bear upon it, and from the Musketry of the Garrison, opened upon them. Heavy as it was, our Loss would have been comparatively trifling, if the Breach had been open, but during the Night, and under our Fire, the Enemy had barricaded it with Hides, so as to render it nearly impracticable. The Night was extremely dark. The Head of the Column missed the Breach, and when it was approached it was so shut up, that it was mistaken for the untouched Wall. In this Situation the Troops remained under a heavy Fire for a Quarter of an Hour, when the Breach was discerned by Captain Renny of the 40th Light Infantry, who pointed it out, and gloriously fell as he mounted it. Our gallant Soldiers rushed to it, and, difficult as it was of Access, forced their way into the Town. Cannon were placed at the Head of the principal Streets, and their Fire, for a short Time, was destructive: but the Troops advanced in all Directions, clearing the Streets and Batteries with their Bayonets, and overturning their cannon. The 40th Regiment, with Colonel Browne, followed. They also missed the Breach, and Twice passed through the Fire of the Batteries, before they found it.

The 87th Regiment was posted near the North Gate, which the Troops who entered at the Breach were to open for them, but their Ardour was so great that they could not wait. They scaled the Walls and entered the Town as the Troops within approached it. At Day-light every Thing was in our Possession except the Citadel, which made a shew of Resistance, but soon surrendered, and early in the Morning the Town was quiet, and the Women were peaceably walking the Streets.

The Gallantry displayed by the Troops during the Assault, and their Forbearance and orderly Behaviour in the Town speak so fully in their Praise, that it is unnecessary for me to say how highly I am pleased with their Conduct. The Service they have been engaged in since we landed, has been uncommonly severe and laborious, but not a murmur has escaped them: every Thing I wished has been effected with order and cheerfulness.

Our Loss during the Siege was trifling, particularly as we were not sheltered by Approaches, and the Enemy's Fire of Shot and Shell was incessant. But it is painful for me to add, that it was great at the Assault. Many most valuable Officers are among the Killed and Wounded. Major Dalrymple of the 40th was the only Field Officer killed. Lieutenant- Colonels Vassal and Brownrigg and Major Tucker are among the wounded. I am deeply concerned to say that the Two former are severely so. The Enemy's Loss was very great, about Eight Hundred killed, Five Hundred wounded, and the Governor Don Pasquil Ruis Huidobro, with upwards of Two Thousand Officers and Men are Prisoners. About Fifteen Hundred escaped in Boats or secreted themselves in the Town.

From Brigadier-General the Honourable W. Lumley and from Colonel Browne, I have received the most able and the most zealous Assistance and Support. The former protected the Line from the Enemy during our March, and covered our Rear during the Siege. The latter conducted it with great Judgement and determined Bravery.

The established Reputation of the Royal Artillery has been firmly supported by the Company under my Orders, and I consider myself much indebted to Captains Watson, Dickson, Carmichael, and Willgress, for their zealous and able Exertions. Captain Fanshaw of the Engineers was equally zealous, and though young in the Service conducted himself with such propriety that I have no doubt of his proving a valuable Officer. Owing to great Fatigue he was taken ill in the midst of our Operations, and Captain Dickson readily undertook his Office, and executed it with the greatest Judgement.

From the Heads of Corps and Departments, from the General Staff of the Army, from the Medical, and from my own personal Staff, I have received the most prompt and cheerful Assistance.

It is insufficient to say, that the utmost Cordiality has subsisted between Rear-Admiral Stirling and myself; I have received from him the most friendly Attention, and every Thing in his Power to grant.

The Captains and Officers of the Navy have been equally zealous to assist us; but I feel particularly indebted to Captains Donnelly and Palmer for their great Exertions. They commanded a Corps of Marines and Seamen that were landed, and were essentially useful to us with the Guns, and in the Batteries, as well as in bringing up the Ordnance and Stores.

This Dispatch will be delivered to you by Major Tucker, who was wounded at the Assault; and as he has long been in my Confidence, I beg Leave to refer you to him for further Particulars.

I have the Honour to be, &c.

S. AUCHMUTY,

Brigadier-General Commanding

Admiralty-Office, April 12, 1807.

CAPTAIN DONNELLY, of His Majesty's Ship Ardent, arrived this Morning with Dispatches from Rear-Admiral Stirling, commanding a Squadron of His Majesty's Ships in the Rio de la Plata, of which the following are Copies:

Diadem, off Monte Video,
8th Feb. 1807.

SIR,

I have peculiar Satisfaction in congratulating my Lords Commissioners of the Admiralty on the Capture of Monte Video, as well from the Importance of the Conquest, as from the Honour which has thereby been acquired by His Majesty's Arms.

Immediately on the Arrival of Brigadier-General Sir Samuel Achmuty, at Maldonado, it was determined to invest this place, and having assembled our Force off the Island of Flores, a Descent was effected on the 16th Ultimo, near Carreta Point, which is about Seven Miles to the Eastward of the Town. The Enemy had assembled in considerable Numbers, and with several Pieces of Artillery seemed determined to oppose our progress.

The Navigation of the Rio de la Plata, with the strong Breezes which we have experienced for several Weeks, rendered the Landing of Troops, and assisting their Operations, very difficult, but the Place chosen was happily adapted to allow the covering Vessels, under the Direction of Captain Hardyman, to approach so close as to command the Beach, and notwithstanding the Weather threatened, and was unfavourable, the Soldiers got all on Shore without a single Accident of any Kind, and were in Possession of the Heights before Six o'Clock, with such Things as the General wanted.

On the 19th the Army moved forwards, and as an Attempt to harass the Rear was expected, I directed Boats to proceed close along Shore to look out for and bring off any wounded Men, whilst the covering Vessels were placed to prevent the Enemy from giving Annoyance, and I had the Happiness to hear that all the Sufferers were brought off, in Despite of well directed Efforts to destroy them.

In the Evening I dropped, with the Fleet, off Chico Bay, near which the Army encamped, within Two Miles of the City.

I had landed about Eight hundred Seamen and Royal Marines, under the Orders of Capt. Donnelly, to act with the Troops; and, as I saw no Advantage could result from any Effort of Ships against a strong Fortress, well defended at all Points, and which, from the Shallowness of the Water, could not be approached within a Distance to allow Shot to be of any use, I disposed the Squadron so as to prevent any Escape from the Harbour, as well as to impede a Communication between Colonna and Buenos Ayres, and confined my whole Attention to give every possible Assistance in forwarding the Siege, by landing Guns from the Line of Battle Ships, with

Ammunition, Stores, Provisions, and every Thing required by the Commander of the Forces.

The Distance which the Ships lay from the Shore, with the almost constant high Winds and swell we had, and the great Way every Thing was to be dragged by the Seamen, up a heavy sandy Road, made the Duty excessively laborious. The Squadron had almost daily Fourteen hundred Men on Shore, and this Ship was often left with only Thirty Men on board.

The Defence made by the Enemy protracted the Siege longer than was expected, and reduced our Stock of Powder so low, that the King's Ships, with all the Transports, and what a Fleet of Merchantmen had for Sale, could not have furnished a further Consumption for more than Two Days, when a practicable Breach was fortunately made, and on the 3d Instant, early in the Morning, the Town and Citadel were most gallantly carried by Storm.

In a Conversation with the General on the preceding Day, I had made such Disposition of the smaller Vessels and armed Boats, as appeared most likely to answer a desired Purpose, and so soon as Fort Saint Philip was in Possession of the British Troops, Lieutenant William Milne, with the armed Launches, took Possession of the Island of Rattones, mounting Ten Guns and garrisoned by Seventy Men, which surrendered without any Resistance, although it is well adapted for Defence, and might have given considerable Annoyance. A very fine Frigate mounting Twenty-eight Guns was set Fire to by her Crew, and blew up with an awful Explosion; as also Three Gun Boats, but the other Vessels in the Harbour were saved by the Exertion of our People.

It has been much the Custom to speak slightly of the Resistance to be expected from the Spaniards in this Country; and with confidence of the Facility which has been given to Naval Operations, by a prior Knowledge of the River, but the Battles lately fought prove the former Opinion to be erroneous, and experience evinces that all the Information hitherto acquired has not prevented the most formidable Difficulties.

The Conduct of the Captains, Officers, Seamen, and Royal Marines of the Ships and Vessels, which I kept with me for this Service, has met with my entire Approbation, and I feel persuaded that I should have had Occasion to express my Satisfaction with the Exertions of the Officers and Crews of the Diomede and Protector, if I had not been obliged to detach them on other Service.

I am much indebted to the able Assistance which Captain Warren has afforded me; and I admire the Zeal, the Patience, and Diligence of every Individual in the Fleet during the incessant Fatigue which I have daily witnessed.

Captain Donnelly will have the Honour to deliver this Dispatch, and is fully able to give their Lordships further Particulars.

I have the Honour to be, &c.
CHARLES STIRLING.

2
DARDANELLES CAMPAIGN

Admiralty-Office, May 4, 1807.

Extracts of a Letter and its Inclosures, which have been received at this Office from Vice-Admiral Lord Collingwood, Commander in Chief of His Majesty's Ships and Vessels in the Mediterranean, addressed to William Marsden, Esq; dated on board His Majesty's Ship Ocean, off Cadiz, the 5th of April 1807.

SIR,

HIS Majesty's Sloop L'Espoir has joined me To-day, bringing Dispatches from Vice-Admiral Sir John T. Duckworth and Mr. Arbuthnot. Copies of the Vice-Admiral's Letters to me, detailing the Proceedings of the Squadron in passing and re-passing the Dardanelles, the burning the Turkish Ships which lay off Point Perquies, with Lists of the Killed and Wounded on the 19th and 27th February, and 3d March, are herewith transmitted.

I am, &c.

COLLINGWOOD.

Royal George, without the Dardanelles, March 6, 1807.

MY LORD,

TOGETHER with this Letter, I transmit to your Lordship Two Letters of the 21st and 26th Ultimo; the former of which will have informed you of my Arrival with the Squadron near Constantinople, and the latter of an unlucky Attempt, in which the Marines and Boats' Crews of the Canopus, Royal George, Windsor Castle, and Standard, had been engaged.

It is now my Duty to acquaint your Lordship with the Result of the Resolution which, for the Reasons I have already detailed, I had adopted of forcing the Passage of the Dardanelles. My Letter of the 21st is dated at an Anchor Eight Miles from

Constantinople, the Wind not admitting of a nearer Approach; but the Endymion, which had been sent ahead with a Flag of Truce, at the Request of the Ambassador, was enabled to anchor within Four Miles. Had it been then in our Power we should have then taken our Station off the Town immediately, but as that could not be done from the current, I was rather pleased than otherwise with the Position we had been forced to take, for in the Conferences between His Majesty's Minister, Mr. Arhuthnot, and the Captain Pacha, of the Particulars of which your Lordship is in Possession, it was promised by Mr Arbuthnot, that even when the Squadron had arrived before Constantinople, the Door to Pacification should remain open, and that he would be willing to negociate on Terms of Equality and Justice. In consideration of this Promise, and as it would convince the Porte of His Majesty's earnest Desire to preserve Peace, as well as possess her Ministers with a Confidence of the Sincerity of our Professions, it was the Opinion of Mr. Arbuthnot, in which I concurred, that it was fortunate we had anchored at a little Distance from the Capital, as a nearer Approach might have given Cause for Suspicion and Alarm, and have cut off the Prospect of an amicable Adjustment of the Differences which had arisen.

At Noon of the 21st, Ysak Bey, a Minister of the Porte, came off; from whose Expressions Mr. Arbuthnot thought it impossible not to believe that, in the Head of the Government (for in the present Instance every Circumstance proved that, between him and the Armed Populace a great Distinction is to be made) there really existed a sincere Desire for Peace; and the Negociation was carried on, as will appear by the Documents transmitted to your Lordship, till the 17th; but from the Moment of our Anchorage till we weighed, on the Morning of the 1st of March, such was the unfortunate State of the Weather, that it was not at any Time in our Power to have occupied a Situation which would have enabled the Squadron to commence offensive Operations against Constantinople. On Sunday the 22d alone, for a few Hours, the Breeze was sufficient to have stemmed the Current where we were placed; but such was the Rapidity on Shore where the Endymion was at Anchor, that Captain Capel thought it very doubtful whether the Squadron could have obtained an Anchorage, though it had been held in preparative Readiness, by Signal, from Day-break; but the peculiarly unsettled State of the Weather, and the Minister's Desire that I should give a few Hours for an Answer to his Letter, through Yska Bey, prevented me from trying. Before Five o'Clock,. P.M. it was nearly calm; and in the Evening the Wind was entirely from the Eastward, and continued light Airs or calm till the Evening of the 28th, when it blew fresh from the N. E. and rendered it impossible to change our Position.

Two Days after our Arrival near Constantinople, the Ambassador found himself indisposed, and has been ever since confined with a fit of Illness, so severe as to prevent him from attending to Business. Under these Circumstances he had delivered in the 22d to the Turkish Minister a Project, as the Basis on which Peace might be preserved, and at his Desire the subsequent Part of the Negociation was carried on in my Name, with his Advice and Assistance; and while I lament most deeply that it has not ended in the re establishment of Peace, I derive Consolation from the Reflection that no Effort has been wanting on the Part of Mr. Arbuthnot and myself to obtain such a Result, which was soon seen from the State of the Preparations at Constantinople could be effected by Negociation only, as the Strength of Current from the Bosphorus with the circuitous Eddies of the Port, rendered it, impracticable to place Ships for an Attack without a commanding breeze which, during the Ten Days I was off the Town, it was not my good Fortune to meet with.

I now come to the Point of explaining to your Lordship the Motives which fixed me to decide in repassing the Channel of the Dardanelles, and relinquishing every Idea of attacking the Capital, and I feel confident it will require no Argument to convince your Lordship of the utter Impracticability of our Force having made any Impression, as at this Time the whole Line of the Coast presented a Chain of Batteries: That Twelve Turkish Line of Battle Ships, Two of them Three Deckers, with Nine Frigates, were with their Sails bent, and apparently in Readiness, filled with Troops; add to this near Two Hundred Thousand were said to be in Constantinople, to march against the Russians; besides there were an innumerable Quantity of small Craft, with Boats; and Fire Vessels had been prepared to act against us. With the Batteries alone we might have coped, or with the Ships, could we have got them out of their strong Hold; but your Lordship will be aware, that after combating the Opposition which the Resources of an Empire had been many Weeks employed in preparing, we should have been in no State to have defended ourselves against them as described, and then repass the Dardanelles. I know it was my Duty, in Obedience to your Lordship's Orders, to attempt every Thing (governed by the Opinion of the Ambassador) that appeared within the Compass of Possibility; but when the unavoidable Sacrifice of the Squadron committed to my Charge which must have arisen, had I waited for a Wind to have enabled me to cannonade the Town, unattended by the remotest Chance of obtaining any Advantage for His Majesty's Service must have been the Consequence of pursuing that Object, it at once became my positive Duty, however wounded in Pride and Ambition, to relinquish it, and if I had not been already satisfied on the Subject, the increased Opposition in the Dardanelles would have convinced me I had done right, when I resolved on the Measure as indispensably necessary. I therefore weighed with the Squadron on the Morning of the first, and as it had been reported that the Turkish Fleet designed to make an effort against us, to give them an Opportunity, if such was really their Intention, I continued to stand on and off during the Day, but they shewed no Disposition to move.

I therefore, as every Hour was of Importance, bore up at Dusk with the Squadron; we arrived off Point Pesquies towards the Evening of the 2d Instant, but the Daylight would not admit of our attempting to pass the Castles, and the Squadron came to Anchor for the Night; we weighed in the Morning, and, when I add that every Ship was in Safety outside of the Passage, about Noon, it is not without the most lively sense of the good Fortune that has attended us.

The Turks had been occupied unceasingly in adding to the Number of their Forts, some had been already completed, and others were in a forward State. The Fire of the Two inner Castles had, on our going up been severe, but, I am sorry to say, the Effects they have had on our Ships returning, has proved them to be doubly formidable: In short, had they been allowed another Week to complete their Defences throughout the Channel, it would have been a very doubtful Point, whether a Return lay open to us at all. The Manner in which they employed the Interval of our Absence has proved their Assiduity.

I transmit your Lordship an Account of the Damage sustained by the respective Ship; as also their Loss in killed and wounded, which your Lordship will perceive is far from trifling. The Mainmast of the Windsor Castle being more than Three Quarters cut through by a Granite Shot of Eight Hundred Weight, we have found great Difficulty in saving it.

I have the Honour to be, &c.
(Signed) J.T. DUCKWORTH.

Royal George, off Constantinople, February 21, 1807.

SIR,

I HAD the Honour of transmitting to your Lordship, by the late First Lieutenant of the Ajax, the various Details relating to the Transactions of the Squadron till the 17th Ultimo. Your Lordship will from thence have been informed of my Resolution of passing the Dardanelles the first fair Wind. A fine Wind from the Southward permitted me to carry it into Effect on the Morning of the 19th.

Information had been given me by His Majesty's Minister, Mr. Arbuthnot, and Sir Thomas Louis, that the Turkish Squadron, consisting of a Sixty-four Gun Ship, Four Frigates, and several Corvetts, had been for some Time at Anchor within the Inner Castle; and conceiving it possible they might have remained there, I had given Orders to Rear Admiral Sir Sydney Smith to bring up with the Thunderer, Standard, and Active, and destroy them, should our Passage be opposed.

At a Quarter before Nine o'Clock the Whole of the Squadron had passed the Outer Castles, without having returned a Shot to their Fire (which occasioned but little Injury). This Forbearance was produced by the Desire of His Majesty's Minister, expressed to preserve every Appearance of Amity, that he might negociate with the strongest Proof of the pacific Disposition of our Sovereign towards the Porte: a second Battery, on the European Side, fired also with as little Effect. At half-past Nine o'Clock, the Canopus, which, on account of Sir Thomas Louis' Knowledge of the Channel, joined to the steady Gallantry which I had before experienced, had been appointed to lead, entered the narrow Passage of Seltos and Abydos, and sustained a very heavy Cannonade from both Castles, within Point-blank Shot of each. They opened their Fire upon our Ships as they continued to pass in Succession, although I was happy in observing that the very spirited Return it met with had so considerably diminished its Force, that the Effect on the sternmost Ships could not have been so severe.

Immediately to the N. E. of the Castles, and between them and Point Pesquies, in which a formidable Battery had been newly erected, the small Squadron which I have already alluded to were at Anchor. The Van Division of our Squadron gave them their

Broadsides as they passed, and Sir Sydney Smith with his Division closed into the Midst, and the Effect of the Fire was such that in Half an Hour the Turks had all cut their Cables to run on shore. The Object of the Rear-Admiral was then to destroy them, which was most rapidly effected; as in less than Four Hours the whole of them had exploded, except a small Corvette, and a Gun-Boat, which it was thought proper to preserve. I inclose to your Lordship a Statement of their Number, and when I add also an Account of the Loss His Majesty's Ships have sustained, I cannot help expressing my Satisfaction that we have suffered so slightly; as, had any of their Stone Shot, some of which exceed Eight Hundred Weight, made such a Breach between Wind and Water, as they have done in our Sides, the Ship must have sunk; or had they struck a lower Mast in the Centre, it must evidently have been cut in two; in the Rigging too, no Accident occurred that was not perfectly arranged in the Course of the next Day. The Sprit-sail Yard of the Royal George, the Gaft of the Canopus, and the Maintop-sail Yard of the Standard, are the only Spars that were injured.

It is with peculiar Pleasure that I embrace the Opportunity, which has been at this Time afforded, of bearing Testimony to the Zeal and distinguished Ability of Sir Sydney Smith; the Manner in which he executed the Service entrusted to him was worthy of the Reputation which he has long since so justly and generally established. The Terms of Approbation in which the Rear Admiral relates the Conduct of Captains Dacres, Talbot, Harvey, and Moubray, which, from my being under the Necessity of passing the Point of Pesquies before the Van could anchor, he had a greater Opportunity of observing than I could, cannot but be highly flattering; but I was a more immediate Witness to the able and officer-like Conduct which Captain Moubray displayed in Obedience to my Signal, by destroying a Frigate with which he had been more particularly engaged, having driven her on Shore on the European Side, after she had been forced to cut her Cables, from under the Fire of the Pompeé and Thunderer. The Sixty-four having run on Shore on Pesquies Point, I ordered the Repulse to work up and destroy her, which Captain Legge, in conjunction with the Boats of the Pompeé, executed with great Promptitude and Judgment. The Battery on the Point, of more than Thirty Guns, which, had it been completely finished, was in a Position to have annoyed the Squadron most severely in passing, was taken Possession of by the Royal Marines and Boats' Crews of the Rear Division; the Turk having retired at their Approach, and the Guns were immediately spiked. This Service was performed under the Direction of Captain Nicholls, of the Standard's Marine, whole Spirit and Enterprize can never be doubted; but as Circumstances rendered it impracticable to effect the entire Destruction of the Redoubt, Orders were given by Sir Sydney Smith to Captain Moubray, which I fully approved, to remain at Anchor near the Pesquies, and to employ Lieutenants Carrol and Arabin, of the Pompeé, and Lieutenant Lawrie, of the Marines, to complete the Demolition of the Redoubt and Guns, which when performed, the Active was to continue in the Passage of the Dardanelles till further Orders.

At a Quarter past Five P. M. the Squadron was enabled to make Sail; and on the Evening of the next Day, the 20th, came to an Anchor, at Ten o'Clock, near the Prince's Islands, about Eight Miles from Constantinople, when I dispatched Captain

Capel, in the Endymion, to anchor near the Town, if the Wind, which was light, would permit the Ship to stem the Current, to convey the Ambassador's Dispatches to the Sublime Porte in the Morning by a Flag of Truce; but he found it impracticable to get within Four Miles, and consequently anchored at Half past Eleven P. M.

I have now the highest Satisfaction to add, that the Conduct of the Officers and Ships' Companies of the Squadron under my Command has fully supported the Character of the British Navy, and is deserving of my warmest Eulogium.

Having endeavoured to pay just Tribute to those whose Duty necessarily called them into this Service, I should feel myself very deficient if I omitted to mention that His Majesty's Minister, Mr. Arbuthnot, and Lord Burghersh (who had requested to take a Cruize with me,) were among the most animated in the Combat. To Captain Blackwood, who after the unfortunate Loss of the Ajax, volunteered to serve in the Royal George, great Praise is due for his able Assistance in regulating the Fire of the Middle and Lower Decks; and when the Royal George anchored, he most readily offered his Services to convey a Message to the Endymion, of great Moment, her Pilot having refused to take Charge of the Ship.

From thence he gave his Assistance to arrange the Landing of the Troops from the Sixty, and setting her on Fire; indeed where active Service was to perform, there was his anxious Desire to be placed. His Officers too requested to serve in the Squadron, and their Services, in passing through the Dardanelles, met with approbation.

I have the Honour to be, &c.
(Signed) J.T. DUCKWORTH.

A List of Turkish Ships and Vessels taken and destroyed by the Squadron under the Command of Vice-Admiral Sir John Thomas Duckworth, K. B. at Anchor off Point Pesquies, the 19th February 1807, *within the Forts of the Dardanelles.*

Burnt
I Line of Battle Ship, 64 Guns 4 Frigates.
3 Corvettes.
1 Brig.
2 Gun Boats.
Taken Possession of. 1 Corvette.
1 Gun Boat.

(Signed)
J.T. DUCKWORTH.

Royal George, at Anchor of Prince's Islands, February 28, 1807

My LORD,

I HAVE to inform your Lordship, that it was perceived at Nine o'Clock Yesterday Morning, that the Turks had landed on the Island of Prota, near which the Squadron was anchored, and were erecting a Battery in a Position to annoy us; I immediately ordered the Marines of the squadron to be prepared for landing, and the Boats to be manned and armed, and the Repulse, with the Lucifer, having been directed to cover them, they proceeded towards the Island. The Turks, on the Ships firing a few Grape to scour the Beach, quitted the Island in their Boats, when all but One Boat with Eleven Men escaped, the which, with Two Guns they had intended to mount, fell into our Possession.

At Half after Two o'Clock in the Afternoon Sir Thomas Louis sent to inform me, that he had received Intelligence of a small Number of Turks being still on the Island, and requesting Permission to send Marines to take them; my Reply was, that no Risk whatever must be run, but if it could be effected without hazarding the People, it might; and a Party of the Canopus's Marines was immediately sent on shore in consequence, with the most positive Orders to Captain Kent, from Sir Thomas Louis, not to pursue the Object if he found it attended with any Hazard. At Four o'clock the Party on shore made the signal for Assistance, and the Marines and Boats manned and armed were directly ordered away from the Royal George, Windsor Castle, and Standard, with particular directions to bring off the Canopus's People, but to avoid being drawn into Danger. A little before Sun-set an Officer was dispatched with Orders for the whole to return on board.

On the Return of the Boats, which was not till after Dark, I heard with the deepest Regret of the Loss we had sustained. To account in some Degree for this unlucky Affair, it appears that the Information of a few Turks only having remained on the Island was entirely false, as nearly an Hundred of them had retired to an old Convent, from Loop-holes in the Walls of which, they defended themselves with Musketry. The People of the Canopus had in the first Instance advanced close under the Walls, and in endeavouring to relieve them from their unpleasant Situation, the others suffered.

In order, if possible, to prevent the Retreat of the Turks from this Island, the Launches of the squadron, armed with their Carronades, were ordered to row Guard during the Night, under the Direction of Captain Elliot, of the Lucifer; but notwithstanding every possible Vigilance, they are supposed to have escaped in the Night, as the next Morning it was represented to me that only Seven Greek Inhabitants of the Place were remaining.

I have the Honour to be, &c.
(Signed) J.T. DUCKWORTH.

3

BATTLE OF BUENOS AIRES

Downing-Street, September 12, 1807.

Lieutenant-Colonel Bourke, Deputy Quarter-Master General to His Majesty's Troops serving in South America, arrived this Morning at the Office of the Viscount Castlreagh, one of His Majesty's principal Secretaries of State, from the Rio de la Plata, with a Dispatch from Lieutenant-General Whitelocke, addressed to the Right Honourable William Windham, of which the following is a Copy

Buenos Ayres, July 10, 1807.

SIR,

I have the Honour, to acquaint you, for the information of His Majesty, that upon being joined at Monte Video on the 15th of June, by the Corps under Brigadier-General Craufurd, not one Moment was lost by Rear-Admiral Murray and myself in making every necessary Arrangement for the Attack of Buenos Ayres. After many Delays, occasioned by foul Winds, a landing was effected, without Opposition, on the 28th of the same Month, at the Entinada de Barragon, a small Bay about Thirty Miles to the Eastward of the Town. The Corps employed on this Expedition were Three Brigades of Light Artillery, under Captain Fraser; the 5th, 38th, and 87th Regiments of Foot, under Brigadier-General Sir Samuel Achmuty; the 17th Light Dragoons, 36th and 88th Regiments, under Brigadier-General the Honourable William Lumley; Eight Companies of the 95th Regiment, and Nine Light Infantry Companies, under Brigadier-General Craufurd; Four Troops of the 6th Dragoon Guards, the 9th Light Dragoons, 40th and 45th Regiments of Foot, under Colonel the Honourable T. Mahon; all the Dragoons being dismounted, except Four Troops of the 17th, under Lieutenant-Colonel Lloyd.

After some fatiguing Marches through a Country much intersected by Swamps and deep muddy Rivulets, the Army reached Reduction, a Village about Nine Miles distant from the Bridge over the Rio Chuelo; on the opposite Bank of which the

Enemy had constructed Batteries, and established a formidable Line of Defence. I resolved, therefore, to turn this Position, by marching in Two Columns from my Left, and crossing the River higher up, where it was represented fordable, to unite my Force in the Suburbs of Buenos Ayres. I sent Directions at the same Time to Colonel Mahon, who was bringing up the greater Part of the Artillery under the Protection of the 17th Light Dragoons and 40th Regiment, to wait for further Orders at Reduction.

Major-General Leveson Gower having the Command of the Right Column, crossed the River at a Pass called the Passo Chico, and falling in with a Corps of the Enemy's, gallantly attacked and defeated it, for the Particulars of which Action, I beg to refer you to the annexed Report. Owing to the Ignorance of my Guide, it was not until the next Day that I joined with the Main Body of the Army, when I formed my Line by placing Brigadier-General Sir Samuel Achmuty's Brigade upon the Left, extending it towards the Convent of the Recoleta, from which it was distant Two Miles. The 36th and 88th Regiments being on its Right; Brigadier-General Craufurd's Brigade occupying the Central and Principal Avenues of the Town, being distant about Three Miles from the Great Square and Fort; and the 6th Dragoon Guards, 9th Light Dragoons and 45th Regiment being upon his Right, and extending towards the Residencia. The Town was thus nearly invested, and this Disposition of the Army, and the Circumstances of the Town and Suburbs being divided into Squares of One Hundred and Forty Yards each Side, together with the Knowledge that the Enemy meant to occupy the Flat Roofs of the Houses, gave rise to the following plan of Attack.

Brigadier-General Sir Samuel Achmuty was directed to detach the 38th Regiment to possess itself of the Plaza de Toros, and the adjacent strong Ground, and there take Post: the 87th, 5th, 36th, and 88th Regiments were each divided into Wings; and each Wing ordered to penetrate into the Street directly in its Front. The Light Battalion divided into Wings, and each followed by a Wing of the 95th Regiment, and a Three Pounder, was ordered to proceed down the Two Streets on the Right of the central One, and the 45th Regiment down the Two adjoining; and after clearing the Streets of the Enemy, this latter Regiment was to take Post at the Residencia. Two Six Pounders were ordered along the central Street, covered by the Carabineers and Three Troops of the 9th Light Dragoons, the Remainder of which was posted as a Reserve in the Centre. Each Division was ordered to proceed along the Street directly in its Front, till it arrived at the Last Square of Houses next the River Plata; of which it was to possess itself, forming on the flat Roofs, and there wait for further Orders.

The 95th Regiment was to occupy Two of the most commanding Situations, from which it could annoy the Enemy. Two Corporals with Tools were ordered to march at the Head of each Column for the Purpose of breaking open the Doors; the Whole were unloaded, and no Firing was to be permitted until the Columns had reached their final Points and formed; a Cannonade in the central Streets was the Signal for the Whole to come forward.

In conformity to this Arrangement, at Half-past Six o'Clock of the Morning of the 5th Instant, the 38th Regiment moving towards its Left, and the 87th straight to its Front, approached the strong Post of the Retiro and Plaza de Toros, and after a most vigorous and spirited Attack, in which these Regiments suffered much from Grape-Shot and Musketry, their gallant Commander, Brigadier-General Sir Samuel Achmuty, possessed himself of the Post, taking Thirty-two Pieces of Cannon, an immense Quantity of Ammunition, and Six Hundred Prisoners. The 5th Regiment meeting with but little Opposition, proceeded to the River, and took Possession of the Church and Convent of St. Catalina. The 36th and 88th Regiments, under Brigadier-General Lumley, moving in the appointed Order, were soon opposed by a heavy and continued Fire of Musketry from the Tops and Windows of the Houses; the Doors of which were barricaded in so strong a Manner, as to render them almost impossible to force. The Streets were intersected by deep Ditches, in the Inside of which were planted Cannon, pouring Showers of Grape on the advancing Columns. In Defiance, however, of this Opposition, the 36th Regiment, headed by the gallant General, reached its final Destination; but the 88th being nearer to the Fort and principal Defences of the Enemy, were so weakened by his Fire as to be totally overpowered and taken. The Flank of the 36th being thus exposed, this Regiment, together with the 5th, retired upon Sir Samuel Auchmuty's Post at the Plaza de Toros; not, however, before Lieutenant-Colonel Burne and the Grenadier Company of the 36th Regiment, had an Opportunity of distinguishing themselves, by charging about Eight Hundred of the Enemy, and taking and spiking Two Guns. The Two Six Pounders moving up the central Streets meeting with a very superiour Fire, the Four Troops of the Carabineers, led on by Lieutenant-Colonel Kingston, advanced to take the Battery opposed to them, but this gallant Officer being unfortunately wounded, as well as Captain Burrell, next in Command, and the Fire both from the Battery and Houses proving very destructive, they retreated to a short Distance, but continued to occupy a Position in Front of the Enemy's principal Defences, and considerably in Advance of that which they had taken in the Morning.

The Left Division of Brigadier-General Craufurd's Brigade, under Lieutenant-Colonel Pack passed on nearly to the River, and turning to the Left, approached the Great Square with the Intention of possessing itself of the Jesuits College, a Situation which commanded the Enemy's principal Line of Defence. But from the very destructive Nature of his Fire, this was found impracticable, and after sustaining a heavy Loss, One Part of the Division throwing itself into a House which was afterwards not found tenable, was shortly obliged to surrender, whilst the remaining Part, after enduring a dreadful Fire with the greatest Intrepidity, Lieutenant-Colonel Pack its Commander being wounded, retired upon the Right Division commanded by Brigadier-General Craufurd himself. This Division having passed quite through to the River Plata, turned also to the Left to approach the Great Square and Fort from the North-East Bastion, of which it was distant about Four Hundred Yards, when Brigadier-General Craufurd, leaving the Fate of his Left Division, thought it most advisable to take possession of the Convent of St. Domingo, near which he then was, intending to proceed onwards to the Franciscan Church which lay still nearer the Fort, if the Attack or Success of any other of our Columns should free him in some Measure from the Host of Enemies which surrounded him. The 45th Regiment being further from the Enemy's Centre, had gained the Residencia without much

Opposition, and Lieutenant-Colonel Guard having it in Possession of his Battalion Companies, moved down with the Grenadier Company towards the Centre of the Town, and joined Brigadier-General Craufurd.

The Enemy, who now surrounded the Convent on all Sides, attempting to take a Three Pounder which lay in the Street, the Lieutenant-Colonel with his Company, and a few Light Infantry under Major Trotter, charged them with great Spirit. In an Instant, the greater Part of his Company and Major Trotter (an Officer of great Merit) were killed, but the Gun was saved. The Brigadier-General was now obliged to confine himself to the Defence of the Convent, from which the Rifle Men kept up a well directed Fire upon such of the Enemy as approached the Post; but the Quantity of Round Shot, Grape, and Musketry to which they were exposed, at last obliged them to quit the Top of the Building, and the Enemy, to the Number of Six Thousand, bringing up Cannon to force the Wooden Gates which fronted the Fort, the Brigadier-General having no Communication with any other Columns, and judging from the cessation of Firing that those next him had not been successful, surrendered at Four o'Clock in the Afternoon. The Result of this Day's Action had left me in Possession of the Plaza de Toros, a strong Post on the Enemy's Right, and the Residencia, another strong Post on his Left, whilst I occupied an advanced Position opposite his Centre; but these Advantages had cost about Two Thousand Five Hundred Men in killed, wounded, and Prisoners. The Nature of the Fire, to which the Troops were exposed, was violent in the Extreme. Grape Shot at the Corners of all the Streets, Musketry, Handgrenades, Bricks, and Stones from the Tops of all the Houses, every Householder with his Negroes defended his Dwelling, each of which was in itself a Fortress, and it is not, perhaps, too much to say, that the whole Male Population of Buenos Ayres was employed in its Defence.

This was the Situation of the Army on the Morning of the 6th Instant, when General Liniers addressed a Letter to me, offering to give up all his prisoners taken in the late Affair, together with the 71st Regiment, and others, taken with Brigadier-General Beresford, if I desisted from any further Attack on the Town, and withdrew His Majesty's Forces from the River Plata, intimating at the same Time, from the exasperated State of the Populace, he could not answer for the Safety of the Prisoners, if I perisisted in offensive Measures. Influenced by this Consideration, (which I knew from better Authority to be founded in Fact,) and reflecting of how little Advantage would be the Possession of a Country, the Inhabitants of which were so absolutely hostile, I resolved to forego the Advantages which the Bravery of the Troops had obtained, and acceded to the annexed Treaty, which I trust will meet the Approbation of His Majesty.

I have nothing further to add, except to mention, in Terms of the highest Praise, the Conduct of Rear-Admiral Murray, whose cordial Co-operation has never been wanting whenever the Army could be benefited by his Exertions. Captain Rowley, of the Royal Navy, commanding the Seamen on Shore, Captain Bayntun, of His Majesty's Ship Africa, who superintended the Disembarkation, and Captain Thompson, of the Fly, who had the Direction of the Gun-Boats, and had previously rendered me much Service by reconnoitring the River, are all entitled to my best Thanks.

As his Character already stands so high, it is almost unnecessary to state that from my Second in Command, Major-General Leveson Gower, I have experienced every zealous and useful Assistance; my Thanks are likewise due to Brigadiers-General Sir Samuel Auchmuty and Lumley, and to Colonel Mahon and Brigadier-General Craufurd commanding Brigades. I cannot sufficiently bring to Notice the uncommon Exertions of Captain Fraser, commanding the Royal Artillery, the Fertility of whose Mind, Zeal and Animation in all Cases left Difficulties behind. Captain Squires of the Royal Engineers is also entitled to my best Thanks; nor should I omit the gallant Conduct of Major Nicholls of the 45th Regiment, who on the Morning of the 6th Instant, being pressed by the Enemy near the Residencia, charged them with great Spirit, and took Two Howitzers and many Prisoners. Lieutenant-Colonel Bradford, Deputy Adjutant General, has likewise a great Claim to my Approbation as a gallant and promising Officer.

The Officers of my personal Staff Lieutenant-Colonel Torrens, Military Secretary, Captains Brawn, Foster, Douglas, and Whittingham, Aides du Camp, must also be mentioned by me in Terms of just Regard; the Knowledge which the latter possesses of the Spanish Language has been eminently useful to me.

This Dispatch will be delivered to you by Lieutenant-Colonel Bourke, Deputy Quarter-Master-General who has afforded me that Assistance which might be looked for from an Officer of his military Talents and Attachment to the Service;to whom I beg to refer you for any further Particulars respecting the military Operations in this Part of the World.

> I have the Honour to be, &c.
> J. WHITELOCKE. Lieut-Gen.

4

BATTLE OF COPENHAGEN

Extracts of a Letter from Lieutenant-General the Honorable Lord Cathcart to Viscount Castlereagh dated Hellerup, before Copenhagen, Aug. 31, 1807.

I HAVE now the Honour of inclosing a Continuation of the Journal from the 22nd of August to the 1st of September.

Journal of the Army under the Command of Lieutenant-General Lord Cathcart, from the Morning of the 22d of August to the Evening of the 1st of September 1807.

Head-Quarters, Copenhagen, Sept.1, 1807.
August 22.

Brigadier-General M Farlane's Division having been landed the preceding Evening, joined the Army and encamped in Rear of Head-Quarters. Lieutenant-General the Earl of Rosslyn's Division marched from the Place of Debarkation to Damhuis and adjacents. Arrangement and Distribution settled for forming the Park, and Progress of providing for Mortar-Batteries.

23d. Lieutenant-General the Earl of Rosslyn's Corps joined the Army, and took its Position in Second Line covering the Center.

The Advanced Squadron of His Majesty's Gun-Brigs and Bomb-Vessels having taken a Position near the Entrance of the Harbour, within the Crown-Battery, were attacked at Ten in the Morning by all the Enemy's Gun-Boats and Praams, supported by the Fire of the Crown-Battery, Block-Ship, and some of the Works; having maintained this Position for several Hours, they at length retired, some of them having been more than once on Fire by Red-hot-Shot. The Batteries near the Mill having acted with Effect upon the Gun-Boats, the latter turned their Fire upon them, but were obliged to retire with considerable Loss.

24th. At Three in the Morning the Army was under Arms; the Center advanced its Position to the Height near the Road which runs in a Direction parallel to the Defences of Copenhagen, to Fredereicksberg, occupying that Road and some Posts beyond it. The Guards at the same Time occupied the Suburbs between Fredereicksberg and Copenhagen, flanked by a Detachment of the 79th. They dislodged a Piquet of the

Enemy, who in their Retreat concealed Thirteen Three-Pounders, which have since been found.

All the Piquets of the Enemy fell back to the Lakes or Inundations in front of the Place; our Piquets occupying their Ground. In the Afternoon the Garrison shewed itself on all the Avenues heading from the Town, apparently with a Design either to recover their Ground, or to burn the Suburbs. The several Generals immediately drove them in, each in his own Front, at the same Time seized all the Suburbs on the North Bank of the Lakes, some of which Posts are within Four Hundred Yards of the Ramparts.

Sir David Baird's Division turned and carried a Redoubt which the Enemy had been some Days constructing, and which was that Night converted into a Work against him.

The Enemy set Fire to the End of the Suburb nearest to the Place, the upper Part of which was occupied by the Guards, and was now defended by them. In consequence of this general Success the Works which had been intended and begun by us, were abandoned, and a new Line was taken, within about Eight Hundred Yards of the Place, and nearer to it on the Flanks.

25th. The Mortar-Batteries in the advanced Line made considerable Progress. A heavy Fire was kept up by the Garrison on the Suburbs and Buildings near the Lake, which were strengthened as much as circumstances would allow. The Navy and Artillery employed in landing Ordnance and Stores, and forwarding them to different Parts of the Line. Lieutenant-General the Earl of Rosslyn's Corps, which had a considerable Share in occupying the Suburbs, relieved the Reserve, which moved into second Line.

The Enemy's Gun-Boats made their Appearance in the Channel between Oinache and Zealand, and cannonaded the Guards in the Suburb. Progress made in preparing a Battery to protect the Right from the Gun-Boats. Frequent Skirmishes with Sharpshooters on the Right and Center, and several Shells thrown from the Lines.

26th. Sir Arthur Wellesley with the Reserve, Eight Squadrons of Cavalry and the Horse Artillery, under Major-General Linsengen, the 6th Battalion of the Line King's German Legion, and the Light Brigade of Artillery belonging to the Reserve, marched to Roskeld Kroe. The Gun Boats made an Attack on the Left of our Position, and were twice driven in by the Wind-Mill Batteries, One Boat having blown up, and several others having suffered considerably. The Guards severely cannonaded by the Gun-Boats; the Enemy likewise attempted a Sortie, but was quickly driven back.

27th. At Daybreak the Battery of Four Twenty-four Pounders opened on the Right, and drove in the Gun-Boats, One of which was much damaged. Sir Arthur Wellesley marched in Two Divisions to attack the Enemy in Front and Rear at Koenerup, but he had moved up towards Kioge, upon which Sir Arthur took a Position to cover the besieging Army. General Peiman applied for an Armistice of Thirty-six Hours to remove the Patients from St. John's Hospital. Four Hours was proposed to him, which offer he did not accept, and several Shots were fired through the said Hospital.

28th. Progress made in landing and bringing forward Ordnance and Stores, as well as in making Batteries and Communications.

29th. Sir Arthur Wellesley marched to Kioge, where he completely defeated and dispersed the Enemy, taking upwards of Sixty Officers and One Thousand Five Hundred Men, Fourteen Pieces of Cannon, and a Quantity of Powder and other Stores. The Patients of St. John's Hospital were removed to the Chapel at Fredereicksberg, and adjacent Houses; his Danish General thankfully acceding to this Removal, and declaring that it was not fired upon by the Order, or with his Knowledge..

30th. Batteries nearly finished, Platforms laid, and Two-thirds of the Ordnance mounted. New Battery planned and begun, near the Chalk Mill Wharf.

31st. The Enemy attempted a Sortie on the Right, before Sunrise, and were stopped by a Piquet of the 50th Regiment, commanded by Lieutenant Light.

They persevered for some Time, and were repulsed by the Piquets with Loss. Sir David Baird twice slightly wounded; but did not quit the Field.

The Danish General Oxholm arrived with his Officers at Head-Quarters, when they were put on Parole, and sent to their respective Homes.

In the Evening One Thousand Five Hundred Prisoners were distributed in the Fleet.

The Batteries in Progress; all armed and completed, except the Chalk-Kiln-Battery, which is close to the Enemy.

The Gun-Boats attacked the In-shore Squadron of Light Vessels; blew up one of them, and obliged them to retire; the Gun-Boats, as well as the Block-Ship, having apparently suffered considerable-Damage from the Batteries at the Wind-Mill.

September 1. The Mortar-Batteries being nearly ready for Action, the Place was summoned. The Answer arriving late, accompanied by a Desire, on his Part, to take the Pleasure of His Danish Majesty, the Reply could not he sent till the following Day: during all these Days the Enemy has fired from the Walls and Outworks with Cannon and Musketry upon the Advanced Posts, and has thrown many Shells on all Parts of the Line, but has had no Success, except in setting Fire to some Houses, and cutting some Trees on his own Side of the Lakes.

(Signed) CATHCART.

Head-Quarters, before Copenhagen,
September 2, 1807.

MY LORD

I HAVE the Honour to transmit herewith the Report of the Expedition undertaken by Brigadier-General Von der Decken; in the Course of which he made a great Number of Troops capitulate, and also took Possession of the Foundery and Powder-Mills at Friedrickswerk. Amongst the Inclosures is the Capitulation, which has been ratified, and the Commanding General in Copenhagen has actually permitted the Artillerymen included in the Capitulation, but who were serving in the Place, to come out of the Town as prisoners on Capitulation.

The Talents, Zeal, and Activity of the Brigadier-General have rendered him extremely useful on every Occasion which has occurred to employ him.

I have the Honour to be, &c.
(Signed) CATHCART.

Jagerberg, Aug. 19, 1807.

MY LORD,

AFTER I had the Honour to state to your Lordship Yesterday the Capture of Six Waggons loaded with Powder, and also of a considerable Quantity of Arms at Friederickstadt, which I have sent to Major-General Von Linsengen, I learned that a Convoy of One Hundred and Eighty Waggons, loaded with Gunpowder, and escorted by upwards of Five Hundred Men, was on its Way to Friederickstadt, after having in vain attempted to enter Copenhagen by Way of Roeskilde, I resolved to attempt to cut it off from Friedrickswerk, and proceed for that Purpose to Krigume. I was informed here that the said Convoy had passed there Two Hours before, that the Escort was very much fatigued, and had begun to desert. I was told that Friedrickswerk was a very strong Position, defended by a Corps called the Volunteers of that Place, raised by the Crown Prince himself for the Protection of the Powder Mills and Arsenal there. Although the Horses of my Detachment (which was composed of One Hundred Light Dragoons of the 1st Light, including Eighteen Dragoons of the 3d,) were very fatigued, yet I thought it advisable to attempt to take the Place by Surprize. I approached Friedrickswerk at One o'clock of the Morning. Captain Krauckenberg, of the 1st Light Dragoons, succeeded in surprizing an advanced Piquet of Nine Men. In arriving near the Entrance, where we expected to find a Battery, we met an Officer, who informed me that the Commanding Officer was willing to capitulate if I would grant him honourable Terms. After some Conversation with Major Tschering, Aid du-Camp to the Prince, and Governor of that Place, he agreed to surrender with his Corps, (Eight Hundred and Sixty strong, including Officers,) under the Condition that he and his whole Corps should not serve during the War, or until an Exchange had taken place.

I found a great Quantity of Powder (about One Thousand Six Hundred Centners) a Number of Guns and small Arms. As I had no Means to carry off the Powder, and even no Time to destroy it, I was obliged to be satisfied with the Promise of the Major and all the Officers upon Honour, that neither Powder nor Stores should be issued to the Danes. As there was no Means of getting Waggons, I was obliged to be satisfied with carrying off the Four Guns, and half the Arms of the Corps which had surrendered, and which I have delivered to Major-General Linsengen.

I left Friederickswerk this Morning at Five o'Clock, and found myself soon after attacked almost in all the Villages by Peasants armed with Forks, delivered for that Purpose by the Danish Government, the greater Part on Foot, but some on Horseback. The Dragoons took about Fifty of these Peasants and Five Horses without any Loss on our Side. On receiving Information that all the roads in the Woods before and behind Friedrickswerk were full of Peasants (some of which were armed with Rifles), I changed my Road by marching to the Left, where the Ground is open, and I discharged the Peasants after explaining to them the Object of our being in this Country.

I cannot conclude this long Report without certifying to your Lordship my great Satisfaction with the Conduct of the Officers and Men which I have had the Honour to command on this Occasion, and to recommend to your Lordship's Notice Captain Krauckenberg of the 1st Light Dragoons.

I have the Honour to be, &c.
FRIED. VON DECKEN,
Brigadier-General.

Head-Quarters, before Copenhagen,
September 2, 1807.

MY LORD,

Having stated to your Lordship in my Dispatch of the 22d the Preparation of Force which was assembling under Lieutenant-General Castenschiold, and my Intention of detaching a Force to disperse them before they should be in a State to undertake any Enterprize; I have now the greatest Pleasure in transmitting the Report I have received from Sir Arthur Wellesley, to whom, with the Assistance of Major-General De Linsengen, and Brigadier-General Stewart, that Service was entrusted.

The Major General marched on the 26th of last Month to Roeskild Kroe, and proceeded on the following Day to attack the Position at Borneruk, which was occupied according to the last Reports by the Danes; Major-General Linsengen having made a long Detour towards the Sea, for the Purpose of cutting off their Retreat, and attacking their Rear.

But finding that the Enemy had moved off by the Right to Kioge, Sir Arthur Wellesley fell back to Roeskild Kroe, extending to his Left to cover the besieging Army until the Cavalry and Infantry, who had made a forced March, had Time to refresh. He then proceeded to attack and to defeat the Enemy in general Action. The Deroute appears to have been complete.

Major-General Oxholm was within a Mile of this Action, in his Way to join General Castenschiold, with a Corps collected in the Southern Islands, which had got over. He endeavoured to stop the Fugitives, but could make no effectual Resistance; this Corps would have endeavoured to connect itself with some Sortie from the Place, and would soon have been troublesome.

Sir Arthur Wellesley has moved into the Center of the Island to disarm and quiet the Country.

The only Corps which appears to have kept together is the Cavalry; but by the last Accounts these have been found by the Patroles, and will be followed up.

The General and his Officers, who are mostly of their Militia; have been released on a very strict Parole; the General being responsible for them; but their Men, One Thousand Five Hundred, to which near One Hundred have since been added, are distributed in His Majesty's Line of Battle Ships; the dread of which will perhaps, induce the remaining Militia of this Description to be averse to quitting their Homes.

I trust it will appear that, the Affair of the 29th, at Kioge, is as useful as it is brilliant.

I have the Honour to be, &c.
(Signed) CATHCART.

Kioge, August 29, 1807.

MY LORD,

ACCORDING to the Intention which I announced to your Lordship on the Evening of the 27th, I moved to Roeskild Kroe, and placed Colonel Reden at Vallensbrek; and General Linsengen marched Yesterday Morning to Roskild; by these different Movements his Force became the Right instead of the Left.

Having had Reason to believe that the Enemy still remained at Kioge, I determined to attack him this Day. I settled with General Linsengen, that he should cross the Kioge Rivulet at Lille Sellyas, and turn the Enemy's Left Flank, while I should move along the Sea Road towards Kioge, and attack him in Front.

Both Divisions broke up this Morning, and marched according to the Plan concerted. Upon my approach to Kioge, I found the Enemy in Force on the North Side of the Town and Rivulet, and they commenced a Cannonade upon the Patroles of Hussars in my Front; they had Three or Four regular Battalions formed in one Line, with Cavalry on both Flanks, and apparently a large Body beyond the Town and Rivulet. At the Time agreed upon with General Linsengen, I formed my Infantry in One Line, with the Left to the Sea, having the Two Squadrons of Hussars upon the Right. There had been some Appearance of a Movement by the Enemy to their Left; and I had not had any Communication with General Linsengen, and was not certain that he had passed the Rivulet, I therefore thought it proper to make the Attack in an Echellon of Battalions from the Left; the whole covered by the Fire of our Artillery.

It fell to the Lot of the 92d Regiment to lead this Attack, and they performed their Part in the most exemplary Manner, and were equally well supported by the 52d and 43d.

The Enemy soon retired to an Entrenchment which they had formed in Front of a Camp on the North Side of Kioge, and they made a Disposition of their Cavalry upon the Sands to charge the 92d in Flank while they should attack this Entrenchment. This Disposition obliged me to move Col. Reden's Hussars from the Right to the Left Flank, and to throw the 43d into a second Line; and then the 93d carried the Entrenchment, and forced the Enemy to retreat into the Town in Disorder. They were followed immediately in the most gallant Style by Col. Reden and his Hussars, and by the 1st Battalion 95th Regiment, and afterwards by the Whole of the Infantry of my Corps. Upon crossing the Rivulet, we found General Linsengen's Corps upon our Right Flank, and the whole joined in the Pursuit of the Enemy.

Major General Ozhoken, the Second in Command, who had joined the Army with Four Battalions last Night from the Southern Island, attempted to stand in the Village of Hersolge but he was attacked briskly by the Hussars, with Detachments of which were Captain Blaquiere and Captain Cotton of the Staff, and by a small Detachment of the 1st of the 95th; and he was compelled to surrender with Count Wedel Jarlsburg, several other Officers, and Four Hundred Men.

The Loss of the Enemy has been very great, many have fallen, and there are nearly Sixty Officers, and One Thousand One Hundred Men Prisoners.

In their Flight they have thrown away their Arms and Cloathing, and many Stands of the former have fallen into our Hands. I believe that we have taken Ten Pieces of Cannon; but I have not yet received all the Reports from the Detachments employed in the Pursuit of the Enemy. I have not seen General Linsengen, as he is still out with his Hussars, but I understand that the Enemy had destroyed the Bridges at Little Salbye, which was the Cause of the Delay of his Operations upon their Flank.

I cannot close this Letter without expressing to your Lordship my Sense of the good Conduct of the Troops; all conducted themselves with the utmost Steadiness; but I cannot avoid to mention particularly the 92d Regiment, under the Command of Lieutenant-Colonel Napier; the 1st Battalion 95th Regiment, under the Command of Lieutenant-Colonel Beckwith; the British Artillery, under the Command of Captain Newhouse; the Hanoverian Hussars under Colonel Reden, and the Hanoverian Light Artillery, under Captain Sympter, as a Corps that had particular Opportunities of distinguishing themselves; I am also much obliged to General Linsengen and to Brigadier-General Stewart, for the Assistance I received from them in the Formation and Execution of the Plan by which the Enemy have been defeated. The Officers of the Staff have also rendered me much Assistance; and I must particularly mention Captain Blaquiere and Captain Campbell.

I have the Honour to be, &c.
(Signed) ARTHUR WELLESLEY.

P.S.   We have taken a large Store of Powder and other Military Stores in this Town, which I propose to destroy, if I should not be able to prevail upon the Captain of one of His Majesty's Ships to take Charge of them.

Head-Quarters before Copenhagen,
September 3, 1807.

MY LORD,

I HAVE the Honour to inclose an Extract of a Letter, dated Brasenborg, September 2, 1807, which has been received from Major-General Sir Arthur Wellesley, covering a Report of Major-General Linsengen's Proceedings on the 29th Ultimo, and containing an Account of the present State of Operations in that Quarter.

Sir Arthur has established his Head Quarters between Ringstedt, Roeskild, and Kioge, from whence he has sent strong Patroles and reconnoitring Parties in different Directions. General Linsengen is at Ringstedt; and they are not without Hopes of finding General Castenschiold and the Cavalry, and of reducing any Assembly of Militia or other Troops that may remain.

A Return of the Ordnance and Stores taken and destroyed, or embarked in His Majesty's Ships, at Kioge, the Amount of which is very considerable, will be transmitted as soon as it can be made up.

I have the Honour to be, &c.
(Signed) CATHCART.

Extract of a letter from Major-General Sir Arthur Wellesley, K.B. dated
Brasenborg, September 2, 1807.
Ringstedt. September 1, 1807.

SIR,

I HAVE the Honour herewith to transmit a detailed Relation of the Engagement before Kioge, on the 29th Instant, in as far as it was connected with the Troops I had the Honour to command on that Day.

I remain, &c.
(Signed) LINSENGEN, Major-General.

Ringstedt, August 31, 1807.

SIR,

THE Right Column, consisting of Six Squadrons of the 1st, 2d, and 3d Light Dragoons, King's German Legion, Five Companies of the 95th, half a Battery of Horse Artillery, the 43d Foot, and the 6th Line Battalion, King's German Legion, broke up from Roskiold by Five o'Clock on the 29th Instant, reached Arstead by Eight o'Clock, when Two Squadrons, that had been sent the Night before from Roskiold to Arstead, did join the Division. This Detachment, under the Command of Major Grote, 1st Light Dragoons, had been sent to Arstead for the Purpose to get Information with regard to the Enemy at and in the Neighbourhood of Ringstedt and Kioge. The Major took Two Prisoners in the Night; the one carrying Dispatches directed to a Danish General, and detailing all our Marches, and ascertaining the Strength of our Corps. The Major likewise took Thirty Waggons with Provisions. The Column again, after a short Halt, moved towards Laddger, on the Road to Eigbye; having reached the former Place, some armed Militia, and small Detachments, were seen towards Eigbye.

As it was my Intention to cross the Rivulet that runs from Gungard to Kioge at Yderholm or Littenge Gaard, I detached One Squadron, One Gun, and Two Companies of the 95th Riflemen, to the Right, to reconnoitre, either Passage, under the Command of Major Plessen of the 1st Light Dragoons. The Grounds between Eigbye and Dalbye being greatly covered with Wood, intersected by a large Morass, and found impracticable for a Column to pass, the Passage at Yderholm was given up, and that of Littenge Gaard forced on. The Detachment under Major Plessen went along the left Bank of the Rivulet by Spanager to protect the Right of the Column, which moved on by Eigbye at about Half past Nine o'Clock A.M. The Cavalry being arrived at the Banks of the Rivulet near Littenge Gaard, the Planks over the Bridge had been taken up, and nothing remained for the Cavalry and Part of the Horse Artillery, but to ford the Rivulet, which they instantly did, and advancing along the Right Bank of it, halted to await the Infantry and the Rest of the Horse Artillery, who by this Time had arrived in close Column at the Bridge. The Pioneers of the 6th Battalion of the Line repaired it so far in Twenty five Minutes' Time, that the Infantry were enabled to pass by single Files (which retarded much the Progress of the Column) whilst the Rest of the Horse Artillery passed through the Ford. Till now the Enemy did not in the least attempt to oppose us. After having passed the Bridge, the Infantry moved on in close Columns through Littenge Gaard on the Road to Kioge between the Rivulet and the Wood. Here I ordered Part of the 95th to clear the Woods to the Right of the Column; the Detachment of the 43d to do the same in front; and forming the 6th Battalion and the Rest of the 43d in Line, advanced with them and the Horse Artillery in the Rear of the Cavalry, Four Squadrons of which had already reached the Plain at the End of the Woods. In the mean while I detached Two Squadrons in the Rear, directing them to cross the Wood on the Right, and to advance upon Swansberg Syllem to the Bridge on the Road between Hortsolge and Soeder. Major Plessen, who took the Command, passed the Wood, which in the meantime had been cleared by the Rifle Corps, and some Sharpshooters of the 6th Battalion, who met with little Opposition, except some Platoon Firing, occasioned by several Divisions of the Enemy's Infantry retreating out of the Woods, the greatest Part of whom were either taken Prisoners or cut to Pieces. It was at this Time that Lieutenant Ruedorss of the 1st Light Dragoons was dangerously wounded, together with Lieutenant Jance of the 3d Light Dragoons, whilst gallantly charging some Infantry at the Entrance of the Kioge.

The Cavalry of Colonel Alten having passed the opening between the Woods, I ordered the Horse-Artillery to play upon a Danish Column of Infantry, retreating from Kioge towards the Shore, which Captain Wetzleben executed with as much Precision as Effect; but a few Shots were fired by the Danish Artillery, the same being soon silenced by the superior Firing of the British. The Cavalry during this had taken Eighteen Waggons with Ammunition, Arms, and Accoutrements, and made a few Prisoners.

The Country being much intersected with high Banks and Ditches, did not allow the 6th Battalion and 43d to advance in Line, they were obliged to cross them, by filing in Divisions before they could reach the Plain before the Wood, where they formed the Line again. By this Time the Squadron of Major Plessen having crossed the Wood in Front of Ashay, and advancing across the Plain, overtook about 50 Waggons, partly laden with Baggage, Ammunition, Arms, &c. and being obliged to leave a good Number of Men with them and the Prisoners, they greatly weakened their Strength, and were necessitated to wait the Arrival of the Center, under Colonel Alten, whom I, after he had passed Clemenhap, ordered to advance speedily upon Helsalze, where Part of a Danish Column of Infantry had taken Possession of the Church-Yard. Colonel Alten inclined to the Right with his Squadrons in order to turn the Village; and whilst the Light Artillery opened a Fire upon the Church, and some Riflemen of the 95th assailed it in Flank, he and Lieutenant Schnuring, of the 2d Light Dragoons, rapidly advanced with Sixteen Hussars, obliged the Danish General Oxenholm, Four Officers, and about One Hundred and Fifty Privates, to lay down their Arms; on this Occasion a Corporal, of the 2d Light Dragoons was shot, and several Horses wounded. The Village having been taken, the Cavalry, joined by the Horse Artillery, followed up their Advantage, by pursuing the Enemy towards Soeder, where many Prisoners were made.

The Infantry being unable to follow the rapid Movements of the Cavalry, took a Position near Swansberg; and perceiving the Enemy completely routed, I took the Road through the Wood by Fuagerod, and from thence to Giersler, in order to pursue the Enemy in the Right Flank, and watch his Movements in his Retreat, protecting at the same Time the Flanks of my Cavalry that had advanced towards the Heights of Soeder, losing Sight of the Enemy. The Cavalry of my Division received Orders, with the 95th Rifle Corps, to fall back to us to take a Position, with their advanced Posts from Lillenge Gaard by Ashay, Swansberg. Sillecrass, and Vinkiold, to cover the Head-Quarters at Kioge.

The 6th Battalion, Part of the 43d Foot, some Horse Artillery, and a few Cavalry, followed me to Giersler, and, with some Detachments, pursued the retreating Enemy towards the Plains of Ringstedt.

The Conduct of both Officers and Men on this Occasion claims my warmest Thanks; and I beg Leave to bring to your Notice Colonel Hohnstedt, who commanded the Infantry, and Colonel Alten, who led the Cavalry, and Lieutenant Wade, at the Head of the Rifle Corps and Light Infantry, who all Three by their Zeal and Attention greatly assisted me.

I have the Honour to be, &c.
(Signed) LINSENGEN, Maj-Gen.

Head-Quarters before Copenhagen,
September 3, 1807.

MY LORD,

FORTY-EIGHT Mortars and Howitzers of different Natures being in Battery, and Twenty Twenty-four Pounders, I proposed to the Admiral to summon the Place on the 1st Instant, offering the Terms which we had agreed to propose at this Period, for the Reasons stated in my Dispatch of the 31st Ultimo.

I have now the Honour to inclose Copies of the Summons, of the Answer thereto, and of our Reply to that Answer; which last was sent as soon as Communication could be had with the Admiral on board, and closed the Correspondence.

At Half past Seven in the Afternoon, all our Batteries opened for the first Time, and the Town was set on Fire by the first general Flight of Shells.

It was afterwards on Fire in another Quarter.

The Navy also threw some Shells, and the Firing continued on Shore Twelve Hours without producing any Overture on the Part of the Garrison.

The Enemy's Fire was very slack during the Night, and Progress has been made in the new Works of Attack.

I have the Honour to be, &c.
(Signed) CATHCART.

5

BATTLE OF ROLIÇA

Downing-Street, September 2, 1808.

DISPATCHES, of which the following are Copies and Extracts, were last Night received from Lieutenant-General Sir Harry Burrard and Lieutenant-General Sir Arthur Wellesley, dated from Head Quarters at Louriiha, addressed to Viscount Castlereagh, one of His Majesty's Principal Secretaries of State, and brought by Captain Campbell, Aid-de-Camp to Sir Arthur Wellesley.

Head Quarters, Villa Verde, August 17, 1808.

MY LORD,

THE French General Laborde having continued in his Position at Roleia, since my arrival at Caldas on the 15th Instant, I determined to attack him in it this Morning. Roleia is situated on an Eminence, having a Plain in its Front, at the End of a Valley, which commences at Caldas, and is closed to the Southward by Mountains, which join the Hills forming the Valley on the Left, Looking from Caldas. In the Centre of the Valley and about Eight Miles from Roleia, is the town and old Moorish Fort of Óbidos, from whence the Enemy's Picquets had been driven on the 15th; and from that Time he had Posts in the Hills on both Sides of the Valley, as well as in the Plain in Front of his Army, which was Posted on the Heights in front of Roleia, its Right resting upon the Hills, its Left upon an Eminence on which was a Windmill, and the Whole covering Four or Five Passes into the Mountains on his Rear.

I have Reason to believe that his Force consisted of at least Six Thousand Men, of which about Five Hundred were Cavalry, with Five Pieces of Cannon; and there was some reason to believe that General Loison, who was at Rio Mayor Yesterday, would join General Laborde by his Right in the Course of the Night. The Plan of Attack was formed accordingly, and the Army, having broken up from Caldas this Morning, was formed into Three Columns. The right, consisting of Twelve Hundred Portuguese Infantry and Fifty Portuguese Cavalry, destined to turn the Enemy's Left, and penetrate into the Mountains in his Rear; the Left, consisting of Major General Ferguson's and Brigadier- General Bowes's Brigade of Infantry, Three Companies of Riflemen, a Brigade of Light Artillery, and Twenty British, and Twenty Portuguese Cavalry, was destined, under the Command of Major General Ferguson, to ascend the Hills at Œbidos, to turn all the Enemy's Posts on the Left of the Valley, as well as the Right of his Post at Roleia. This Corps was also destined to watch the Motions of General Loison on the Enemy's Right, who, I had heard, had moved from Rio Mayor towards Alcoentré last Night. The Centre Column, consisting of Major-General Hill's, Brigadier-General Nightingale's, Brigadier-General Craufurd's, and Brigadier-General Fane's Brigades (with the Exception of the Riflemen detached with Major General Ferguson), and Four Hundred Portuguese Light Infantry, the British and Portuguese Cavalry, a Brigade of Nine-Pounders, and a Brigade of Six-Pounders, was destined to attack General Laborde's Position in the Front.

The Columns being formed, the Troops moved from Œbidos about Seven o'clock in the Morning. Brigadier-General Fane's Riflemen were immediately detached into the Hills on the Left of the Valley, to keep up the Communication between the Centre and Left Columns, and to protect the March of the former along the Valley, and the Enemy's Posts were successively driven in. Major-General Hill's Brigade, formed in Three Columns of Battalions, moved on the Right of the Valley, supported by the Cavalry, in order to Attack the Enemy's Left; and Brigadier-Generals Nightingale and Craufurd moved with the Artillery along the high Road, until at length the Former formed in the Plain immediately in the Enemy's Front, supported by the Light Infantry Companies, and the 45th Regiment of Brigadier-General Craufurd's Brigade; while the Two other Regiments of this Brigade (the 50th and 91st), and Half of the Nine-pounder Brigade, were kept up as a Reserve in the Rear.

Major-General Hill and Brigadier-General Nightingale advanced upon the Enemy's Position, and at the same Moment Brigadier-General Fane's Riflemen were in the Hills on his Right, the Portuguese in a Village upon his Left, and Major-General Ferguson's Column was descending from the Heights into the Plain. From this Situation the Enemy retired by the Passes into the Mountains with the utmost Regularity and the greatest Celerity; and notwithstanding the rapid Advance of the British Infantry, the want of a sufficient Body of Cavalry was the Cause of his Suffering but little Loss on the Plain.

It was then necessary to make a Disposition to Attack the formidable Position which he had taken up.

Brigadier-General Fane's Riflemen were already in the Mountains on his Right; and no Time was lost in attacking the different Passes, as well to support the Riflemen as to defeat the Enemy completely.

The Portuguese Infantry were ordered to move up a Pass on the Right of the whole; the Light Companies of Major-General Hill's Brigade, and the 5th Regiment, moved up a Pass next on the Right; and the 29th Regiment, supported by the 9th Regiment, under Brigadier-General Nightingale, a third Pass; and the 45th and 82d Regiments, Passes on the Left.

These Passes were all difficult of Access, and some of them were well defended by the Enemy, particularly that which was attacked by the 29th and 9th Regiments. These Regiments attacked with the utmost Impetuosity, and reached the Enemy before those whose Attacks were to be made on their Flanks: the Defence of the Enemy was desperate; and it was in this Attack principally that we sustained the Loss which we have to lament, particularly of that gallant Officer, the Honourable Lieutenant-Colonel Lake, who distinguished himself upon this Occasion. The Enemy was, however, driven from all the Positions he had taken in the Passes of the Mountains, and our Troops were advanced in the Plains on their Tops. For a considerable Length of Time the 29th and 9th Regiments alone were advanced to this Point, with Brigadier-General Fane's Riflemen at a Distance on the Left, and they were afterwards supported by the 5th Regiment, and by the Light Companies of Major-General Hill's Brigade, which had come upon their Right, and by the other Troops ordered to ascend the Mountains, who came up by Degrees.

The Enemy here made Three most gallant Attacks upon the 29th and 9th Regiments, supported as I have above stated, with a View to cover the Retreat of his defeated Army, in all of which he was, however, repulsed; but he succeeded in effecting his Retreat in good Order, owing principally to my Want of Cavalry, and, secondly, to the Difficulty of bringing up the Passes of the Mountains, with celerity, a sufficient number of Troops and of Cannon to support those which had first ascended. The Loss of the Enemy has, however, been very great, and he left Three Pieces of Cannon in our Hands.

I cannot sufficiently applaud the Conduct of the Troops throughout this Action. The Enemy's Positions were formidable, and he took them up with his usual Ability and Celerity, and defended them most gallantly. But I must observe, that although we had such a Superiority of Numbers employed in the operations of this day, the troops actually engaged in the Heat of the Action were, from unavoidable Circumstances, only the 5th, 9th, 29th, the Riflemen of the 95th and 60th, and the Flank Companies of Major-General Hill's brigade; being a Number by no means equal to that of the Enemy - their Conduct therefore deserves the highest Commendation.

I cannot avoid taking this Opportunity of expressing my Acknowledgments for the Aid and Support I received from all the general and other Officers of this Army. I am particularly indebted to Major-General Spencer for the Advice and Assistance I received from him; to Major-General Ferguson, for the Manner in which he led the Left Column; and to Major-General Hill, and Brigadier-Generals Nightingale and Fane, for the Manner in which they conducted the different Attacks which they led. I derived most material assistance also from Lieutenant-Colonel Tucker and Lieutenant-Colonel Bathurst, in the Offices of Deputy-Adjutant and Deputy Quarter-Master General, and from the Officers of the Staff employed under them. I must also mention that I had every Reason to be satisfied with the Artillery under Lieutenant-Colonel Robe.

I have the honor to be, &c.

(Signed)ARTHUR WELLESLEY.

6

BATTLE OF VIMEIRO

Head-Quarters Maceira,21 August, 1808.

MY LORD,

THE Report which I have the Honour to inclose to your Lordship, made at my Request by Lieutenant-General Sir Arthur Wellesley, conveys Information which cannot but prove highly gratifying to His Majesty.

On my landing this Morning, I found that the Enemy's Attack had already, commenced, and I was fortunate enough to reach the Field of Action in Time to witness and approve of every Deposition that had been, and was afterwards made by Sir Arthur Wellesley, his comprehensive Mind furnishing a ready Resource in every Emergency, and rendering it quite unnecessary to direct any Alteration.

I am happy on this Occasion to bear Testimony to the great Spirit and good Conduct displayed by the troops composing this gallant Army in this well contested Action.

I send this Dispatch by Captain Campbell, Aid-de-Camp to Sir Arthur Wellesley, no Person being better qualified to give your Lordship Information.

I have the Honour to be, &c.

(Signed) HARRY BURRARD,
Lieutenant-General.

To Lieut. General Sir H. Burrard, Bart Vimeira, 21st August, 1808.

SIR,

I HAVE the honor to inform you, that the Enemy attacked us in our Position at Vimeira this Morning. The Village of Vimiera stands in a Valley, through which, runs the River Maceira; at the Back, and to the Westward and Northward of this Village, is a Mountain, the Western Point of which touches the Sea, and the Eastern is separated by a deep ravine from the Heights, over which passes the Road which leads from Lourinha, and the Northward to Vimeira. The greater Part of the Infantry, the 1st, 2d, 3d, 4th, 5th, and 8th Brigades, were posted on this Mountain, with Eight

Pieces of Artillery, Major-General Hill's Brigade being on the Right, and Major-General Ferguson's on the Left, having one battalion on the heights separated from the Mountain. On the Eastern and Southern side of the Town is a Hill, which is entirely commanded, particularly on its Right, by the Mountain to the Westward of the Town, and commanding all the Ground in the neighbourhood to the Southward and Eastward, on which Brigadier-General Fane was posted with his Riflemen, and the 50th Regiment, and Brigadier-General Anstruther with his Brigade, with half a Brigade of Six-pounders, and half a Brigade of Nine-pounders, which had been ordered to the Position in the Course of last Night. The Ground over which passes the Road from Lourinha commanded the Left of this Height, and it had not been occupied, excepting by a Picquet, as the camp had been taken up only for one night, and there was no Water in the Neighbourhood of this Height.

The Cavalry and the Reserve of Artillery were in the Valley, between the Hills on which the Infantry stood, both flanking and supporting Brigadier-General Fane's Advanced Guard.

The Enemy first appeared about Eight o'clock in the Morning, in large Bodies of Cavalry on our left, upon the Heights on the Road to Lourinha; and it was soon obvious that the Attack would be made upon our Advanced Guard and the Left of our Position; and Major-General Ferguson's Brigade was immediately moved across the Ravine to the Heights on the Road to Lourinha, with Three Pieces of Cannon; he was followed successively by Brigadier-General Nightingale, with his Brigade and Three pieces of Cannon; Brigadier-General Acland, and his Brigade, and Brigadier-General Bowes, with his Brigade. These Troops were formed (Major General Ferguson's Brigade in the first Line, Brigadier-General Nightingale's in the Second, and Brigadier-General Bowes's and Acland's, in Columns in the Rear) on those Heights, with their Right upon the Valley which leads into Vimeira, and their Left upon the other Ravine, which separates these Heights from the Range which terminates at the Landing Place at Maceira. On the last mentioned Heights the Portuguese Troops, which had been in the Bottom near Vimeira, were posted in the first Instance, and they were supported by Brigadier-General Craufurd's Brigade.

The Troops of the Advanced Guard, on the Heights to the Southward and Eastward of the Town, were deemed sufficient for its Defence, and Major-General Hill was moved to the Centre of the Mountain, on which the great Body of the Infantry had been posted, as a Support to these Troops, and as a Reserve to the whole Army; in addition to this Support, these Troops had that of the Cavalry in the Rear of their Right.

The Enemy's Attack began in several Columns upon the whole of the Troops on this Height; on the Left they advanced, notwithstanding the Fire of the Riflemen, close to the 50th Regiment, and they were checked and driven back only by the Bayonets of that Corps. The 2d Battalion, 43d Regiment was likewise closely engaged with them in the Road which leads into Vimeira; a Part of that Corps having been ordered into the Churchyard, to prevent them from penetrating into the Town. On the Right of the Position they were repulsed by the Bayonets of the 97th Regiment, which

Corps was successfully supported by the 2d battalion 52d, which, by an Advance in Column, took the Enemy in Flank.

Besides this Opposition given to the Attack of the Enemy on the Advanced Guard by their own Exertions, they were attacked in Flank by Brigdier-General Acland's Brigade, in its Advance to its Position on the Heights on the Left, and a Cannonade was kept up on the Flank of the Enemy's Columns by the Artillery on those Heights.

At length, after a most desperate Contest, the Enemy was driven back in Confusion from this Attack, with the Loss of Seven Pieces of Cannon, many Prisoners, and a great Number of Officers and Soldiers killed and wounded. He was pursued by the Detachment of the 20th Light Dragoons, but the Enemy's Cavalry were so much superior in Numbers, that this Detachment has suffered much, and Lieutenant-Colonel Taylor was unfortunately killed.

Nearly at the same Time the Enemy's Attack commenced upon the Heights on the Road to Lourinha. This Attack was supported by a large Body of Cavalry, and was made with the usual impetuosity of French Troops. It was received with Steadiness by Major-General Ferguson's Brigade, consisting of the 36th, 40th, and 71st Regiments, and these Corps charged as soon as the Enemy approached them, who gave Way, and they continued to advance upon him, supported by the 82d, one of the Corps of Brigadier-General Nightingale's Brigade, which, as the Ground extended, afterwards formed a Part of the first Line by the 29th Regiment, and by Brigadier-General Bowes's and Acland's Brigades, whilst Brigadier-General Craufurd's Brigade and the Portuguese Troops, in two Lines, advanced along the Height on the Left. In the Advance of Major-General Ferguson's Brigade, six Pieces of Cannon were taken from the Enemy, with many Prisoners, and vast Numbers were killed and wounded.

The Enemy afterwards made an attempt to recover Part of his Artillery, by attacking the 71st and 82d Regiments, which were halted in a Valley in which it had been taken. These Regiments retired from the Low Grounds in the Valley to the Heights, where they halted, faced about, and fired, and advanced upon the Enemy, who had by that Time arrived in the Low Ground, and they thus obliged him again to retire with great Loss.

In this Action, in which the whole of the French Force in Portugal was employed, under the Command of the Duc D'Abrantes in person, in which the Enemy was certainly superior in Cavalry and Artillery, and in which not more than Half of the British Army was actually engaged, he has sustained a signal Defeat, and has lost Thirteen Pieces of Cannon, Twenty-three Ammunition Waggons, with Powder, Shells, Stores of all Descriptions, and Twenty Thousand rounds of Musket Ammunition. One General Officer has been wounded (Beniere) and taken prisoner, and a great many Officers and Soldiers have been killed, wounded, and taken.

The Valor and Discipline of His Majesty's Troops have been conspicuous upon this Occasion, as you, who witnessed the greatest Part of the Action, must have observed; but it is a Justice to the following Corps to draw your Notice to them in a particular Manner: viz., the Royal artillery, commanded by Lieutenant-Colonel Robe; the 20th Dragoons, which has been commanded by Lieutenat-Colonel Taylor; the 50th Regiment, commanded by Colonel Walker; the 2d Battalion 95th foot, commanded by Major Travers; the 5th Battalion 60th Regiment, commanded by Major Davy; the 2d Battalion 43d, commanded by Major Hull; the 2d Battalion 52d, commanded by Lieutenant-Colonel Ross; the 97th Regiment, commanded by Lieutenant-Colonel Lyon; the 36th Regiment, commanded by Colonel Burne; the 40th, commanded by Lieutenant-Colonel Kemmis; the 71st, commanded by Lieutenat-Colonel Pack; and the 82d Regiment, commanded by Major Eyre.

In mentioning Colonel Burne and the 36th Regiment upon this Occasion, I cannot avoid adding that the regular and orderly Conduct of this Corps throughout the Service, and their Gallantry and Discipline in Action, have been conspicuous.

I must take this Opportunity of acknowledging my Obligations to the General and Staff Officers of the Army. I was much indebted to Major-General Spencer's Judgment and Experience in the Decision which I formed in respect to the Number of Troops allotted to each Point of Defence, and for his Advice and Assistance throughout the Action. In the Position taken up by Major-General Ferguson's Brigade, and in its Advances upon the Enemy, that Officer showed equal Bravery and Judgment; and much Praise is due to Brigadier-General Fane and Brigadier-General Anstruther for their gallant Defence of their Position in Front of Vimeira, and to Brigadier-General Nightingale, for the Manner in which he supported the Attack upon the Enemy made by Major-General Ferguson.

Lieutenant-Colonel G. Tucker, and Lieutenant-Colonel Bathurst, and the Officers in the Departments of the Adjutant and Quarter-Master-General, and Lieutenant-Colonel Torrens and the Officers of my personal Staff, rendered me the greatest Assistance throughout the Action.

> I have the honor to be, &c.
> (Signed) ARTHUR WELLESLEY.

7

BATTLE OF CORUNNA

Downing-Street, January 24, 1809.

THE Honourable Captain Hope arrived late last Night with a Dispatch from Lieutenant-General Sir David Baird to Lord Viscount Castlereagh, one of His Majesty's Principal Secretaries of State, of which the following is a Copy.

His Majesty's Ship Ville de Paris, at Sea, January 18, 1809.

MY LORD

BY the much lamented Death of Lieutenant-General Sir John Moore, who fell in Action with the Enemy on the 16th Instant, it has become my Duty to acquaint your Lordship, that the French Army attacked the British Troops in the Position they occupied in Front of Corunna, at about Two o'Clock in the Afternoon of that Day.

A severe Wound, which compelled me to quit the Field a short Time previous to the Fall of Sir John Moore, obliges me to refer your Lordship for the Particulars of the Action, which was long and obstinately contested, to the inclosed Report of Lieutenant-General Hope, who succeeded to the Command of the Army, and to whose Ability and Exertions in Direction of the ardent Zeal and unconquerable Valour of His Majesty's Troops, is to be attributed, under Providence, the Success of the Day, which terminated in the complete and entire Repulse and Defeat of the Enemy at every Point of Attack.

The Honourable Captain Gordon, my Aide-de-Camp, will have the Honour of delivering this Dispatch, and will be able to give your Lordship any further Information which may be required.

I have the Honour to be, &c.
D. BAIRD, Lieut. Gen.

His Majesty's Ship Audacious off Corunna
January 18, 1809.

SIR,

IN compliance with the Desire contained in your Communication of Yesterday, I avail myself of the first Moment I have been able to command, to detail to you the Occurrences of the Action which took place in Front of Corunna on the 16th Instant.

It will be in your Recollection, that about One in the Afternoon of that Day the Enemy, who had in the Morning received Reinforcements, and who had placed some Guns in Front of the Right and Left of his Line, was observed to be moving Troops towards his Left Flank, and forming various Columns of Attack at that Extremity of the strong and commanding Position which on the Morning of the 15th he had taken in our immediate Front.

This Indication of his Intention was immediately succeeded by the rapid and determined Attack which he made upon your Division which occupied the Right of our Position. The Events which occurred during that Period of the Action you are fully acquainted with. The first Effort of the Enemy was met by the Commander of the Forces, and by yourself, at the Head of the 42d Regiment, and the Brigade under Major-General Lord William Bentinck.

The Village on your Right became an Object of obstinate Contest.

I lament to say, that soon after the severe Wound which deprived the Army of your Services, Lieutenant-General Sir John Moore, who had just directed the most able Disposition, fell by a Cannon-Shot. The Troops, though not unacquainted with the irreparable Loss they had sustained, were not dismayed, but by the most determined Bravery not only repelled every Attempt of the Enemy to gain Ground, but actually forced him to retire, although he had brought up fresh Troops in support of those originally engaged.

The Enemy, finding himself foiled in every Attempt to force the Right of the Position, endeavoured by Numbers to turn it. A judicious and well timed Movement which was made by Major-General Paget, with the Reserve, which Corps had moved out of its Cantonments to support the Right of the Army, by a vigorous Attack, defeated this Intention. The Major-General, having pushed forward the 95th (Rifle Corps) and 1st Battalion 52d Regiments, drove the Enemy before him and in his rapid and judicious Advance, threatened the Left of the Enemy's Position. This Circumstance, with the Position of Lieutenant-General Fraser's Division, (calculated to give still further Security to the Right of the Line) induced the Enemy to relax his Efforts in that Quarter.

They were however more forcibly directed towards the Centre, where they were again successfully resisted by the Brigade under Major-General Manningham, forming the Left of your Division, and a Part of that under Major General Leith, forming the Right of the Division under my Orders. Upon the Left, the Enemy at first contented himself with an Attack upon our Piquets, which however in general maintained their Ground. Finding however his Efforts unavailing on the Right and Centre, he seemed determined to render the Attack upon the Left more serious, and had succeeded in obtaining Possession of the Village through which the great Road to Madrid passes, and which was situated in Front of that Part of the Line. From this Post, however, he was soon expelled, with considerable Loss, by a gallant Attack of some Companies of the 2d Battalion 14th Regiment, under Lieutenant-Colonel Nicholls; before Five in the Evening, we had not only successfully repelled every Attack made upon the Position, but had gained Ground in almost all Points, and occupied a more forward Line, than at the Commencement of the Action, whilst the Enemy confined his Operations to a Cannonade, and the Fire of his Light Troops, with a View to draw off his other Corps. At Six the Firing entirely ceased. The different Brigades were re-assembled on the Ground they occupied in the Morning, and the Piquets and Advanced Posts, resumed their original Stations.

Notwithstanding the decided and marked Superiority which at this Moment the Gallantry of the Troops had given them over an Enemy, who from his Numbers and the commanding Advantages of his position, no doubt expected an easy Victory, I did not, on reviewing all Circumstances conceive that I should be warranted in departing from what I knew was the fixed and previous Determination of the late Commander of the Forces to withdraw the Army on the Evening of the 16th, for the Purpose of Embarkation, the previous Arrangements for which had already been made by his Order, and were in fact far advanced at the Commencement of the Action. The Troops quitted their Position about Ten at Night, with a Degree of Order that did them credit. The whole of the Artillery that remained unembarked, having been withdrawn, the Troops followed in the Order prescribed, and marched to their respective Points of Embarkation in the Town and Neighbourhood of Corunna. The Piquets remained at their Posts until Five on the Morning of the 17th, when they were also withdrawn with similar Orders, and without the Enemy having discovered the Movement.

By the unremitted Exertion of Captains the Honourable H. Curzon, Gosselin, Boys, Rainier, Serret, Hawkins, Digby, Carden, and Mackenzie, of the Royal Navy, who, inpursuance of the Orders of Rear Admiral de Courcy, were entrusted with the Service of embarking the Army; and in consequence of the Arrangements made by Commissioner Bowen, Captains Bowen and Shepherd, and the other Agents for Transports, the Whole of the Army was embarked with an Expedition which has seldom been equalled. With the Exception of the Brigades under Major Generals Hill and Beresford, which were destined to remain on Shore, until the Movements of the Enemy should become manifest, the whole was afloat before Day-Light.

The Brigade of Major-General Beresford, which was alternately to form our Rear-Guard, occupied the Land Front of the Town of Corunna; that under Major-General Hill was stationed in Reserve on the Promontory in Rear of the Town.

The Enemy pushed his Light Troops toward the Town soon after Eight o'Clock in the Morning of the 17th, and shortly after occupied the Heights of St. Lucia, which command the Harbour. But notwithstanding this Circumstance, and the manifold Defects of the Place; there being no Apprehension that the Rear-Guard could he forced, and the Disposition of the Spaniards appearing to be good, the Embarkation of Major-General Hill's Brigade was commenced and completed by Three in the Afternoon; Major-General Beresford, with that Zeal and Ability which is so well known to yourself and the whole Army, having fully explained, to the Satisfaction of the Spanish Governor, the Nature of our Movement, and having made every previous Arrangement, withdrew his Corps from the Land Front of the Town soon after Dark, and was, with all the wounded that had not been previously moved, embarked before One this Morning.

Circumstances forbid us to indulge the Hope, that the Victory with which it has pleased Providence to crown the Efforts of the Army, can be attended with any very brilliant Consequences to Great Britain. It is clouded by the Loss of one of her best Soldiers. It has been atchieved at the Termination of a long and harassing Service. The superior Numbers, and advantageous Position of the Enemy, not less than the actual Situation of this Army, did not admit of any Advantage being reaped from Success. It must be however to you, to the Army, and to our Country, the sweetest Reflection that the Lustre of the British Arms has been maintained, amidst many disadvantageous Circumstances. The Army which had entered Spain, amidst the fairest Prospects, had no sooner compleated its Junction, than owing to the multiplied Disasters that dispersed the Native Armies around us, it was left to its own Resources. The Advance of the British Corps from the Duero, afforded the best Hope that the South of Spain might be relieved, but this generous Effort to save the unfortunate People, also afforded the Enemy the Opportunity of directing every Effort of his numerous Troops, and concentrating all his principal Resources for the Destruction of the only regular Force in the North of Spain.

You are well aware with what Diligence this System has been pursued.

These Circumstances produced the Necessity of rapid and harassing Marches, which had diminished the Numbers, exhausted the Strength, and impaired the Equipment of the Army. Notwithstanding all these Disadvantages, and those more immediately attached to a defensive Position, which the imperious Necessity of covering the Harbour of Corunna for a Time had rendered indispensable to assume, the native and undaunted Valour of British Troops was never more conspicuous, and must have exceeded what even your own Experience of that invaluable Quality, so inherent in them may have taught you to expect. When every one that had an Opportunity seemed to vie in improving it, it is difficult for me, in making this Report, to select particular Instances for your Approbation. The Corps chiefly engaged were the Brigades under Major-Generals Lord William Bentinck, and Manningham and Leith; and the Brigade of Guards under Major-General Warde.

To these Officers, and the Troops under their immediate Orders, the greatest Praise is due. Major-General Hill and Colonel Catlin Crauford, with their Brigades on the Left of the Position, ably supported their Advanced Posts. The Brunt of the Action fell upon the 4th, 42d, 50th, and 81st Regiments, with Parts of the Brigade of Guards, and the 26th Regiment. From Lieutenant-Colonel Murray, Quarter-Master-General, and the Officers of the General Staff, I received the most marked Assistance. I had Reason to regret, that the Illness of Brigadier-General Clinton, Adjutant-General, deprived me of his Aid. I was indebted to Brigadier-General Slade during the Action, for a zealous Offer of his personal Services, although the Cavalry were embarked.

The greater Part of the Fleet having gone to Sea Yesterday Evening, the whole being under Weigh, and the Corps in the Embarkation necessarily much mixed on board, it is impossible at present to lay before you a Return of our Casualties. I hope the Loss in Numbers is not so considerable as might have been expected. If I was obliged to form an Estimate I should say, that I believe it did not exceed in Killed and Wounded from Seven to Eight Hundred; that of the Enemy must remain unknown, but many Circumstances induce me to rate it at nearly double the above Number. We have some Prisoners, but I have not been able to obtain an Account of the Number; it is not, however, considerable. Several Officers of Rank have fallen or been wounded, among whom I am only at present enabled to state the Names of Lieutenant-Colonel Napier, 92d Regiment, Majors Napier and Stanhope, 50th Regiment, killed; Lieutenant-Colonel Winch, 4th Regiment, Lieutenant-Colonel Maxwell, 26th Regiment, Lieutenant-Colonel Fane, 59th Regiment, Lieutenant-Colonel Griffith, Guards, Majors Miller and Williams, 81st Regiment, wounded.

To you, who are well acquainted with the excellent Qualities of Lieutenant General Sir John Moore, I need not expatiate on the Loss the Army and his Country have sustained by his Death. His Fall has deprived me of a valuable Friend, to whom long Experience of his Worth had sincerely attached me. But it is chiefly on public Grounds that I must lament the Blow. It will be the Conversation of every one who loved or respected his manly Character, that, after conducting the Army through an arduous Retreat with consummate Firmness, he has terminated a Career of distinguished Honour by a Death that has given the Enemy additional Reason to respect the Name of a British Soldier. Like the immortal Wolfe, he is snatch'd from his Country at an early Period of a Life spent in her Service; like Wolfe, his last Moments were gilded by the Prospect of Success, and cheared by the Acclamation of Victory; like Wolfe also, his Memory will for ever remain sacred in that Country which he sincerely loved and which he had so faithfully served.

It remains for me only to express my Hope, that you will speedily be restored to the Service of your Country, and to lament the unfortunate Circumstance that removed you from your Station in the Field, and threw the momentary Command Into far less able Hands.

I have the Honour to be, &c.
JOHN HOPE, Lieut. Gen,

8

CAPTURE OF MARTINIQUE

Admiralty-Office, April 12, 1809.

CAPTAIN JOSEPH SPEAR, of HIS Majesty's Sloop the Wolverene, arrived at this Office this Morning with Dispatches fiom Rear-Admiral the Honourable Sir Alexander Cochrane, C.B. Commander in Chief of His Majesty's Ships and Vessels at the Leeward Islands, addressed to the Honourable William Wellesley Pole, of which the following are Copies.

Neptune, Fort-Royal Bay, Martinique, February 25, 1809.

SIR,

BY my letter of the 18th, a duplicate of which accompanies this, together with one of the 4th, the Lords Commissioners of the Admiralty will have been informed, that it was intended to open a fire on the enemy from four-batteries on the succeeding day, in addition to his own guns turned, upon him from Fort Edward, which was accordingly done at half past four in the afternoon, the time appointed.

The enemy at first returned the fire with spirit, but it gradually slackened until the following morning, and then entirely ceased, except at long Intervals, which made it evident he was beaten from his guns.

While the batteries were kept constantly firing on the (Enemy from the Western Side, Captains Barton and Nesham, of the York and Intrepid, with about four hundred seamen and marines, continued to be employed in getting the heavy cannon, mortars, and howitzers, up to Mount Surirey from the Eastern Side of the fort, which was a service of the utmost labour and difficulty, owing to the rains and deepness of the roads, but notwithstanding which, a battery of four twenty-four pounders and four mortars was finished by the 22d, and the guns mounted ready for service.

On the following day several more guns were got up, and ready to be placed in an advanced battery, intended to consist of eight twenty-four-pounders; a similar battery was preparing to the Westward, and the whole would have been in a state to open on the enemy by the 26th, had not a flag of truce been sent from the fort on the 23d, with proposals for a surrender, on the principle of being sent to France on parole; but Lieutenant-General Beckwith, the Commander of the Forces, and myself not judging it proper to accede to such terms, the batteries, which had before opened their fire, recommenced the attack, at half past eight o'Clock in the evening, and continued It without intermission during the night. The next morning; a little past six o'clock, one of the magazines in the Fort blew up with a great explosion, and soon afterwards. Three flags of truce were hoisted, by the enemy, and Hostilities ceased on our Part.

A Letter was then received from the Captain General Villaret Joyeuse requesting that Commissioners might be appointed on both sides to settle the Terms of Capitulation, to which was agreed to and Lieutenant-General Sir George Prevost and Major-General Maitland were named by the Commander of the Forces, and Commodore Cockburn by me. These Officers were met by the General of Artillery Villaret, (the Captain General's Brother) and Colonels Montfort and Boyer, in a tent erected for the purpose between the advanced Piquets on each side, when the terms were settled and ratified before midnight; a copy, of which I have the Honour to enclose.

This morning a detachment of troops took possession of the Bouille Redoubt, and the Ravelines and Gateway of Fort Bourbon on the land side; and the Garrison (a Return of which, as well as the rest of the prisoners taken since the Commencement of the Siege, is enclosed) will be embarked in the course of eight days in transports, and His Majesty's ships Belleisle and Ulysses will proceed with them as a guard to Europe. I now beg Leave to congratulate their Lordships on the happy termination of a Siege, which was by the uncommon exertions of the Army and Navy, brought to a close within twenty-eight days from the failing of the expedition from Barbadoes.

The fire kept up by the batteries was irresistible, the enemy was driven from his defences, his cannon dismounted, and the whole of the interior of the work ploughed up by the shot and shells, within five days after the batteries opened.

Never did more unanimity prevail between the two services than on the present occasion, one sentiment, one Wish pervaded the whole; and they looked with Confidence to a speedy and glorious termination of their toils.

I had on this service the happiness to act with Lieutenant-General Beckwith, an Officer I have long been in the habits of intimacy with, from whose zeal 1 had everything to expect, and which the recent events have so fully realized. He did me the Honour to consult me on various occasions, and his Communications and Co-operation were friendly and cordial, which, on all conjunct Expedition, is the surest Pledge of Success.

I have already informed their Lordships, that I entrusted the whole of the Naval arrangements on shore to Commodore Cockburn. His exertions have been unremitting, and his merit beyond my praise. He speaks in Terms of high approbation of the able support and assistance he received from Captains Barton, Nefham, and Brenton, whom I had selected to act with him. To all these Officers, and the Lieutenants and other Officers, Petty Officers,

Seamen and Marines immediately under their Commands, I feel truly obliged for performing the arduous duties imposed upon them. The seven-gun battery at Folville was entirely fought by Seamen, from which the Enemy suffered severely. I have also the fullest reason to be thankful to the other Officers and Men of the Squadron employed on the blockade and reduction of the Island, for their general activity and emulation.

I subjoin a List of the several Returns and Papers which I have been able to collect, and send herewith.

For any other Information I beg to refer their Lordships to Captain Spear, of the Wolverene, an old and deserving Commander; whom I have entrusted with this Dispatch. I have the Honour to be, &c.

(Signed) ALEX. COCHRANE.

SIR,

HAVING on the 20th January received a Letter from Lieutenant-General Beckwith, informing me that in consequence of some Alteration of Circumstances he was induced to proceed on the Attack of Martinique, and expressing a Wish to see me at Barbadoes, in order to make the final Arrangements, I lost no Time in meeting him there for that Purpose; and having embarked all the Troops, I committed the principal Landing of the Army intended to be put on Shore at Bay Robert, to Captain Beaver, of His Majesty's Ship Acasta, who had Lieutenant-General Beckwith, the Commander of the Forces, with him; Major-General Sir George Prevost, commanding the Division, being embarked on board the Penelope. By the inclosed Letter from Captain Beaver their Lordships will see that he completed this Service, with his usual Ability, on the 30th of January, and Morning of the 31st, whilst the other Division, under Major-General Maitland, was landed on the 30th at Saint Luce, under the Superintendance of captain Fahie, of the Belleisle, who had formed the most judicious Arrangements for the Purpose.

About Six Hundred Men were detached on board His Majesty's Ship York, under the Command of Major Henderson of the Royal York Rangers, to take Possession of the Battery at Point Solomon, in order to secure a safe Anchorage for the Men of War and Transports: after effecting this the Rangers pushed on, and invested the Fort of Pigeon Island, on which a Mortar was brought to bear so early as the 1st Initant, but not finding the Fire of that sufficient, Nine others, including Howitzers, were landed, Five of which were got up to the Top of a commanding Height, by the very great Exertions of Captain Cockburn of the Pompée, and the Seamen under his Orders, who ably gave Support to Brigadier-Generals
Sir Charles Shipley and Scehelin in completing the Batteries, which opened last Night, at Six o'Clock, with such Effect as to oblige the Enemy to capitulate this Morning; and One Hundred and Thirty-six Persons that were in the Fort, surrendered themselves Prisoners of War. Our Less consisted of Two Seamen killed, and One Soldier of the Royal York Rangers wounded. The Enemy's of Five killed and several wounded.

In order to cut off the Retreat of the Enemy, I previously sent the Æolus and

Cleopatra, Frigates, and the Recruit, Sloop of War, to the upper Part of Fort Royal Bay; when this was perceived, the Enemy set Fire to, and destroyed the Amphitrite Frigate, of Forty-four Guns, and all the Shipping in the Harbour; having, on our first Landing, burnt the Carnation at Marin, also a Corvette at St. Pierres on the following Night.

The Army under Lieutenant-General Beckwith having advanced towards the Heights of Surrey, fell in with the Enemy on the 1st Instant, who was defeated with considerable Loss; since then two Actions have taken place, which has given to His Majesty's Forces Possession of the before-mentioned Heights, commanding Fort Bourbon. The Enemy upon this abandoned the lower Fort, or Fort de France, having destroyed the Guns, and from the different Explosions I suppose they have blown up the Magazines.

Major-General Maitland reached Samantin on the 2d without Opposition, and has since formed a Junction with the Lieutenant-General. I am now moving the Squadron to the Fort Royal Side of the Bay, so as to embrace the double View of an early Communication with the Head Quarters of the Army, and affording the Supplies necessary for the Siege of Fort Bourbon on both Sides.

From the Zeal which has manifested itself in each Service, I make no doubt but the Batteries will soon be in a Fit State to open upon the Enemy, and I hope before long, that I shall have the Satisfaction to communicate to their Lordships that, the Fort has surrendered.

The Militia who were forced to serve, have re-turned to their Homes.

I have the Honour to be, &c.
(Signed) ALEX. COCHRANE.

9

BATTLE OF THE BASQUE ROADS

Admiralty-Office, April 21, 1809.

Sir Harry Neale, Bart. First Captain to Admiral Gambier, Commander in Chief of
His Majesty's Ships and Vessels employed in the Channel Soundings &c. arrived
here this Morning with a Dispatch from His Lordship to the Honourable William
Wellesley Pole, of which, the following is a Copy:

Caledonian at Anchor, in Basque Roads, April 14,1809.

SIR,

THE Almighty's Favour to His Majesty and the Nation has been strongly marked in
the Success he has been pleased to give to the Operations of His Majesty's Fleet under
my Command; and I have the Satisfaction to acquaint you, for the Information of the
Lords Commissioners of the Admiralty that the Four Ships of the Enemy named in
the Margin* have been destroyed at their Anchorage, and several others, from getting
on Shore, if not rendered altogether unserviceable, are at least disabled for a
considerable Time.

The Arrangement of the Fire Vessels placed under the Direction of Captain the
Right Honourable Lord Cochrane were made as fully as the State of the Weather
would admit, according to his Lordship's Plan, on the Evening of the 11th Inst.; and
at Eight o'Clock on the same Night they proceeded to the Attack under a favourable
strong Wind from the Northward, and Flood Tide, (preceded by some Vessels filled
with Powder and Shells, as proposed by his Lordship, with a View to Explosion,)
and led on in the most undaunted and determined Manner by Captain Wooldridge, in
the Mediator Fire-Ship, the others following in Succession, but owing to the Darkness
of the Night several Mistook their Course and failed.

On their Approach to the Enemy's Ships, it was discovered that a Boom was placed
in Front of their Line for Defence. This however the Weight of the Mediator soon
broke and the usual Intrepidity and Bravery of British Seamen overcame all

Difficulties. Advancing under a heavy Fire from the Forts in the Isle of Aix, as well as from the Enemy's Ships, most of which cut or slipt their cables and from the confined Anchorage, got on Shore; and thus avoided taking Fire.

At Daylight the following Morning, Lord Cochrane communicated to me by Telegraph, that Seven of the Enemy's Ships were on Shore, and might be destroyed. I immediately made the Signal for the Fleet to unmoor and weigh, intending to proceed with it to effect their Destruction. The Wind however being fresh from the Northward, and the Flood Tide running, rendered it too hazardous to run into Aix Roads (from its shallow Water), I therefore anchored again at the Distance of about Three Miles from the Forts on the Island.

As the Tilde suited, the enemy evinced great Activity in endeavouring to warp their Ships (which had grounded) into deep Water, and succeeded in getting all but Five of the Line towards the Entrance of the Charente before it became practical to attack them.

I gave Orders to Captain Bligh of the Valiant to proceed with that ship, the Revenge, Frigates, Bombs and small Vessels, named in the Margin** to anchor near the Boyant Shoal, in Readiness for the Attack. At Twenty Minutes past Two P.M., Lord Cochrane advanced in the Imperieuse with his accustomed Gallantry and Spirit, and opened a well-directed Fire upon the Calcutta, which struck her Colours to the Imperieuse; the Ships and Vessels above mentioned Soon after joined in the Attack upon the Ville de Varsovie and Aquilon, and obliged them, before Five o'Clock, after sustaining a heavy Cannonade, to strike their Colours, when they were taken Possession of by the Boats of the advanced Squadron. As soon as the Prisoners were removed, they were set on Fire, as was also the Tonnerre, a short Time after by the Enemy.

I afterwards detached Rear-Admiral the Honourable Robert Stopford in the Cæsar with the Theseus, three additional Fire Ships (which were hastily prepared in the Course of the Day), and all the Boats of the Fleet, with Mr. Congreve's Rockets, to conduct the further Operations of the Night against any of the Ships which lay exposed to an Attack. On the Morning of the 13th, the Rear-Admiral reported to me, that as the Caesar and other Line of Battle Ships had grounded, and were in a dangerous Situation, he thought it adviseable to order them all out, particularly as the remaining Part of the Service could be performed by Frigates and small Vessels only; and, I was happy to find that they were extricated from their perilous Situation.

Captain Bligh has since informed me, that it was found impracticable to destroy the Three-decked Ship, and the others which were lying near the Entrance of the Charente, as the former, being the outer one, was protected by Three Lines of Boats placed in advance from her.

This Ship and all the others, except Four of the Line and a Frigate, have now moved up the River Charente. If any further Attempt to destroy them is practicable, I shall not fail to use every Means in my Power to accomplish it.

I have great Satisfaction in stating to their Lordships how much I feel obliged to the zealous Cooperation of Rear-Admiral Stopford, under whose Arrangement the Boats of the Fleet were placed; and I must also express to their Lordships the high

Sense I have of the Assistance I received from the Abilities and unremitted Attention of Sir Harry Neale, Bart. the Captain of the Fleet, as well as of the Animated Exertions of the Captains, Officers, Seamen, and Marines under my Command, and their Forwardness to volunteer upon any Service that might be allotted to them; particularly the Zeal and Activity shewn by the Captains of Line of Battle Ships in preparing the Fire Vessels.

I cannot speak in sufficient Terms of Admiration and Applause, of the vigorous and gallant Attack made by Lord Cochrane upon the French Line of Battle Ships which were on Shore, as well as of his judicious Manner of approaching them, and placing his Ship in the Position most advantageous to annoy the Enemy, and preserve his own Ship; which could not be exceeded by any Feat of Valour hitherto achieved by the British Navy.

It is due to Rear-Admiral Stopford, and Sir Harry Neale, that I should here take the Opportunity of acquainting their Lordships of the handsome and earnest Manner in which both these meritorious Officers had volunteered their Services before the Arrival of Lord Cochrane to undertake an Attack upon the Enemy with Fire Ships; and that, had not their Lordships fixed upon him to conduct the Enterprize, I have full Confidence that the Result of their Effort would have been highly creditable to them.

I should feel that I did not do Justice to the Services of Captain Godfred of the Ætna in bombarding the Enemy's Ships op the 12th, and nearly all the Day of the 13th, if I did not recommend him to their Lordships' Notice; and I cannot omit bearing due Testimony to the anxious Desire expressed by Mr. Congreve to be employed wherever I might conceive his Services in the Management of his Rockets would be useful; some of them were placed in the Fire Ships with Effect, and I have every Reason to be satisfied with the Artillerymen and others who had the Management of them, under Mr. Congreve's Direction.

I send herewith a Return of the Killed, Wounded, and Missing of the Fleet, which I am happy to observe, is comparatively small. I have not yet received the Returns of the Number of Prisoners taken, but I conceive they amount to between Four and Five Hundred.

I have charged Sir Harry Neale with this Dispatch (by the Imperieuse) and I beg Leave to refer their Lordships to him, as also to Lord Cochrane, for any further Particulars of which they may wish to be informed.

I have the Honour to be, &c.
(Signed) GAMBIER.

15th April.

P.S.   This Morning Three of the Enemy's Line of Battle Ships are observed to be still on Shore under Fouras, and One of them is in a dangerous Situation. One of their Frigates (L'lndienne), also on Shore, has fallen over, and they are now dismantling her. As the Tides will take off in a Day or Two, there is every Probability that she will be destroyed.

Since writing the foregoing, I have learnt that the Honourable Lieutenant-Colonel Cochrane (Lord Cochrane's Brother) and Lieutenant Bissett of the Navy, were Volunteers in the Imperieuse, and rendered themselves extremely useful, the former by commanding some of her Guns on the Main Deck, and the latter in conducting one of the Explosion Vessels.

Ville de Varsovie, of 80 Guns; Tonnerre of 74 Guns; Aquilon of 74 Guns; and Calcutta of 54 Guns

Indefatigable, Aigle, Emerald, Pallas, Beagle, Ætna Bomb, Insolent Gun-Brig, Conflict, Encounter, Fervent, and Growler.

10

BATTLE OF OPORTO

Downing-Street, May 24, 1809.

A DISPATCH, of which the following is a Copy, was received this Evening from Lieutenant-General the Right Honourable Sir Arthur Wellesley, by Viscount Castlereagh, one of His Majesty's Principal Secretaries of State.

Oporto, 12th May, 1809.

MY LORD,

I HAD the Honour to apprise your Lordship on the 7th Instant, that I intended that the Army should march on the 9th from Coimbra, to dispossess the Enemy of Oporto.

The Advanced Guard and the Cavalry had marched on the 7th, and the whole had halted on the 8th, to afford Time for Marshal Beresford with his Corps to arrive upon the Upper Douro.

The Infantry of the Army was formed into Three Divisions for this Expedition, of which Two, the Advanced Guard, consisting of the Hanoverian Legion, and Brigadier-General R. Stewart's Brigade, with a Brigade of Six-Pounders, and a Brigade of Three-Pounders, under Lieutenant-General Paget, and the Cavalry under Lieutenant-General Payne, and the Brigade of Guards, Brigadier-General Campbell's and Brigadier-General [Sontag's- *no name in the original*] Brigades of Infantry, with a Brigade of Six-Pounders, under Lieutenant-General Sherbrooke, moved by the High Road from Coimbra to Oporto: and one, composed of Major-General Hill's and Brigadier-General Cameron's Brigades of Infantry, and a Brigade of Six-Pounders, under the Command of Major-General Hill, by the Road from Coimbra to Aveiro.

On the 10th in the Morning, before Daylight, the Cavalry and Advanced Guard crossed the Vouga, with the Intention to surprise and cut off Four Regiments of French Cavalry, and a Battalion of Infantry and Artillery, cantoned in Albergaria Nova and the neighbouring Villages, about Eight Miles from that River, in the last of which we failed; but the superiority of the British Cavalry was evident throughout the Day; we took some Prisoners and their Cannon from them; and the Advanced Guard took up the Position of Oliveira.

On the same Day Major General Hill, who had embarked at Aveiro on the Evening of the 9th, arrived at Ovar, in the Rear of the Enemy's Right; and the Head of Lieutenant-General Sherbrooke's Division passed the Vouga on the same Evening.

On the 11th, the Advanced Guard and Cavalry continued to move on the High Road towards Oporto, with Major General Hill's Division in a parallel Road which leads to Oporto from Ovar.

On the Arrival of the Advanced Guard at Vendas Novas, between Sonto Redondo and Grijon, they fell in with the Outposts of the Enemy's Advanced Guard, which were immediately driven in; and shortly afterwards we discovered the Enemy's Advanced Guard, consisting of about Four Thousand Infantry and some Squadrons of Cavalry, strongly posted on the Heights above Grijon, their Front being covered by Woods and broken Ground. The Enemy's Left Flank was turned by a Movement well executed by Major-General Murray, with Brigadier-General Langwerth's Brigade of the Hanoverian Legion; while the 16th Portuguese Regiment of Brigadier-General Richard Stewart's Brigade attacked their Right, and the Riflemen of the 95th, and the Flank Companies of the 29th, 43d, and 52d of the same Brigade, under Major Way, attacked the Infantry in the Woods and Village in their Centre.

These Attacks soon obliged the Enemy to give way; and the Honourable Brigadier-General Charles Stewart led two Squadrons of the 16th and 20th Dragoons, under the Command of Major Blake, in Pursuit of the Enemy, and destroyed many and took several Prisoners.

On the Night of the 11th the Enemy crossed the Douro, and destroyed the Bridge over that River.

It was important, with a View to the Operations of Marshal Beresford, that I should cross the Douro immediately; and I had sent Major-General Murray in the Morning with a Battalion of the Hanoverian Legion, a Squadron of Cavalry, and Two Six-Pounders, to endeavor to collect Boats, and, if possible, to cross the River at Avintas, about Four Miles above Oporto; and I had as many Boats as could be collected brought to the Ferry, immediately above the Towns of Oporto and Villa Nova.

The Ground on the Right Bank of the River at this Ferry is protected and commanded by the Fire of Cannon, placed on the Height of the Serra Convent at Villa Nova, and there appeared to be a good Position for our Troops on the opposite Side of the River, till they should be collected in sufficient Numbers.

The Enemy took no Notice of our Collection of Boats, or of the Embarkation of the Troops, till after the First Battalion (the Buffs) were landed, and had taken up their Position, under the Command of Lieutenant General Paget, on the opposite Side of the River.

They then commenced an Attack upon them, with a large Body of Cavalry, Infantry, and Artillery, under the Command of Marshal Soult, which that Corps most gallantly sustained till supported successively by the 48th and 66th Regiments, belonging to Major General Hill's brigade, and a Portuguese Battalion, and afterwards by the First Battalion of Detachments belonging to Brigadier-General Richard Stewart's Brigade.

Lieutenant-General Paget was unfortunately wounded soon after the Attack commenced, when the Command of these gallant Troops devolved upon Major General Hill.

Although the French made repeated Attacks upon them, they made no Impression, and at last, Major General Murray having appeared on the Enemy's Left Flank on his March from Ovintre, where he had crossed, and Lieutenant-General Sherbrooke, who by this Time had availed himself of the Enemy's weakness in the Town of Oporto, and had crossed the Douro at the Ferry between the Towns of Villa Nova and Oporto, having appeared upon their Right with the Brigade of Guards, and the 29th Regiment; the whole retired in the utmost Confusion towards Amarante, leaving behind them Five Pieces of Cannon, Eight Ammunition Tumbrils, and many Prisoners.

The Enemy's loss in killed and wounded in this Action has been very large, and they have left behind them in Oporto 700 sick and wounded.

Brigadier-General the Honourable Charles Stewart then directed a Charge by a Squadron of the 14th Dragoons, under the Command of Major Hervey, who made a successful Attack on the Enemy's Rear Guard.

In the different Actions with the Enemy, of which I have above given your Lordship an Account, we have lost some, and the immediate Services of other valuable Officers and Soldiers.

In Lieutenant-General Paget, among the latter, I have lost the Assistance of a Friend, who had been most useful to me in the few Days which had elapsed since he had joined the Army.

He had rendered a most important Service at the Moment he received his Wound, in taking up the Position which the Troops afterwards maintained, and in bearing the first Brunt of the Enemy's Attack.

Major Hervey also distinguished himself at the Moment he received his Wound in the Charge of the Cavalry on this Day.

I cannot say too much in Favour of the Officers and Troops. They have marched in Four Days over Eighty Miles of most difficult Country, have gained many important Positions, and have engaged and defeated Three different Bodies of the Enemy's Troops.

I beg particularly to draw your Lordship's Attention to the Conduct of Lieutenant-General Paget, Major-General Murray, Major-General Hill, Lieutenant-General Sherbrooke, Brigadier-General the Honourable Charles Stewart. Lieutenant-Colonel Delancey, Deputy Quarter-Master-General, and Captain Mellish, Assistant Adjutant-General, for the Assistance they respectively rendered General the Honourable Charles Stewart in the Charge of the Cavalry this day and on the 11th, Major Colin Campbell, Assistant Adjutant-General, for the Assistance he rendered Major-General Hill in the Defence of his Post, and Brigadier-General the Honourable-Charles Stewart in the Charge of the Cavalry this Day, and Brigade-Major Fordyce, Captain Currie, and Captain Hill, for the Assistance they rendered General Hill.

I have also to request your Lordship's Attention to the Conduct of the Riflemen and of the Flank Companies of the 29th, 43d, and 52d Regiments, under the Command of Major Way of the 29th; that of the 16th Portuguese Regiment, commanded by Colonel Machado, of which Lieutenant-Colonel Doyle is Lieutenant-Colonel, that of the Brigade of the Hanoveran Legion, under the Command of Brigadier-General Langwerth; and that of the Two Squadrons of the 16th and 20th Light Dragoons, under the Command of Major Blake of the 20th in the Action of the 11th: and the Conduct of the Buffs, commanded by Lieutenant-Colonel Drummond; the 48th, commanded by Colonel Duckworth; and 66th, commanded by Major Murray, who was wounded; and of the Squadron of the 14th Dragoons, under the command of Major Hervey, in the Action of this Day.

I have received the greatest Assistance from the Adjutant-General and Quarter-Master-General Colonel Murray, and from all the Officers belonging to those Departments respectively throughout the Service, as well as from Lieutenant-Colonel Bathurst and the Officers of my personal Staff, and I have every Reason to be satisfied with the Artillery and Officers of Engineers.

I send this Dispatch by Captain Stanhope, whom I beg to recommend to your Lordship's Protection: his brother the Honourable Major Stanhope, was unfortunately wounded by a Sabre whilst leading a Charge of the 16th Light Dragoons on the 10th Instant.

I have the honor to be, &c.
(Signed)ARTHUR WELLESLEY.

11

BATTLE OF TALAVERA

Downinng-Street, August 15, 1809.

DISPATCHES, of which the following are Copies and Extracts, were this Day received at the Office of the Lord Viscount Castlereagh, One of His Majesty's Principal Secretaries of State, from Lieutenant-General the Right Honourable Sir Arthur Wellesley, K.B. dated Talavera, 29th July 1809.

Talavera de la Reyna, 29th July, 1809.

MY LORD,

GENERAL CUESTA followed the Enemy's March with his Army from the Alberché, on the Morning of the 24th, as far as Santa Olalla, and pushed forward his Advanced Guard as far as Torrijos. For the Reasons stated to your Lordship in my Dispatch of the 24th, I moved only Two Divisions of Infantry and a Brigade of Cavalry across the Alberche to Cazalegas, under the Command of Lieutenant-General Sherbrooke, with a View to keep up the Communication between General Cuesta and me, and with Sir Robert Wilson's Corps at Escalona.

It appears that General Venegas had not carried into Execution that Part of the Plan of Operations which related to his Corps, and that he was still at Damiel, in La Mancha; and the Enemy, in the Course of the 24th, 25th, and 26th, collected all his Forces in this Part of Spain, between Torrijos and Toledo, leaving but a small Corps of Two Thousand men in that Place.

This united Army thus consisted of the Corps of Marshal Victor, of that of General Sebastiani, and of Seven or Eight Thousand Men, the Guards of Joseph Buonaparte, and the Garrison of Madrid, and it was commanded by Joseph Buonaparte, aided by Marshals Jourdan and Victor, and by General Sebastiani.

On the 26th, General Cuesta's Advanced Guard was attacked near Torrijos and obliged to fall back; and the General retired with his Army on that Day to the left Bank of the Alberché, General Sherbrooke continuing at Cazalegas, and the Enemy at Santa Olalla.

It was then obvious that the Enemy intended to try the Result of a general Action, for which the best Position appeared to be in the Neighbourhood of Talavera; and General Cuesta having consented to take up this Position on the Morning of the 27th, I ordered General Sherbrooke to retire with his Corps to its Station in the Line, leaving General Mackenzie with a Division of Infantry and a Brigade of Cavalry as an Advanced Post in the Wood, on the Right of the Alberché, which covered our Left Flank.

The Position taken up by the Troops at Talavera extended rather more than Two Miles; the Ground was open upon the Left, where the British Army was stationed, and it was commanded by a Height, on which was placed in Echellonand Second Line, a Division of Infantry under the Orders of Major General Hill.

There was a Valley between the Height and a Range of Mountains still farther upon the Left, which Valley was not at first occupied, as it was commanded by the Height before mentioned; and the Range of Mountains appeared too distant to have any Influence on the expected Action.

The Right, consisting of Spanish Troops, extended immediately in Front of the Town of Talavera, down to the Tagus. This Part of the Ground was covered by Olive Trees, and much intersected by Banks and Ditches. The high Road leading from the Bridge over the Alberché was defended by a heavy Battery in Front of a Church, which was occupied by Spanish Infantry.

All the Avenues of the Town were defended in a similar Manner; the Town was occupied, and the Remainder of the Spanish infantry was formed in Two Lines behind the Banks on the Road which led from the Town and the Right to the Left of our Position.

In the Centre, between the two Armies, there was a commanding Spot of Ground, on which we had commenced to construct a Redoubt, with some open Ground in its Rear.

Brigadier-General Alexander Campbell was posted at this Spot with a Division of Infantry, supported in his Rear by General Cotton's Brigade of Dragoons and some Spanish Cavalry.

At about Two o'clock on the 27th, the Enemy appeared in Strength on the Left Bank of the Alberché, and manifested an Intention to attack General Mackenzie's division.

The Attack was made before they could be withdrawn; but the Troops, consisting of General Mackenzie's and Colonel Donkin's Brigades, and General Anson's Brigade of Cavalry, and supported by General Payne with the other Four Regiments of Cavalry in the Plain between Talavera and the Wood, withdrew in good Order, but with some Loss, particularly by the 2d Battalion 87th Regiment, and the 2d Battalion 31st Regiment, in the Wood.

Upon this Occasion, the Steadiness and Discipline of the 45th Regiment, and the 5th Battalion 60th Regiment, were conspicuous, and I had particular Reason for being satisfied with the Manner in which Major-General Mackenzie withdrew this Advanced Guard.

As the Day advanced, the Enemy appeared in larger Numbers on the Right of the Alberché, and it was obvious that he was advancing to a general Attack upon the

Combined Army. Major-General Mackenzie continued to fall back gradually upon the Left of the Position of the Combined Armies, where he was placed in the Second Line in the Rear of the Guards, Colonel Donkin being placed in the same Situation farther upon the Left, in the rear of the King's German Legion.

The Enemy immediately commenced his Attack, in the Dusk of the Evening, by a Cannonade upon the Left of our Position, and by an Attempt with his Cavalry to overthrow the Spanish Infantry, Posted, as I have before stated, on the Right. This Attempt entirely failed.

Early in the Night, he pushed a Division along the Valley on the Left of the Height occupied by General Hill, of which he gained a momentary Possession; but Major-General Hill attacked it instantly with the Bayonet, and regained it.

This Attack was repeated in the Night, but failed, and again, at Daylight on the Morning of the 28th, by Two Divisions of Infantry, and was repulsed by Major General Hill.

Major General Hill has reported to me, in a particular Manner, the Conduct of the 29th Regiment, and of the 1st Battlion 48th Regiment, in these different Affairs, as well as that of Major General Tilson and Brigadier-General Richard Stewart.

We have lost many brave Officers and Soldiers in the Defence of this important Point in our Position; among others, I cannot avoid mentioning Brigade-Major Fordyce and Brigade-Major Gardner; and Major General Hill was himself wounded, but I am happy to say but slightly.

The Defeat of this Attempt was followed about Noon by a general Attack with the Enemy's whole Force upon the whole of that Part of the Position occupied by the British Army.

In consequence of the repeated Attempts upon the Height upon our Left by the Valley, I had placed Two Brigades of British Cavalry in that Valley, supported in the Rear by the Duc d'Alburquerque's Division of Spanish Cavalry.

The Enemy then placed Light Infantry in the Range of Mountains on the Left of the Valley, which were opposed by a Division of Spanish Infantry, under Lieutenant-General De Bassecourt.

The general Attack began by the March of several Columns of Infantry into the Valley, with a view to attack the Height occupied by Major-General Hill. These Columns were immediately charged by the 1st German Light Dragoons and 23d Dragoons, under the Command of General Anson, directed by Lieutenant-General Payne, and supported by General Fane's Brigade of heavy Cavalry; and although the 23d Dragoons suffered considerable Loss, the Charge had the Effect of preventing the Execution of that Part of the Enemy's Plan.

At the same Time, he directed an Attack upon Brigadier-General Alexander Campbell's Position in the Centre of the Combined Armies, and on the Right of the British.

This Attack was most successfully repulsed by Brigadier-General Campbell, supported by the King's Regiment of Spanish Cavalry and two Battalions of Spanish Infantry; and Brigadier-General Campbell took the Enemy's Cannon.

The Brigadier General mentions particularly the Conduct of the 97th, the 2d

Battalion 7th, and of the 2d Battlion of the 53d Regiment, and I was highly satisfied with the Manner in which this Part of the Position was defended.

An attack was also made at the same Time upon Lieutenant-General Sherbrooke's Division, which was in the Left and Centre of the First Line of the British Army. This Attack was most gallantly repulsed by a Charge with Bayonets by the whole Division, but the Brigade of Guards, which were on the Right, having advanced too far, they were exposed on their Left Flank to the Fire of the Enemy's Batteries, and of their retiring Columns, and the Division was obliged to retire towards the original Position, under Cover of the Second Line of General Cotton's Brigade of Cavalry, which I moved from the Centre, and of the 1st Battalion 48th Regiment.

I had moved this Regiment from its original Position on the Height as soon as I observed the Advance of the Guards, and it was formed in the Plain, and advanced upon the Enemy, and covered the Formation of Lieutenant-General Sherbrooke's Division.

Shortly after the Repulse of this general Attack, in which apparently all the Enemy's Troops were employed, he commenced his Retreat across the Alberché, which was conducted in the most regular Order, and was effected during the Night, leaving in our Hands Twenty Pieces of Cannon, Ammunition, Tumbrils, and some Prisoners.

Your Lordship will observe, by the enclosed Return, the great Loss which we have sustained of valuable Officers and Soldiers in this long and hard fought Action with more than double our Numbers. By all Accounts their Loss is Ten Thousand Men. Generals Lapisse and Morlot are killed; Generals Sebastiani and Boulet wounded.

I have particularly to lament the loss of Major-General Mackenzie, who had distinguished himself on the 27th; and of Brigadier-General Langwerth, of the King's German Legion, and of Brigade Major Beckett, of the Guards.

Your Lordship will observe that the Attacks of the Enemy were principally, if not entirely, directed against the British Troops. The Spanish Commander in Chief, his Officers and Troops, manifested every Disposition to render us Assistance, and those of them who were engaged did their Duty; but the Ground which they occupied was so important, and its Front at the same Time so difficult, that I did not think it proper to urge them to make any Movement on the Left of the Enemy while he was engaged with us.

I have Reason to be satisfied with the Conduct of all the Officers and Troops. I am much indebted to Lieut. General Sherbrooke for the Assistance I received from him, and for the Manner in which he led on his Division to the Charge with Bayonets.

To Lieutenant-General Payne and the Cavalry, particularly General Anson's Brigade, to Major-Generals Hill and Tilson, Brigadier-Generals Alexander Campbell, Richard Stewart, and Cameron, and to the Divisions and Brigades of Infantry under their Commands respectively; particularly to the 29th Regiment, commanded by Colonel White, to the 1st Battalion 48th, commanded by Colonel Donellan; afterwards when that Officer was wounded, by Major Middlemore; to the 2d Battalion 7th, commanded by Lieutenant Colonel Sir William Myers; to the 2d Battalion 53d, commanded by Lieutenant-Colonel Bingham; to the 97th, commanded by Colonel

Lyon; to the 1st Battalion of Detachments, commanded by Lieutenant Colonel Bunbury; to the 2d Battalion 30th, commanded by Major Watson; the 45th, commanded by Lieutenant-Colonel Guard; and to the 5th Battalion 60th, commanded by Major Davy.

The Advance of the Brigade of Guards was most gallantly conducted by Brigadier-General Campbell, and, when necessary, that Brigade retired and formed again in the best Order.

The Artillery, under Brigadier-General Howorth, was also throughout these Days of the greatest Service, and I had every Reason to be satisfied with the Assistance I received from the Chief Engineer, Lieutenant-Colonel Fletcher, the Adjutant-General, Brigadier-General the Honourable C. Stewart, the Quarter-Master-General, Colonel Murray, and the Officers of those Departments respectively; and from Colonel Bathurst, and the Officers of my personal Staff.

I also received much Assistance from Colonel O'Lawlor, of the Spanish Service, and from Brigadier-General Whittingham, who was wounded in bringing up the Two Spanish Battalions to the Assistance of Brigadier-General Alexander Campbell.

I send this by Captain Fitzroy Somerset, who will give your Lordship any further Information, and who, I beg Leave to recommend.

> I have the honor to be, &c.
> (Signed) ARTHUR WELLESLEY.

12

THE STORMING
OF FLUSHING

Downing-Street, August 20th 1809.

A DISPATCH of which the following is a Copy, has been received at, the Office of Viscount Castlereagb, one of His Majesty's Principal Secretaries of State, from Lieutenant-General the Earl of Chatham, K. G. dated Head-Quarters, Middleburg, August 11, 1809.

Head-Quarters, Middleburg,
11th August 1809.

MY LORD,

I RECEIVED Yesterday Evening your Lordship's Dispatch of the 8th instant, by the Messenger Mills; and I must entreat of your Lordship, to offer my most dutiful Acknowledgements to His Majesty, for the gracious Approbation he has been pleased to express of my humble Endeavours in his Service; and I shall feel the greatest: Satisfaction in communicating to Lieutenant General Sir Eyre Coote, and the General and other Officers, and the Troops employed here under my Command, the Sense which His Majesty entertains of their meritorious Conduct in the Services in which they have been engaged, as well as the Confidence His Majesty feels in their future good Conduct, and which 1 trust, they will not disappoint.

The Enemy has continued to give what Interruption he could to the Progress of our Works; but since the Date of my last Letter, he has attempted no Sortie in any Force. He has endeavoured to cause us some Embarrassment by opening the Sluices at Flushing, and letting in the Salt Water, but this has been attended as yet with little Inconveniences as the necessary Precautions for letting off the Water through the Sluices in our Possession at this Place and at Veer, I have no doubt will be found effectual. The several Batteries will probably be ready to open on the Place either the

12th or 13th; and I shall look with great Anxiety to the Result, as the speedy Reduction of Flushing (particularly under present Appearances) is of the last Importance, as till then so very large a Portion of the Force under my Command is unavoidably detained before it.

The Divisions of Lieutenant-General Lord Rosslyn and Lieutenant-General Lord Huntly, were according to the Intention I mentioned in my last Letter, landed in South Beveland, on the Morning of the 9th Instant, but I am sorry to say that the Division of Transports, with the Cavalry and Artilery Horses, the Heavy Ordnance, Ammunition, and Stores of all Descriptions, have not yet been brought through the Slow Passage. The Moment they appear, it is my Intention to proceed towards Batz; but as till then no Operation can be undertaken, I have thought my Presence here was more useful.

A large Portion of the Flotilla has proceeded up the River to Batz, on which Place I learn that the Enemy had again made an Attack but had been repulsed by the Guns of the Fort.

I have the Honour to be, &c.
(Signed) CHATHAM.

A DISPATCH of which the following is a Copy, was this Day received at the Office of Viscount Castlereagh, one of His Majesty's Principal Secretaries of State, from Lieutenant-General the Earl of Chatham, K. G. dated Head-Quarters, Middleburgh, August 16, 1809.

Head-Quarters, Middleburg, August 16, 1809.

MY LORD,

I HAVE the Honour of acquainting your Lordship, that on the 13th Instant, the Batteries before Flushing being completed, (and the Frigates, Bombs, and Gun Vessels, having at the same Time taken their Stations) a Fire was opened at about Half-past One P.M. from Fifty-two Pieces of Heavy Ordinance, which was vigorously returned by the Enemy. An additional Battery of Six Twenty-four Pounders was completed the same Night, and the whole continued to play upon the Town with little or no Intermission till late on the following Day.

On the Morning of the 14th Instant, about Ten o'Clock, the Line of Battle Ships at Anchor in the Durloo Passage, Led by Rear Admiral Sir Richard Strachan got under weigh, and ranging up along the Sea Line of Defence, kept up as they passed a tremendous Cannonade on the Town for several Hours with the greatest Gallantry and Effect.

About Four in the Afternoon, perceiving that the Fire of the Enemy had entirely ceased, and the Town presenting a most awful Scene of Destruction, being on Fire in almost every Quarter, I directed Lieutenant-General Sir Eyre Coote to send in to summons the Place; General Monnet returned for Answer, that he would reply to the

Summons as soon as he had consulted a Council of War, an Hour had been allowed him for the Purpose, but a Considerable Time beyond it having lapsed without an Answer being received, Hostilities were ordered to recommence with the utmost vigour, and about Eleven o'Clock at Night, one of the Enemy's Batteries, advanced upon the Sea Dyke in Front of Lieutenant-General Fraser's Position, was most gallantly carried at the Point of the Bayonet, by Detachments from the 36th, 71st, and Light Battalions of the King's German Legion, under Lieutenant-Colonel Pack, opposed to great superiority of Numbers; they took Forty Prisoners, and killed and wounded a great many of the Enemy.

I must not omit to mention, that on the preceding Evening, an Intrenchment in Front of Major-General Graham's Position, was also forced in a Manner equally undaunted, by the 14th Regiment, and Detachments of the King's German Legion, under Lieutenant-Colonel Nicolls, who drove the Enemy from it, and made a Lodgement within Musket-Shot of the Walls of the Town, taking One Gun and Thirty Prisoners.

About Two in the Morning, the Enemy demanded a Suspension of Arms for Forty-eight Hours which was refused, and only Two Hours granted, when he agreed to surrender according to the Summons sent in, on the Basis of the Garrison becoming Prisoners of War.

I have now the Satisfaction of acquainting your Lordship, that these Preliminaries being acceded to; as soon as the Admiral landed in the Morning, Colonel Long, Adjutant-General, and Captain Cockburn of the Royal Navy, were appointed to negociate the further Articles of Capitulation, which I have now the Honour to enclose. They were ratified about Three this Morning, when Detachments of the Royals on the Right, and of His Majesty's 71st Regiment on the Left, took Possession of the Gates of the Town. The Garrison will march out Tomorrow, and will be embarked as speedily as possible.

I may also congratulate your Lordship on the fall of a Place so Indispensibly necessary to our future Operations, as so large a proportion of our Force being required to carry on the Siege with that degree of Vigour and dispatch, which the means of defence the Enemy possessed, and particularly his powers of Inundation (which was rapidly spreading to an alarming extent) rendered absolutely necessary.

Having hoped, had Circumstances permitted, to have proceeded up the River at an earlier Period. I had committed to Lieutenant General Sir Eyre Coote, the direction of the Details of the Siege, and of the Operations before Flushing, and I cannot sufficiently express my Sense of the unremitting Zeal and Exertion with which he has conducted the arduous Service entrusted to him in which he was ably assisted by Lieutenant-Colonels Walsh and Offerey attached to him, as assistants in the Adjutant and Quarter-Master Generals Department.

I have every reason to be satisfied with the judicious manner in which the General Officers have directed the several Operations as well as with the spirit and intelligence manifested by the Commanding Officers of Corps, and the Zeal and ardour of all Ranks of Officers.

It is with great pleasure, I can report the uniform good conduct of the Troops, who have not only on all occasions shewn the greatest intrepidity in presence of the Enemy, but have sustained, with great pleasure and chearfulness, the laborious duties they have had to perform.

The active and persevering Exertions of the Corps of Royal Engineers have been conducted with much skill and judgement by Colonel Fyers, aided by Lieutenant Colonel D'Arcey, and it is impossible for me to do sufficient Justice to the distinguished Conduct of the Officers and Men of the Royal Artillery, under the able Direction and animating Example of Brigadier General McLeod.

The Seamen, whose Labours had already been so useful to the Army, sought their Reward in a further Opportunity of distinguishing themselves, and One of the Batteries was accordingly entrusted to them, and which they served with admirable Vigor and Effect.

I must here beg to express my strong Sense of the constant and cordial Co-operation of the Navy on all Occasions, and my warmest Acknowledgments are most particularly due to Captain Cockburn of the Belleisle, commanding the Flotilla, and to Captain Richardson of the Cæsar, commanding the Brigade of Seamen landed with the Army.

I have the Honor to enclose a Return of the Garrison of Flushing, in Addition to which I have learned that, besides the Number killed, which was considerable, upwards of One Thousand wounded Men were transported to Cadsand, previous to the complete Investment of the Town.

I also subjoin a Statement of Deserters and Prisoners, exclusive of the Garrison of Flushing.

This Dispatch will be delivered to your Lordship by my First Aid-de-Camp Major Bradford, who is fully qualified to give your Lordship every further Information, and whom I beg Leave earnestly to recommend to His Majesty's Protection.

I have the Honour to be, &c.
(Signed) CHATHAM.

13

INVASION OF GUADELOUPE

Downing-Street, March 15, 1810.

CAPTAIN WILBY, Aid-de-Camp to Lieutenant-General Sir George Beckwith, K. B., commanding His Majesty's Forces in the Windward and Leeward Islands, arrived this Morning with a Dispatch from the Lieutenant-General to the Earl of Liverpool, one of His Majesty's Principal Secretaries of State, of which the following is a Copy.

Guadaloupe, Feb. 9, 1810

MY LORD,

IN obedience to the King's Command to attack this Island, as pointed out in your Lordship's Dispatch of the 2d November last, I have the Honour to report, for His Majesty's Information, that having taken the necessary Measures to collect such a Force as Circumstances admitted, and as I judged adequate to this important Service, and having made every necessary Arrangement with Vice-Admiral Sir Alexander Cochrane, I sailed from Martinique on the 22d Ult. to the Place of general Rendezvous, at Prince Rupert's, Dominica, where we were detained Forty-eight Hours, some of the Transports having fallen to Leeward.

The Army was formed into Five Brigades. The First Brigade, under the Command of Brigadier-General Harcourt, was composed of Five Hundred Light Infantry, Three Hundred of the 15th Foot, including their Flank Companies, and Four Hundred Battalion Men of the 3d West India Regiment.

The Second Brigade, commanded by Brigadier-General Barrow, consisted of Three Hundred Grenadiers, Six Hundred Men of the 25th Regiment, including their Flank Companies, and Three Hundred and Fifty Men of the 6th West India Regiment, including their Flank Companies.

The Third brigade, commanded by Brigadier-General Maclean, consisted of Five Hundred Light Infantry, Five Hundred Men of the 90th Foot, including their Flank

Companies, and Four Hundred Men of the 8th West India Regiment, including their Flank Companies.

The Fourth Brigade, commanded by Brigadier-General Skinner, was composed of a Battalion of Six Hundred Men formed from the 13th and 63d Regiments, a Detachment of Two Hundred Men of the York Light Infantry Volunteers, and the 4th West India Regiment.

The Fifth Brigade, under the Command of Brigadier-General Wale, consisted of Three Hundred Grenadiers, Nine Hundred Men of the Royal York Rangers; to this Force was added Three Hundred Artillery, under the Command of Colonel Burton, with a Company of Military Artificers. These Brigades were formed into Two Divisions and a Reserve.

The First Division, commanded by Major-General Hislop, was composed of the Third and Fourth Brigades; the Second Division, under the Command of Brigadier-General Harcourt, consisted of the First and Second Brigades.

The Fifth Brigade under the Command of Brigadier-General Wale, formed the Reserve.

The Second Division sailed from Dominica on the Morning of the 26th, and anchored at the Saintes. The First Division, with the Reserve, sailed in the course of the Afternoon, and anchored on the 27th at Isle Gosier Grande Terre, and early in the Morning of the 28th, proceeded across the Bay to St. Mary's in Capesterre, in the smaller Vessels of War, other Craft and Flat Boats, where a Landing was effected without Opposition in the course of the Day, and in the Afternoon, the First Division, under the Command of Major-General Hislop, moved forward, the Third Brigade to Capesterre, the Fourth Brigade to Grande Riviere, the Reserve remained to cover the Landing of the necessary Provisions, and other Objects.

On the 29th the First Division marched to the Bannaniers River, where it took Post. The Reserve at the same Time abandoned the Landing-Place at St. Mary's, and reached the Grande Riviere that Night, with Two Days Provisions for the Corps acting to Windward. On the 30th, the First Division advanced by the strong Pass of Trou au Chien, which was not defended, and the Head of the Column reached Three Rivers about Eleven o'Clock, pushing small Detachments on the Enemy with the Light Troops. The Reserve marched early in the Morning from its Position, gaining Three Rivers about Sunset.

The Enemy marked a Disposition to defend the Heights, D'Olot and other Places-strengthened with Field Artillery, but in the Afternoon he abandoned all his Posts with Precipitation, leaving his Ordnance behind.

It became necessary for the First Division and the Reserve to remain at Three Rivers until, the Morning of the 2d Instant, to land Five Days Provisions from the Fleet, which, owing to the uncommon Exertions of Commodore Fahie, Captains Dilkes and Dowers, with other Naval Officers, (whose Activity on this Occasion, as well as at the landing at Saint Mary's, was most Conspicuous,) was promptly effected.

The Corps marched in Two Columns, the Reserve forming the Right, and advancing by the Mountains took Possession of Palmiste, at his upper Extremity, whilst the First Division marching by D'Olet, and the great Road to Basseterre, subdivided at the Foot of this Height, the Fourth Brigade ascending it near the Centre, the Third Brigade at its lower Extremity the Reserve found the Posts of Langlais abandoned, and the Guns spiked. The Possession of Morne Hoüel being of the highest Importance, I directed Brigadier-General Wale to March with the Reserve at Four o'Clock in the Afternoon, who occupied it without Resistance about Eight at Night, the Cannon being spiked and dismounted, and the Ammunition in general wasted or destroyed.

On the Morning of the 3d, the First Division marched from Palmiste, crossing the River Galion in one Column at the only practicable Pass, the Fourth Brigade taking Post in the Centre, about a Mile from the Bridge of Noziere on the River Noire, and the Third Brigade occupied Mr. Peltier's House, where the Enemy abandoned a Magazine of Provisions.

In the course of the 29th, the Second Division, under the Command of Brigadier-General Harcourt, weighed from the Saintes, and standing across towards Three Rivers, gave the Enemy some Jealousy in that Quarter, facilitating the Advance of the Rest of the Army, but in the Night bore up, landing the next Morning to Leeward near the River du Plessis; and marching immediately towards the Enemy's Right, inclining to his Rear, excited his Attention to such a Degree as to induce him to abandon his Defences at Three Rivers, Palmiste, Morne Hoüel, and to retire beyond the Bridge of Noziere, putting the River in his Front, and expending his Left in such Manner into the Mountains as in his Opinion to secure his Position.

The Second Division was enabled, from the Nature of the Country, to land two Royal Howitzers and-two Field Pieces and to mount them in Battery, to which two Eight-inch Howitzer Mortars were afterwards added.

The Enemy being now compressed within narrow Limits, the Difficulty, (and that a considerable one,) was the Passage of the River Noire, to the Defence of which he had paid the utmost Attention; it appeared me to be necessary to turn his Left by the Mountains, notwithstanding all the Obstructions of Nature and of Art which opposed this Decision. I therefore gave the necessary Orders to Brigadier-General Wale, commanding the Reserve, to carry this important Service into Execution during the Night of the 3d; but, after my separating from the Brigadier-General, he obtained Intelligence of a Nature so important as not, in his Opinion, to admit of consulting me upon an Alteration in the Time; and he proceeded to execute his Orders, although by a shorter Rouse than we possessed the Knowledge of at the Period of my quitting him.

I entirely approve of the Brigadier-General's Determination on the Grounds on which he decided, although it created a temporary Embarrassment.

Commissioners appointed on both Sides having met the next Morning (the 5th), a Capitulation was agreed upon, which was ratified on the Morning of the 6th, and which I trust will be honoured with His Majesty's Approbation.

GEO. BECKWITH, Commander of Forces.

14

BATTLE OF
GRAND PORT

Admiralty-Office, December 15, 1810.

Copy of a Letter from William Shield, Esq, Commissioner of His Majesty's Navy at the Cape of Good Hope to John Wilson Croker, Esq; dated at the Cape, the 24th September 1810.

SIR,

IT is with the deepest Regret I acquaint you, for the Information of the Right Honourable the Lords Commissioners of the Admiralty with the Loss of a Part of His Majesty's Squadron on this Station.

The Account I have now the Honour to present to you, came to my Knowledge by His Excellency Lord Caledon having had the Goodness to send for my Perusal, Dispatches he received last Night by the late Master of the Sirius from the Governor of Bourbon, I have transcribed and inclosed such Part thereof as may lead their Lordships' Judgment to the Extent of this disastrous Event.

The Isle de la Passe had fallen by Assault from a Party leaded by Two of the Frigates; subsequent to which the Bellona, Minerva, and Victor arrived ran into Port South East, with their Prize the Honourable East India Company's Ship Ceylon, taken in Company with the Windham, after a gallant Resistance, on their Way from the Cape to Madras with a Part of the 24th Regiment on board.

The Windham was turned from Fort South East and recaptured by the Sirius, but the Troops had been removed to the Bellona.

Captain Pym appears to have immediately determined on attacking these Ships, and to his not being aware of the Difficulties of the Navigation within the Port is to be attributed his Failure and the Loss of the King's Ships. The Sirius and Magicienne were burnt by their Crews, after doing every Thing that was possible to extricate the Ships from the Situation they had fallen into. The Nereide after every Officer and Man on board were either killed or wounded, fell on shore a mere Wreck, and was taken possession of by the Enemy.

I am sorry to add to this List of Misfortunes, that the Ranger Transport, laden with provisions for the Squadron, and having some Stores on board, has also fallen into the Hands of the Enemy.

The Transports having the Troops on board, and which were to have sailed Yesterday from hence without Convoy, will be prevented putting to Sea by the Arrival of this lamented Intelligence.

If it should prove that I have not been exactly correct in the Information I have now given, I hope for their Lordships' Indulgence, and that they will impute it to my Anxiety to give them the most early Intimation of so important an Event.

I have the Honour to be, &c.
(Signed) W. SHIELD

P. S. Captain Willoughby has lost an Eye, and is otherwise wounded, and is in the Hands of the Enemy.

Copy of a Letter from Captain Pym, of His Majesty's late Ship the Sirius, addressed to Captain Rowley, of the Boadicea.

L'Isle de la Passe, August 24, 1810.

SIR,

BY my last you were informed of my Intention to attack the Frigates, Corvette, and Indiamen in this Port.

Magicienne having joined just as the recaptured Ship was about to make Sail, I sent Captain Lambert Orders to bring her and the Gun-Brig with Dispatch off L'Isle de la Passe; and that the Enemy in Port Louis, should not be alarmed, I made all Sail round the South Side, and although blowing very hard, reached L'lsle de la Passe next Day.

At Noon Nereide made Signal ready for Action; I then, closed, and from the Situation of the Enemy decided on an immediate Attack; and when her Master came on board as Pilot, made Signal to weigh, but when within about a Quarter of an Hour's Run of the Enemy, he unfortunately run me on the Edge of the inner narrow Passage. We did not get off (and that with wonderful Exertion) until Eight o'Clock next Morning. At Noon on the 23d the Iphigenia and Magicienne came in Sight; the Enemy having moved further in, and making several Batteries, as also, manning the East India Ship, and taking many Men on board the Frigates, I called them to assist in the Attack, having all the Captains and Pilot onboard, and being assured were past all Danger and could run direct for the Enemy's Line,we got under Weigh, and pushed for our Stations, viz. Sirius alongside the Bollona, Nereide between her and the Victor, Iphigenia alongside La Minerva, and Magicienne between her and the East India Ship; and just as their Shot began to pass over us, sad to say, Sirius grounded on a small Bank, not known; Captain Lambert joined his Post, and had hardly given the third Broadside before his Opponent cut her Cable. Magicienne, close to Iphigenia, ran on a Bank which prevented her bringing more than Six Guns to bear; poor Nereide nearly gained her Post, and did in the most gallant Manner maintain that and the one intended for Sirius, until Bellona cut. All the Enemy's Ships being on shore, and finding Sirius could not get off, the whole of them opened their Fire on Nereide; and even in this unequal Contest, and being a-ground, she did not cease firing until Ten o'Clock, and sorry am I to say, that the Captain, every officer and Man on board, are killed or wounded.

Captain Lambert would have immediately run down with the Enemy, but there was a Shoal a very little Distance from and between him and them; he did all that could be done, by keeping open a heavy, although distant Fire; nothing was wanting to make a most complete Victory, but one of the other Frigates to close with La Bellona.

I must now inform you, that the Moment we took the Ground, every possible Exertion was made to get the Ship off, by carrying out Stream and Kedge Anchors but both Anchors came home together. I then got a whole Bower Cable and Anchor hauled out, (not a common Exertion for a Frigate) as also the Stream, and although having the one with the Capstan, and the other with Purchase on Purchase, we could not move her one Inch from the Nature of the Ground and the very heavy Squalls at that time. We continued lightening every Thing from forward, and made many severe but fruitless Attempts to heave the Ship off before Daylight, but all to no Effect. At that Time the Nereide was a perfect Wreck, Magicienne in as bad a Situation as Sirius, no Possibility of Iphigenia closing with the Enemy, the whole of the Enemy on shore in a Heap. We then tried last Resource by warping the Iphigenia to heave us off, but could not get her in a proper Situation until the 25th in the Forenoon.

I had a Survey by the Captain, Masters, and Carpenters, in which they agreed it was impossible to get the Ship off; I had the same Report Yesterday from Captain Curtis, and that his Men were falling very fast, I ordered her to be abandoned at Dusk and burnt and, as the Enemy's Frigates cannot get off, I thought it most prudent to preserve L'Isle de Passe, by warping Iphigenia for its support; and, having no Prospect of any other immediate Support, I thought it most prudent to quit my Ship, then within Shot of all the Enemy's Posts and Ships, and only being able to return their Fire from Two Guns, After seeing every Man safe from the Ship, Lieutenant Watling and myself set her on Fire; and I trust Sir, although my Enterprise has been truly unfortunate, that no possible Blame can be attached to any one and never did Captains, Officers, and Men go into Action with a greater Certainty of Victory; and I do aver, that if I could have got alongside the Bellona, all the Enemy's Ships would have been in our Possession in less than Half an Hour. My Ship being burnt, I have given up the Command to Captain Lambert, and I have recommended his supporting and protecting this Island with his Ship and Ships' Companies of Sirius and Magicienne. Provisions and Water will be immediately wanted.

I have, &c.
(Signed) S.PYM.

15

BATTLE OF BUSACO

Downing-Street, October 14, 1810.

A DISPATCH, of which the following is a Copy, was received this Day at the Earl of Liverpool's Office, addressed to his Lordship, from Lieutenant-General Lord Viscount Wellington, K.B.dated Coimbra the 30th September 1810.

MY LORD,

WHILE the Enemy was advancing from Celorico and Francolo upon Vizeu, the different Divisions of Militia and Ordenanza were employed upon their Flanks and Rear; and Colonel Trant with his Division attacked the Escort of the Military Chest and Reserve Artillery near Tojal, on the 20th Instant. He took Two Officers and One Hundred Prisoners, but the Enemy collected a Force from the Front and Rear, which obliged him to retire again towards the Douro.

I understand that the Enemy's Communication with Almeida is completely cut off, and he possesses only the Ground upon which his Army stands.

My Dispatch of the 20th Instant will have informed you of the Measures which I had adopted and which were in progress to collect the Army in this Neighbourhood, and, if possible, to prevent the Enemy from obtaining Possession of this Town.

On the 21st the Enemy's Advanced Guard pushed on to St Combadao, at the Junction of the Rivers Criz and Dao; and Brigadier-General Pack retired across the former and joined Brigadier-General Craufurd at Mortagoa, having destroyed the Bridges over those Two Rivers. The Enemy's Advanced Guard crossed the Criz, having repaired the Bridge, on the 23rd, and the whole of the 6th Corps was collected on the other side of the River; I therefore withdrew the Cavalry through the Sierra de Busaco, with the Exception of Three Squadrons, as the Ground was unfavorable for the Operation of that Arm.

On the 25th, the whole of the 6th and of the 2nd Corps crossed the Criz in the Neighbourhood of St. Combadao; and Brigadier-General Pack's Brigade and Brigadier-General Craufurd's Division retired to the Position which I had fixed upon for the Army on the top of the Seirra de Busaco. These Troops were followed in this Movement by the whole of the Corps of Ney and Regnier (the 6th and the 2nd); but it was conducted by Brigadier-General Craufurd with great Regularity, and the Troops took their Position without sustaining any Loss of Importance.

The 4th Portuguese Caçadores, which had retired on the Right of the other Troops, and the Piquets of the 3rd Division of Infantry, which were posted at St. Antonio de Cantaro, under Major Smyth of the 45th Regiment, were engaged with the Advance of Regnier's Corps in the Afternoon, and the former showed that Steadiness and Gallantry which others of the Portuguese Troops have since manifested.

The Sierra de Busaco is a high Ridge which extends from the Mondego in a North-Easterly direction about Eight Miles.

At the highest Point of the Ridge, about Two Miles from its Termination, is the Convent and Garden of Busaco. The Sierra de Busaco is connected by a mountainous Tract of Country with the Sierra de Caramula, which extends in a North-Easterly Direction beyond Viseu, and separates the Valley of the Mondego from the Valley of the Douro. On the Left of the Mondego, nearly in a Line with the Sierra de Busaco, is another Ridge of the same description, called the Serra da Murcella covered by the River Alva, and connected by other mountainous Tracks with the Serra d'Estrella.

All the Roads to Coimbra from the Eastward lead over the one or the other of these Sierras. They are very difficult for the Passage of an Army, the approach to the Top of the Ridge on both sides being mountainous. As the Enemy's whole Army was on the Right of the Mondego, and it was evident that he intended to force our Position, Lieutenent General Hill crossed that river by a short movement to his left, on the morning of the 26th, leaving Colonel Le Cor with his brigade on the Sierra da Murcella, to cover the Right of the Army, and Major General Fane, with his Division of Portuguese Cavalry and the 13th Light Dragoons, in Front of the Alva, to observe and check the Movements of the Enemy's Cavalry on the Mondego. With this Exception, the whole Army was collected upon the Sierra de Busaco, with the British Cavalry observing the Plain in the Rear of its Left, and the Road leading from Mortagoa to Oporto, through the mountainous tract which connects the Sierra de Busaco with the Sierra de Caramula.

The 8th Corps joined the Enemy in our Front on the 26th, but he did not make any serious Attack on that Day. The Light Troops on both Sides were engaged throughout the Line.

At Six in the Morning of the 27th the Enemy made Two desperate Attacks upon our Position, the one on the Right, the other on the Left of the highest Point of the Sierra. The Attack upon the Right was made by Two Divisions of the 2nd Corps, on that Part of the Sierra occupied by the 3rd Division of Infantry. One Division of French Infantry arrived at the Top of the Ridge, where it was attacked in the most gallant Manner by the 88th Regiment, under the command of Lieutenant Colonel Wallace; and the 45th Regiment, under the Command of the Honourable Lieutenant Colonel Meade, and by the 8th Portuguese Regiment, under the command of Lieutenant Colonel Douglas, directed by Major General Picton.

These three Corps advanced with the Bayonet, and drove the Enemy's Division from the advantageous Ground which they had obtained. The other Division of the 2nd Corps attacked farther on the Right, by the Road leading by St Antonio de Cantaro, also in front of Major General Picton's Division. This Division was repulsed before they could reach the Top of the Ridge, by the 74th Regiment, under the

Command of the Hon. Lieut. Colonel Trench, and the Brigade of Portuguese Infantry of the 9th and 21st Regiments, under the command of Colonel Champelmond, directed by Colonel Mackinnon. Major General Leith also moved to his Left to the support of Major General Picton, and aided in the Defeat of the Enemy by the 3rd Battalion Royals, the 1st Battalion, and the 2nd Battalion of the 38th Regiment. In these Attacks Major Generals Leith and Picton, Colonels Mackinnon and Champelmond, of the Portuguese service, who was wounded, Lieutenant Colonel Wallace, the Honourable Lieutenant Colonel Meade, Lieutenant Colonel Sutton, of the 9th Portuguese, Major Smith of the 45th Regiment, who was unfortunately killed, Lieutenant Colonel Douglas, and Major Birmingham of the 8th Portuguese Regiment, distinguished themselves. Major General Picton reports the good Conduct of the 9th and 21st Portuguese Regiments, commanded by Lieutenant Colonel Sutton and Lieutenant Colonel Aroujé Bacellar, and of the Portuguese Artillery, commanded by Major Arentschildt. I have also to mention, in a particular Manner, the Conduct of Captain Dansey of the 88th Regiment.

Major General Leith reports the good Conduct of the Royals, 1st Battalion 9th, and 2nd Battalion 38th Regiment; and I beg to assure your Lordship that I have never witnessed a more gallant Attack than that made by the 88th, 45th, and 8th Portuguese Regiment, on the Enemy's Division which had reached the Ridge of the Sierra.

On the Left the Enemy attacked with Three Divisions of Infantry of the 6th Corps, on the Part of the Sierra occupied by the Light Division of Infantry commanded by Brigadier General Craufurd, and by the Brigade of Portuguese Infantry commanded by Brigadier General Pack.

One Division of Infantry only made any progress to the Top of the Hill, and they were immediately charged with the Bayonet by Brigadier General Craufurd, with the 43rd, 52nd, and 95th Regiments and the 3rd Portuguese Caçadores, and driven down with immense Loss.

Brigadier General Coleman's Brigade of Portuguese Infantry, which was in Reserve, was moved up to the Right of Brigadier General Craufurd's Division, and a Battalion of the 19th Portuguese Regiment, under the Command of Lieutenant Colonel MacBean, made a gallant and successful Charge upon a Body of another Division of the Enemy, which was endeavoring to penetrate in that quarter.

In this Attack, Brigadier General Craufurd, Lieutenant Colonels Beckwith, of the 95th and Barclay of the 52nd, and the commanding Officers of the Regiments, distinguished themselves.

Besides these Attacks, the Light Troops of the Two Armies were engaged throughout the 27th, and the 4th Portuguese Caçadores, and the 1st and 16th Regiments, directed by Brigadier General Pack, and commanded by Lieutenant Colonel de Reyo Barreto, Lieutenant Colonel Hill, and Major Armstrong, showed great Steadiness and Gallantry.

The Loss sustained by the Enemy in his Attack of the 27th has been enormous.

I understand that the General of Division Merle and General Macune are wounded, and General Simon was taken Prisoner by the 52nd Regiment, and Three Colonels, and 250 men.

The Enemy left Two Thousand killed upon the Field of Battle, and I understand from the Prisoners and Deserters that the Loss in wounded is immense.

The Enemy did not renew his Attack, excepting by the Fire of his Light Troops on the 28th, but he moved a large Body of Infantry and Cavalry from the Left of his Centre to the Rear, from whence I saw his Cavalry in march on the Road from Mortagoa over the Mountains towards Oporto.

Having thought it probable that he would endeavor to turn our Left by that Road, I had directed Colonel Trant, with his Division of Militia, to march to Sardao, with the intention that he should occupy the Mountains, but unfortunately he was sent round by Oporto, by the General Officer commanding in the North, in consequence of a small Detachment of the Enemy being in Possession of St. Pedro do Sul; and, notwithstanding the Efforts which he made to arrive in Time, he did not reach Sardao till the 28th at Night, after the Enemy were in Possession of the Ground.

As it was probable that, in the Course of the Night of the 28th, the Enemy would throw the whole of his Army upon the Road, by which he could avoid the Sierra de Busaco and reach Coimbra by the High Road of Oporto, and thus the Army would have been exposed to be cut off from that Town or to a general Action in less favorable Ground, and as I had Reinforcements in my Rear, I was induced to withdraw from the Sierra de Busaco.

The Enemy did break up in the Mountains at Eleven at Night of the 28th, and he made the March I expected. His Advanced Guard was at Avelans, on the Road from Oporto to Coimbra, Yesterday, and the whole Army was seen in March through the Mountains: that under my Command, however, was already in the Low Country, between the Sierra de Busaco and the Sea; and the whole of it, with the Exception of the Advanced Guard, is this Day on the left of the Mondego.

Although, from the unfortunate Circumstance of the Delay of Colonel Trant's Arrival at Sardao, I am apprehensive that I shall not succeed in effecting the Object which I had in view in passing the Mondego and in occupying the Serra de Busaco, I do not regret my having done so. This Movement has afforded me a favorable Opportunity of showing the Enemy the Description of troops of which this Army is composed; it has brought the Portuguese Levies into Action with the Enemy for the first Time in an advantageous Situation; and they have proved that the Trouble which has been taken with them has not been thrown away, and that they are worthy of contending in the same Ranks with British Troops in this interesting Cause, which they afford the best Hopes of saving.

Throughout the Contest on the Sierra, and in all the previous Marches, and those which we have since made, the whole Army have conducted themselves in the most regular Manner. Accordingly all the Operations have been carried on with Ease, the Soldiers have suffered no Privations, have undergone no unnecessary Fatigue, there has been no Loss of Stores, and the Army is in the highest spirits.

I have received throughout the Service the greatest Assistance from the General and Staff Officers. Lieutenant General Sir Brent Spencer has given the Assistance his Experience enables him to afford me, and I am particularly indebted to the Adjutant and the Quarter-Master-General, and the Officers of their Departments and to Lieutenant Colonel Bathurst, and the Officers of my personal Staff, to Major General Howorth and the Artillery, and particularly to Lieutenant Colonel Fletcher, Captain Chapman, and the Officers of the Royal Engineers.

I must likewise mention Mr. Kennedy, and the Officers of the Commissariat, which Department has been carried on most successfully.

I should not do Justice to the Service, or to my own Feelings, if I did not take this Opportunity of drawing your Lordship's attention to the Merits of Marshal Beresford. To him exclusively, under the Portuguese Government, is due the merit of having raised, formed, disciplined, and equipped the Portuguese Army, which has now shown itself capable of engaging and defeating the Enemy.

I have besides received from him all the Assistance which his Experience and Abilities, and his Knowledge of this Country, have qualified him to afford me.

The Enemy have made no Movement in Estremadura, or in the Northern Provinces, since I addressed your Lordship last.

I send this dispatch by my Aide-de-Camp, Captain Burgh, to whom I beg to refer your Lordship for any further Details, and I recommend him to your Lordship's Notice.

> I have the honor to be, &c.
> (Signed) WELLINGTON.

16

BATTLE OF BARROSA

Dispatches, of which the following are copies, were last Night received at the Earl of Liverpool's Office, addressed to His Lordship by Lieutenant-General Graham, dated 6th and 10th of March 1811.

Isla de Leon, March 6, 1811.

MY LORD

CAPTAIN HOPE, my first Aid-de-camp, will have the Honor of delivering this Dispatch, to inform your Lordship of the glorious Issue of an Action fought Yesterday by the Division under my Command, against the Army commanded by Marshal Victor, composed of the two Divisions Ruffin and Laval.

The Circumstances were such as compelled me to attack this very superior Force. In order as well to explain to your Lordship the Circumstances of peculiar Disadvantage under which the Action was began, as to justify myself from the Imputation of Rashness in the Attempt, I must state to your Lordship, that the allied Army, after a Night March of Sixteen Hours from the camp near Veger, arrived in the Morning of the Fifth on the low Ridge of Barossa, about Four Miles to the Southward of the Mouth of the Santi Petri River. This Height extends inland about a Mile and a Half, continuing on the North the the extensive heathy Plain of Chiclana. A great Pine Forest skirts the Plain, and circles round the Height at some Distance, terminating down to Santi Petri; the intermediate Space between the North Side of the Height and the Forest being uneven and broken.

A well-conducted and successful Attack on the Rear of the Enemy's Lines near Santi Petri, by the Vanguard of the Spanish Army, under Brigadier General Lardizabal, having opened the Communication with the Isla de Leon, I received General La Peña's Directions to move down from the Position of Barossa to that of the Torre de Bermesa, bout half way to the Santi Petri River, in order to secure the Communication across the River, over which a Bridge had been lately established. This latter Position occupies a narrow woody Ridge, the Right on the Sea-Cliff, the Left falling down to the Almanza Creek, on the Edge of the Marsh. A hard Sandy Beach gives an easy Communication between the Western Points of these Two Positions.

My Division being halted on the Eastern Slope of the Barossa Height, was marched about 12 o'clock through the wood towards the Bermesa, (Cavalry Patrols having previously been sent towards Chiclana, without Meeting with the Enemy). On the March I received Notice that the Enemy had appeared in Force on the Plain, and was advancing towards the Height of Barossa.

As I considered that Position as the Key of that of Santi Petri, I immediately countermarched, in order to support the Troops left for its Defence, and the Alacrity with which this manoeuvre was executed served as a favourable Omen. It was however impossible, in such intricate and difficult Ground, to preserve Order in the Columns, and there never was Time to restore it entirely.

But before we could get ourselves quite disentangled from the Wood, the Troops on the Barossa Hill were seen returning from it, while the Enemy's Left Wing was rapidly ascending. At the same Time his Right Wing stood on the Plain, on the Edge of the Wood, within Cannon Shot. A Retreat in the Face of such an Enemy, already within Reach of the easy Communication by the Sea Beach, must have involved the whole Allied Army in all the Danger of being attacked during the unavoidable Confusion of the different Corps arriving on the narrow Ridge of Bermesa nearly at the same Time.

Trusting to the known Heroism of British Troops, regardless of the Numbers and Position of their Enemy, an immediate Attack was determined on. Major Duncan soon opened a powerful Battery of Ten Guns in the Centre. Brigadier General Dilkes, with the Brigade of Guards, Lieutenant Colonel Browne's (of the 28th) Flank Battalion, Lieutenant Colonel Norcott's Two Companies of the 2nd Rifle Corps, and Major Acheson, with a Part of the 67th Foot, (separated from the Regiment in the Wood) formed on the Right.

Colonel Wheatley's Brigade, with Three Companies of the Coldstream Guards, under Lieutenant Colonel Jackson (separated likewise from his Battalion in the Wood), and Lieutenant Colonel Barnard's Flank Battalion, formed on the Left.

As soon as the Infantry was thus hastily got together, the Guns advanced to a more favourable Position, and kept up a most destructive Fire.

The Right Wing proceeded to the Attack of General Ruffin's Division on the Hill, while Lieutenant Colonel Barnard's Battalion and Lieutenant Colonel Bushe's Detachment of the 20th Portuguese, were warmly engaged with the Enemy's Tirailleurs on our Left.

General Laval's Division, notwithstanding the havoc made by Major Duncan's Battery, continued to advance in very imposing Masses, opening his Fire of Musketry, and was only checked by that of the Left Wing. The Left Wing now advanced, firing; a most determined charge, by the Three Companies of the Guards, and the 67th Regiment, supported by all the remainder of the Wing, decided the defeat of General Laval's Division.

The Eagle of the Eighth regiment of Light Infantry, which suffered immensely, and a Howitzer, rewarded this Charge, and remained in Possession of Major Gough, of the 87th Regiment. These attacks were zealously supported by Colonel Belsen with the 28th Regiment, and Lieutenant Colonel Prevost with a Part of the 67th.

A Reserve formed beyond the narrow Valley, across which the Enemy was closely pursued, next shared the same Fate, and was routed by the same means.

Meanwhile the Right Wing was not less successful; the Enemy confident of Success, met General Dilkes on the Ascent of the Hill, and the Contest was sanguinary, but the undaunted Perseverance if the Brigade of Guards, of Lieutenant Colonel's Browne's Battalion, and of Lieutenant Colonel Norcott's and Major Acheson's Detachment, overcame every Obstacle, and General Ruffin's Division was driven from the Heights in Confusion; leaving Two Pieces of Cannon.

No expression of mine could do Justice to the Conduct of the Troops throughout. Nothing less than the almost unparalleled Exertions of every Officer, the invincible Bravery of every Soldier, and the most determined Devotion of the honor of his majesty's Arms in all, could have achieved this brilliant Success, against such a formidable Enemy, so posted.

In less than an Hour and a Half from the Commencement of the Action, the Enemy was in full Retreat. The retiring Divisions met, halted, and seemed inclined to form: a new and more advanced Position of our Artillery quickly dispersed them.

The exhausted State of our Troops made Pursuit impossible. A Position was taken on the Eastern side of the Hill; and we were strengthened on our Right by the Return of the Two Spanish battalions that had been attached before to my Division, but which I had left on the Hill, and which had been ordered to retire.

These Battalions (Walloon Guards and Ciudad Real) made every Effort to come back in Time, when it was known that we were engaged.

I understand, too, from General Whittingham, that with the Three Squadrons of Cavalry he kept in check a Corps of Infantry and Cavalry that attempted to turn the Barossa Height by the Sea. One Squadron of the 2nd Hussars, King's German Legion, under Captain Busche, and directed by Lieutenant Colonel Ponsonby, (both had been attached to the Spanish Cavalry), joined in time to make a brilliant and most successful Charge against a Squadron of French Dragoons, which was entirely routed.

An Eagle, Six Pieces of Cannon, the General of Division Ruffin, and the the General of Brigade, Rosseau, wounded and taken, Chief of the Staff General Bellegrade, an Aide-de-Camp of Marshal Victor, and the Colonel of the 8th Regiment, with many other Officers, killed, and several wounded and taken Prisoners; the Field covered with the dead Bodies and Arms of the Enemy, attest that my Confidence in this Division was nobly repaid.

Where all have so distinguished themselves, it is scarcely possible to discriminate any as the most deserving of Praise. Your Lordship will, however, observe how gloriously the Brigade of Guards, under Brigadier General Dilkes, with the Commanders of the Battalions Lieutenant Colonel the Honourable C. Onslow, and the Lieutenant Colonel Sebright wounded, as well as the Three separated Companies under Lieutenant Colonel Jackson, maintained the high Character of his majesty's Household Troops. Lieutenant Colonel Browne, with his Flank Battalion, Lieutenant Colonel Norcott, and Major Acheson, deserve equal Praise.

And I must equally recommend to your Lordship's Notice Colonel Wheatley, with Colonel Belson, Lieutenant Colonel Prevost, and Major Gough, and the Officers of the respective Corps composing his Brigade.

The animated Charges of the 87th Regiment were conspicuous; Lieutenant Colonel

Barnard (twice wounded), and the Officers of his Flank Battalion, executed the Duty of Skirmishing in advance with the Enemy in a masterly Manner, and were ably seconded by Lieutenant Colonel Busche, of the 20th Portuguese, who (likewise twice wounded), fell into the Enemy's Hands, but was afterwards rescued. The detachment of this Portuguese Regiment behaved admirably throughout the whole Affair.

I owe too much to Major Duncan, and the Officers and Corps of the Royal Artillery, not to mention them in the highest Approbation; never was Artillery better served.

The Assistance I received from the unwearied Exertions of Lieutenant Colonel Macdonald, and the Officers of the Adjutant General's Department, of Lieutenant Colonel the Honourable C. Cathcart, and the officers of the Quarter Master General's department, of Captain Birch and Captain Nicholas, and the Officers of the Royal Engineers, of Captain Hope, and the Officers of my Personal Staff (all animating by their Example) will ever be most gratefully remembered. Our Loss has been severe: as soon as it can be ascertained by the proper Return, I shall have the Honour of transmitting it; but much as it is to be lamented, I trust it will be considered as a necessary Sacrifice, for the Safety of the whole Allied Army.

Having remained some Hours on the Barossa Heights, without being able to procure any Supplies for the exhausted Troops, the Commissariat Mules having been dispersed on the Enemy's First Attack of the Hill, I left Major Ross, with the Detachment of the 3rd Battalion of the 95th, and withdrew the rest of the Division, which crossed the Santi Petri River early the next Morning.

I cannot conclude this dispatch without earnestly recommending to His Majesty's gracious Notice for Promotion, Brevet Lieutenant-Colonel Browne, Major of the 28th Foot, Brevet Lieutenant-Colonel Norcott, Major of the 95th, Major Duncan Royal Artillery, Major Gough of the 87th, Major the Honourable E. Acheson of the 67th, and Captain Birch of the Royal Engineers, all in the Command of Corps or Detachments on this memorable Service; and I confidently trust that the Bearer of this Dispatch, Captain Hope, (to whom I refer your Lordship for further details) will be promoted, on being permitted to lay the Eagle at his Majesty's Feet.

I have the honour to be, etc.
THOMAS GRAHAM, Lieutenant-General

P.S. I beg leave to add, that Two Spanish officers, Captain Miranda and Naughton, attached to my Staff, behaved with the utmost Intrepidity.

17

BATTLE OF FUENTES DE OÑORO

Downing-Street, May 25, 1811.

Dispatches, of which the following are Copies, were this Day, received at the Earl of Liverpool's Office, addressed to His Lordship by Lieutenant-General Lord Viscount Wellington K.B., dated Villa Formosa, 8th and 10th May.

Villa Fermosa, 8th May, 1811.

MY LORD,

THE Enemy's whole Army, consisting of the 2d, 6th, and 8th Corps, and all the Cavalry which could be collected in Castille and Leon, including about Nine Hundred of the Imperial Guard, crossed the Agueda at Ciudad Rodrigo on the 2d instant.

The Battalions of the 9th Corps had been joined to the Regiments to which they belonged in the other Three Corps, excepting a Division consisting of Battalions belonging to Regiments in the Corps doing Duty in Andalusia; which Division likewise formed Part of the Army.

As my Object in maintaining a Position between the Coa and the Agueda, after the Enemy had retired from the former, was to blockade Almeida, which Place I had learned from intercepted Letters, and other Information, was ill supplied with Provisions for its Garrison, and as the Enemy were infinitely superior to us in Cavalry, I did not give any Opposition to their March, and they passed the Azava on that Evening, in the Neighborhood of Espeja, Carpio, and Gallegos.

They continued their March on the 3d, in the Morning, towards the Duos Casas, in Three Columns, Two of them, consisting of the 2d and 8th Corps, to the Neighborhood of Almeida and Fort Concepcion, and the Third Column, consisting of the whole of the Cavalry, and the 6th and that Part of the 9th Corps which had not already been drafted into the other Three.

The Allied Army had been cantoned along the River Duos Casas, and on the Sources of the Azava, the Light Division at Gallegos and Espeja. This last fell back upon Fuentes de Honor, on the Duos Casas, with the British Cavalry, in Proportion as the Enemy advanced, and the 1st, 3d, and 7th Divisions were collected at that place; the 6th Division, under Major-General Campbell, observed the Bridge at Alameda; and Major General Sir William Erskine, with the 5th Division, the Passages of the Duos Casas at Fort Concepcion and Aldea d'Obispo. Brigadier-General Pack's Brigade, with the Queen's Regiment from the 6th Division, kept the Blockade of Almeida; and I had prevailed upon Don Julian Sanchez to occupy Nave d'Aver with his Corps of Spanish Cavalry and Infantry.

The Light Division were moved in the evening to join General Campbell, upon finding that the Enemy were in strength in that Quarter; and they were brought back again to Fuentes de Honor on the Morning of the 5th, when it was found that the 8th Corps had joined the 6th on the Enemy's Left.

Shortly after the Enemy had formed on the Ground on the Right of the Duos Casas, on the afternoon of the 3d, they attacked with a large force the village of Fuentes de Honor, which was defended in a most gallant Manner by Lieutenant-Colonel Williams, of the 5th Battalion 60th regiment, in command of the Light Infantry Battalions belonging to Major-General Picton's Division, supported by the Light Infantry Battalion in Major-General Nightingall's Brigade, commanded by Major Dick of the 42d Regiment, and the Light Infantry battalion in Major-General Howard's brigade, commanded by Major McDonnell of the 92d, and the Light Infantry Battalion of the King's German Legion, commanded by Major Ally, of the 5th Battalion of the Line, and by the 2d Battalion of the 83d Regiment, under Major Carr. These Troops maintained their Position; but having observed the repeated Efforts which the Enemy were making to obtain Possession of the Village, and being aware of the Advantage which they would derive from the Possession in their subsequent Operations, I reinforced the Village successively with the 71st Regiment under the Honourable Lieutenant-Colonel Cadogan, and the 79th under Lieutenant-Colonel Cameron, and the 24th under Major Chamberlain. The former, at the Head of the 71st Regiment, charged the Enemy, and drove them from a Part of the Village of which they had obtained a momentary Possession.

Nearly at this Time Lieutenant-Colonel Williams was unfortunately wounded, but I hope not dangerously, and the Command devolved upon Lieutenant-Colonel Cameron of the 79th Regiment. The Contest continued till Night, when our Troops retained in possession of the whole.

I then withdrew the Light Infantry Battalions, and the 83d Regiment, leaving the 71st and 79th Regiments only in the Village, and the 2d battalion 24th Regiment to support them.

On the 4th the Enemy reconnaitred the Positions which, we had occupied on the Duos Casas River, and during that Night they moved General Junot's Corps from Alameda to the Left of the Position occupied by the 6th Corps, opposite to Fuentes de Honor.

From the Course of the Reconnaissance on the 4th I had imagined that the Enemy would endeavor to obtain Possession of Fuentes de Honor, and of the Ground occupied by the Troops behind that Village, by crossing the Duos Casas at Poya

Velho, and in the Evening I moved the 7th Division, under Major General Houstoun, to the Right, in order, if possible, to protect that Passage.

On the Morning of the 5th, the 8th Corps appeared in two Columns, with all the Cavalry, on the opposite Side of the Valley of the Duos Casas and Poya Velho; and as the 6th and 9th Corps also made a Movement to their Left, the Light Division, which had been brought back from the Neighborhood of Alameda, were sent with the Cavalry, under Sir Stapleton Cotton, to support Major-General Houstoun, while the 1st and 3d Divisions made a Movement to their Right, along the Ridge between the Turon and Duos Casas Rivers, corresponding to that of the 6th and 9th Corps, on the Right of the Duos Casas.

The 8th Corps attacked Major-General Houstoun's Advanced Guard, consisting of the 85th Regiment, under Major Macintosh, and the 2d Portuguese Caçadores, under Lieutenant-Colonel Nixon, and obliged them to retire; and they retired in good Order, although with some Loss. The 8th Corps being thus established in Poya Velho, the Enemy's Cavalry turned the Right of the 7th Division, between Poya Velho and Nave d'Aver, from which last Place Don Julian Sanchez had been obliged to retire; and the Cavalry charged.

The charge of the Advanced Guard of the Enemy's Cavalry was met by Two or Three Squadrons of the different Regiments of British Dragoons, and the enemy were driven back; and Colonel La Motte, of the 13th Chasseurs, and some Prisoners, taken.

The Main Body were checked and obliged to retire by the Fire of Major-General Houstoun's Division; and I particularly observed the Chasseurs Britanniques, under Lieutenant-Colonel Eustace, as behaving in the most steady Manner, and Major-General Houstoun mentions in high Terms the Conduct of a detachment of the Duke of Brunswick's Light Infantry.

Notwithstanding that this Charge was repulsed, I determined to concentrate our Force towards the Left, and to move the 7th and Light Divisions and the Cavalry from Poya Velho towards Fuentes de Honor, and the other Two Divisions.

I had occupied Poya Velho and that Neighborhood, in hopes that I should be able to maintain the Communication across the Coa by Sabugal, as well as provide for the Blockade, which Objects it was now obvious were incompatible with each other, and I therefore abandoned that which was the least important, and placed the Light division in Reserve in the Rear of the Left of the 1st Division, and the 7th Division on some commanding Ground beyond the Turon, which protected the right Flank and Rear of the 1st Division, and covered the Communication with the Coa, and prevented that of the Enemy with Almeida by the Roads between the Turon and that river.

The Movement of the Troops upon this Occasion was well Conducted, although under very critical Circumstances, by Major-General Houstoun, Brigadier-General Craufurd, and Lieutenant- General Sir Stapleton Cotton. The 7th division was covered in its Passage of the Turon by the Light Division, under Brigadier-General Craufurd, and this last, in its March to join the 1st Division, by the British Cavalry.

Our Position thus extended on the high Ground from the Turon to the Duos Casas. The 7th Division, on the Left of the Turon, covered the Rear of the Right; the 1st

Division, in Two Lines, were on the Right; Colonel Ashworth's Brigade, in Two Lines, in the Centre; and the 3d Division, in Two Lines, on the Left. The Light Division and British Cavalry in reserve; and the village of Fuentes de Honor in Front of the Left. Don Julian's Infantry joined the 7th Division in Freneda; and I sent him with his Cavalry to endeavor to intercept the Enemy's Communication with Ciudad Rodrigo. The Enemy's Efforts on the Right Part of our Position, after it was occupied as I have above described, were confined to a Cannonade, and to some Charges with his Cavalry, upon the advanced Posts.

The Picquets of the 1st Division, under Lieutenant-Colonel Hill of the 3d Regiment of Guards, repulsed one of these; but as they were falling back they did not see the Direction of another in sufficient time to form to oppose it, and Lieutenant- Colonel Hill was taken Prisoner, and many Men were wounded, and some taken, before a Detachment of the British Cavalry could move up to their support.

The 2d Battalion, 42d Regiment, under Lord Blantyre, also repulsed a Charge of the Cavalry directed against them.

They likewise attempted to push a Body of Light Infantry upon the Ravine of the Turon, to the right of the 1st Division which were repulsed by the Light Infantry of the Guards under Lieutenant-Colonel Guise, aided by Five Companies of the 95th under Captain O'Hare.

Major-General Nightingall was wounded in the Course of the Cannonade, but I hope not severely.

The Enemy's principal Effort was throughout this Day again directed against Fuentes de Honor; and, notwithstanding that the whole of the 6th Corps were at different Periods of the Day employed to attack this Village, they could never gain more than a temporary Possession of it. It was defended by the 24th, 71st, and 79th Regiments, under the command of Colonel Cameron; and these Troops were supported by the Light Infantry Battalions of the 3d Division, Commanded by Major Woodgate; the Light Infantry Battalions of the 1st Division, commanded by Major Dick, Major McDonald, and Major Aly; the 6th Portuguese Caçadores, commanded by Major Pinto; by the Light Companies in Colonel Champelmond's Portuguese Brigade, under Colonel Sutton; and those in Colonel Ashworth's Portuguese Brigade, under Lieutenant-Colonel Pynn, and by the Piquets of the 3d Division, under the command of the Honourable Lieutenant-Colonel Trench. Lieutenant-Colonel Cameron was severely wounded in the Afternoon, and the Command in the Village devolved upon the Hon. Lieutenant-Colonel Cadogan.

The Troops in Fuentes were besides supported, when pressed by the Enemy, by the 74th Regiment, under Major Russell Manners, and the 88th Regiment, under Lieutenant-Colonel Wallace, belonging to Colonel Mackinnon's Brigade; and on one of these Occasions, the 88th, with the 71st and 79th, under the Command of Colonel Mackinnon, charged the Enemy, and drove them through the Village; and Colonel Mackinnon has reported particularly the conduct of Lieutenant-Colonel Wallace, Brigade Major Wilde, and Lieutenant and Adjutant Stewart of the 88th Regiment.

The Contest again lasted in this Quarter till Night, when our Troops still held their Post; and from that Time the Enemy have made no fresh Attempt on any Part of our Position.

The Enemy manifested an Intention to attack Major-General Sir W. Erskine's Post at Aldea del Bispo on the same morning, with a Part of the 2d Corps; but the Major-General sent the 2d Battalion of the Lusitanian Legion across the ford of the Duos Casas, which obliged them to retire.

In the Course of last Night the Enemy commenced retiring from their Position on the Duos Casas; and this Morning, at Daylight, the whole was in Motion. I cannot yet decide whether this Movement is preparatory to some fresh Attempt to raise the Blockade of Almeida, or is one of decided Retreat; but I have every Reason to hope that they will not succeed in the First, and that they will be obliged to have Recourse to the last.

Their Superiority in Cavalry is very great, owing to the weak State of our Horses, from recent Fatigue and Scarcity of Forage, and the Reduction of Numbers in the Portuguese Brigade of Cavalry with this Part of the Army, in exchange for a British Brigade sent into Estremadura with Marshal Sir William Beresford, owing to the Failure of the Measures reported to have been adopted to supply Horses and Men with Food on the Service.

The Result of a general Action, brought on by an Attack upon the Enemy by us, might, under those Circumstances, have been doubtful; and if the Enemy had chosen to avoid it, or if they had met it, they would have taken Advantage of the Collection of our Troops to fight this Action, and throw relief into Almeida.

From the great Superiority of Force to which we have been opposed upon this Occasion, your Lordship will judge of the Conduct of the Officers and Troops. The Actions were partial, but very severe, and our Loss has been great. The Enemy's Loss has also been very great, and they left Four Hundred killed in the Village of Fuentes, and we have many Prisoners.

I particularly request your Attention to the Conduct of Lieutenant Colonel Williams, and Lieutenant-Colonel Cameron, and Lieutenant-Colonel Cadogan; and to that of Colonel Mackinnon and Lieutenant Colonel Kelly, 24th Regiment; of several Officers commanding Battalions of the Line and of Light Infantry, which supported the Troops in Fuentes de Honor; likewise to that of Major Macintosh of the 85th and of Lieutenant-Colonel Nixon, of the 2d Caçadores, and of Lieutenant-Colonel Eustace, of the Chasseurs Britanniques, and of Lord Blantyre.

Throughout these operations I have received the greatest Assistance from Lieutenant-General Sir Brent Spencer and all the General Officers of the Army; and from the Adjutant and Quarter Master-General, and the Officers of their several Departments, and those of my personal Staff.

From Intelligence from Marshal Sir William Beresford, I learn that he has invested Badajoz, on the Left of the Guadiana, and is moving their Stores for the Attack of the Place.

I have the Honour to inform you that the Intelligence has been confirmed, and that Joseph Bonaparte passed Valladolid, on his Way to Paris, on the 27th of April. It is not denied by the French Officers that he is gone to Paris.

I have the honor to be, &c.
(Signed) WELLINGTON

18

BATTLE OF ALBUERA

Extract of a letter from Marshal Beresford to Lord Wellington, dated Albuera May18, 1811.

MY LORD,

I HAVE infinite Satisfaction in communicating to Your Lordship that the allied Army, united here under my Orders, obtained, on the 16th Instant, after a most sanguinary Contest, a complete Victory over that of the Enemy, commanded by Marshal Soult; and I shall proceed to relate to your Lordship the Circumstances.

In a former Report I have informed your Lordship of the Advance of Marshal Soult from Seville, and I had in consequence judged it wise entirely to raise the Siege of Badajoz, and prepare to meet him with our united Forces, rather than, by looking to Two Objects at once, to risk the Loss of both.

Marshal Soult, it appears, had been long straining every Nerve to collect a Force which he thought fully sufficient to his Object for the Relief of Badajoz; and for this Purpose he had drawn considerable Numbers from the Corps of Marshal Victor and General Sebastiani, and also, I believe, from the French Army of the Centre. Having thus completed his Preparations, he marched from Seville on the 10th Instant, with a Corps then estimated at Fifteen or Sixteen Thousand Men, and was joined on descending into Estremadura by the Corps under General Latour Maubourg, stated to be Five Thousand men. His Excellency General Blake, as soon as he learned the Advance of Marshal Soult, in strict Conformity to the Plan proposed by Your Lordship, proceeded to form his Junction with the Corps under my Orders, and arrived at Valverde in Person on the 14th Instant, where, having consulted with His Excellency and General Castanos, it was determined to meet the Enemy and to give him Battle.

On finding the Determination of the Enemy to relieve Badajoz, I had broken up from before that Place, and marched the Infantry to the Position in front of Valverde, except the Division of The Honourable Major-General G.L. Cole, which, with Two Thousand Spanish Troops, I left to cover the Removal of our Stores.

The Cavalry, which had, according to Orders, fallen back as the Enemy advanced, was joined at Santa Marta by the Cavalry of General Blake; that of General Castanos, under the Conde de Penne Villamur, had been always with it.

As remaining at Valverde, though a stronger Position, left Badajoz entirely open, I determined to take up a Position (such as could be got, in this widely open Country) at this Place, thus standing directly between the Enemy and Badajoz.

The Army was therefore assembled here on the 15th Instant. The Corps of General Blake, though making a forced March to effect it, only joined in the Night, and could not be placed in its Position till the Morning of the 16th Instant, when General Cole's Division, with the Spanish Brigade under Don Carlos d'Espana, also joined, and a little before the Commencement of the Action. Our cavalry had been forced on the Morning of the 15th Instant to retire from Santa Martha, and joined here. In the Afternoon of that Day the Enemy appeared in Front of us. The next Morning our Disposition for receiving the Enemy was made, being formed in Two Lines, nearly parallel to the river Albuera, on the Ridge of the gradual Ascent rising from that River, and covering the Roads to Badajoz and Valverde, though your Lordship is aware that the whole Face of this Country is every-where passable for all Arms. General Blake's Corps was on the Right in Two Lines; its left, on the Valverde Road, joined the Right of Major General the Honourable William Stewart's Division, the Left of which reached the Badajoz Road, where commenced the Right of Major-General Hamilton's Division, which closed the Left of the Line. General Cole's Division, with one Brigade of General Hamilton's, formed the Second Line of the British and Portuguese Army.

The Enemy, on the Morning of the 16th, did not long delay his Attack. At Eight o'Clock he was observed to be in Movement, and his Cavalry was seen passing the Rivulet of Albuera, considerably above our Right; and shortly after he marched out of the Wood opposite to us a strong Force of Cavalry, and Two heavy Columns of Infantry, pointing them to our Front, as if to Attack the Village and Bridge of Albuera. During this Time, under Cover of his vastly superior Cavalry, he was filing the principal Body of his Infantry over the River beyond our Right; and it was not long before his Intention appeared to be to turn us by that Flank, and to cut us off from Valverde. Major General Cole's Division was therefore ordered to form an oblique Line to the Rear of our Right, with his own Right thrown back; and the Intention of the Enemy to attack our Right becoming evident, I requested General Blake to form Part of his First Line, and all his Second, to that Front, which was done.

The Enemy commenced his Attack at Nine o'clock, not ceasing at the same Time to menace our Left; and after a strong and gallant Resistance of the Spanish Troops, he gained the Heights upon which they had been formed. Meanwhile the Division of the Honourable Major-General William Stewart had been brought up to support them; and that of Major-General Hamilton brought to the Left of the Spanish Line, and formed in contiguous close Columns of Battalions, to be moveable in any Direction. The Portuguese Brigade of Cavalry, under Brigadier General Otway, remained at some Distance on the Left of this, to check any Attempt of the Enemy below the Village.

As the Heights the Enemy had gained raked and entirely commanded our whole Position, it became necessary to make every Effort to retake and maintain them; and a noble one was made by the Division of General Stewart, headed by that gallant Officer.

Nearly at the beginning of the Enemy's Attack a heavy Storm of Rain came on, which, with the Smoke from the Firing, rendered it impossible to discern anything distinctly. This, with the Nature of the Ground, had been extremely favorable to the Enemy in forming his Columns, and in his subsequent Attack.

The Right Brigade of General Stewart's Division, under Lieutenant-Colonel Colborne, first came into Action, and behaved in the most gallant Manner; and finding that the Enemy's Column could not be shaken by Fire, proceeded to Attack it with the Bayonet; and, while in the Act of Charging, a Body of Polish Lancers (cavalry), which the thickness of the Atmosphere and the Nature of the Ground had concealed (and which was, besides, mistaken by those of the Brigade, when discovered, for Spanish Cavalry, and therefore not fired upon), turned it; and, being thus attacked unexpectedly in the Rear, was unfortunately broken, and suffered immensely. The 31st Regiment, being the Left one of the Brigade, alone escaped this Charge, and, under the command of Major L'Estrange, kept its Ground until the Arrival of the 3d Brigade, under Major-General Hoghton. The Conduct of this Brigade was most conspicuously gallant; and that of the 2d Brigade, under the Command of the Honourable Lieutenant-Colonel Abercrombie, was not less so. Major-General Hoghton, cheering on his Brigade to the Charge, fell pierced by Wounds. Though the Enemy's principal Attack was on this Point of the Right, he also made a continual Attempt upon that Part of our original Front at the Village and Bridge, which were defended in the most gallant Manner by Major-General Baron Alten, and the Light Infantry Brigade of the German Legion, whose Conduct was, in every Point of View, conspicuously good. This Point now formed our Left, and Major-General Hamilton's Division had been brought up there; and he was left to direct the Defence of that Point, whilst the Enemy's Attack continued on our Right, a considerable Proportion of the Spanish Troops supporting the defence of this Place. The Enemy's Cavalry, on his Infantry attempting to force our Right, had endeavored to turn it; but, by the able Manoeuvres of Major-General the Honourable William Lumley, commanding the Allied Cavalry, though vastly inferior to that of the Enemy in Number, his Endeavors were foiled. Major-General Cole, seeing the Attack of the Enemy, very judiciously bringing up his Left a little, marched in line to attack the Enemy's Left, and arrived most opportunely to contribute, with the Charges of the Brigades of General Stewart's Division, to force the Enemy to abandon his Situation, and retire precipitately, and to take Refuge under his Reserve. Here the Fusilier Brigade particularly distinguished itself. He was pursued by the Allies to a considerable Distance, and as far as I thought it prudent, with his immense Superiority of Cavalry; and I contented myself with seeing him driven across the Albuera.

I have every reason to speak favorably of the Manner in which our Artillery was served, and fought: and Major Hartman, commanding the British, and Major Dickson, commanding the Portuguese, and the Officers and Men, are entitled to my Thanks. The Four Guns of the Horse Artillery, commanded by Captain Le Fevre, did great Execution on the Enemy's Cavalry; and one Brigade of Spanish Artillery (the only one in the field) I saw equally gallantly and well served. We lost in the Misfortune which occurred to the Brigade commanded by Lieutenant Colonel Colborne (whom

General Stewart Reports to have acted, and was then acting, in a most noble Manner, leading on the Brigade in admirable Order) one Howitzer, which the Enemy, before the Arrival of the gallant General Hoghton's Brigade, had time to carry off with Two Hundred or Three Hundred prisoners of that Brigade. After he had been beaten from this his principal Attack he still continued that near the Village, on which he never could make any Impression, or cross the Rivulet, though I had been obliged to bring a very great Proportion of the Troops from it, to support the principal Point of Attack; but the Enemy seeing his main Attack defeated, relaxed in his Attempt there also. The Portuguese Division of Major-General Hamilton in every Instance evinced the utmost Steadiness and Courage, and manoeuvred equally well with the British.

Brigadier-General Harvey's Portuguese Brigade, belonging to General Cole's Division, had an opportunity of distinguishing itself when marching in Line across the Plain, by repulsing, with the utmost Steadiness, a Charge of the Enemy's Cavalry.

It is impossible to enumerate every Instance of Discipline and Valor shown on this severely contested Day; but there never were Troops that more valiantly or more gloriously maintained the Honour of their respective Countries. I have not been able to particularize the Spanish Divisions, Brigades, or Regiments, that were particularly engaged, because I am not acquainted with their Denominations or Names; but I have great pleasure in saying that their Behaviour was most gallant and honorable: and though, from the superior Number and Weight of the Enemy's Force, that Part of them that were in the Position attacked were obliged to cede the Ground, it was after a gallant Resistance, and they continued in good Order to support their Allies; and I doubt not his Excellency General Blake will do ample Justice on this Head, by making Honorable Mention of the deserving.

The Battle commenced at Nine o'clock, and continued without Interruption till Two in the Afternoon, when, the Enemy having been driven over the Albuera, for the Remainder of the Day there was but cannonading and skirmishing.

It is impossible by any Description to do justice to the distinguished Gallantry of the Troops; but every Individual most nobly did his Duty, which will be well proved by the great Loss we have suffered, though repulsing the Enemy; and it was observed that our Dead, particularly the 57th Regiment, were lying as they had fought in Ranks, and every Wound was in Front.

The Honourable Major General William Stewart most particularly distinguished himself, and conduced much to the Honor of the Day; he received Two contusions, but would not quit the Field. Major General the Honourable G.L. Cole is also entitled to every Praise; and I have to regret being deprived for some Time of his Services by the Wound he has received. The Honourable Lieutenant-Colonel Abercrombie, commanding the 2d Brigade, 2d Division, and Major L'Estrange, 31st Regiment, deserve to be particularly mentioned; and nothing could exceed the Conduct and Gallantry of Colonel Inglis at the Head of his Regiment. To the Honourable Major-General William Lumley, for the very able Manner in which he opposed the numerous Cavalry of the Enemy, and foiled him in his Object, I am particularly indebted. To Major-General Hamilton, who commanded on the Left during the severe Attack upon our Right, I am also much indebted; and the Portuguese Brigade of Brigadier General

Fonseca and Archibald Campbell deserve to be mentioned. To Major-General Alten, and to the excellent Brigade under his Orders, I have much Praise to give; and it is with great Pleasure I assure your Lordship that the good and gallant Conduct of every Corps, and of every Person, was in Proportion to the Opportunity that offered for distinguishing themselves. I know not an Individual who did not do his Duty. I have, I fear, to regret the Loss to the Service of Colonel Collins, commanding a Portuguese Brigade, his Leg having been carried off by a Cannon Shot. He is an Officer of great Merit; and I deeply lament the Death of Major General Hoghton, and of those two promising Officers, Lieutenant-Colonel Sir William Myers and Lieutenant-Colonel Duckworth.

It is most pleasing to me to inform Your Lordship, not only of the steady and gallant Conduct of our Allies, the Spanish Troops under his Excellency General Blake, but also to assure you that the most perfect Harmony has subsisted between us; and that General Blake not only conformed in all Things to the general Line proposed by Your Lordship, but in the Details and in whatever I suggested to his Excellency I received the most immediate and cordial Assent and Co-operation; nothing was omitted on his Part to ensure the Success of our united Efforts; and during the Battle he most essentially, by his Experience, Knowledge, and Zeal, contributed to its fortunate Result.

His Excellency the Captain-General Castanos, who had united the few Troops he had in a State to be brought into the Field to those of General Blake and placed them under his Orders, assisted in Person in the Field; and not only on this, but on all occasions, I am much indebted to General Castanos, who is ever beforehand in giving whatever can be beneficial to the Success of the common Cause.

Though I unfortunately cannot Point out the Corps, or many of the Individuals of the Spanish Troops, that distinguished themselves, yet I will not omit to mention the Names of General Vallesteros, whose Gallantry was most conspicuous, as of the Corps he had under his Command; and the same of General Zayas and of Don Carlos d'Espana. The Spanish Cavalry have behaved extremely well; and the Count de Penne Villamur is particularly deserving to be mentioned.

I annex the Return of our Loss in this hard contested Day: it is very severe; and in Addition to it is the Loss of the Troops under his Excellency General Blake, who are Killed, Missing, and Wounded, but of which I have not the Return. The Loss of the Enemy, though I cannot know what it is, must be still more severe. He has left on the Field of Battle about Two Thousand Dead, and we have taken from Nine Hundred to One Thousand Prisoners. He has had Five Generals Killed and Wounded: of the former, Generals of Division, Werle and Pesim; and Gazan and Two others amongst the latter. His Force was much more considerable than we had been informed of, as I do not think he displayed less than from Twenty to Twenty-Two Thousand infantry, and he certainly had Four Thousand Cavalry, with a numerous and heavy Artillery. His overbearing Cavalry cramped and confined all our Operations, and, with his Artillery, saved his Infantry after its Rout.

He Retired after the Battle to the Ground he had been previously on, but occupying it in Position; and on this Morning, or rather during the Night, commenced his Retreat on the Road he came, towards Seville, and has abandoned Badajoz to its Fate. He left a Number of his Wounded on the Ground he had retired to, and to whom we are administering what Assistance we can. I have sent our Cavalry to follow the Enemy; but in that Arm he is too powerful for us to attempt any Thing against him in the Plains he is traversing.

Thus we have reaped the Advantage we proposed from our Opposition to the Attempts of the Enemy; and, whilst he has been forced to abandon the object for which he has almost stripped Andalusia of Troops, instead of having accomplished the haughty Boasts with which Marshal Soult harangued his Troops on leaving Seville, he returns there with a curtailed Army, and, what perhaps may be still more hurtful to him, with a diminished Reputation.

In enumerating the Services received from the Officers of my own Staff, I must particularly call Your Lordship's Attention to those of Brigadier-General d'Urban, Quarter Master General to the Portuguese Army; and which I cannot sufficiently praise, though I can appreciate. On all Occasions I have felt the benefits of his Talents and Services, and more particularly on this, where they very essentially contributed to the Success of the Day: and I cannot here omit the name of Lieutenant-Colonel Hardinge, Deputy Quarter Master General to the Portuguese Troops, whose Talents and Exertions deserve my Thanks. To Brigadier-General Mozinho, Adjutant General of the Portuguese Army, and to Lieutenant-Colonel Rooke, Assistant Adjutant General to the united British and Portuguese Force, and to Brigadier-General Lemos, and to the Officers of my own personal Staff, I am indebted for their Assistance.

To the Services of Lieutenant-Colonel Arbuthnot (Major in His Majesty's Service) I am also much indebted; and he is the Bearer of this to Your Lordship, and is fully enabled to give you any further Information you may desire, and is most deserving of any Favor your Lordship may be pleased to recommend him for to His Royal Highness the Prince Regent.

I have the honor to be, &c.
(Signed) W.C.BERESFORD.
Marshal and Lieut. Gen.

P.S.   Major General Hamilton's division, and Brigadier General Madden's Brigade of Portuguese Cavalry, march To-morrow morning to reinvest Badajoz on the South Side of the Guadiana. W. C. B.

Admiral Sir John Thomas
Duckworth (1748-1817), by
William Beechey.

"Combat de Grand Port", by Pierre-Julien Gilbert.

Vice Admiral Cuthbert Collingwood, 1st Baron Collingwood (26 September 1748 – 7 March 1810), by Henry Howard.

The destruction of the French Fleet in Basque Roads by Thomas Sutherland, after a painting by Thomas Whitcombe.

Sir Samuel Auchmuty
(1756-1822), artist
unknown.

Sir John Moore, by
Sir Thomas
Lawrence.

Second Siege of Ciudad Rodrigo, artist unknown.

"The Devil's Own, 88th Regiment at the Siege of Badajoz". Watercolour en grisaille by Richard Caton Woodville.

William Carr Beresford,
Viscount Beresford, by Sir
William Beechey.

Battle of Bussaco, a print after Major Thomas S. St. Clair, engraved by C. Turner.

The Battle of Barrosa, by William Heath.

Thomas Graham,
Baron Lynedoch, by Sir
George Hayter.

The Battle of the Nivelle, by W. Heath.

British infantry exchanges fire with the French across the Languedoc Canal during the Battle of Toulouse, print after Henri Dupray.

Sir Arthur Wellesley
Duke of Wellington,
by Thomas Lawrence.

Battle of Waterloo 1815, by William Sadler.

19

BATTLE OF ARROYO DOS MOLINES

Downing-Street, December 1, 1811.

Captain Hill, Aid-de-Camp to Lieutenant-General Hill, arrived this Day at the Earl of Liverpool's Office, with a Dispatch, addressed to his Lordship by General Viscount Wellington, dated Freneda, 6th November, 1811.

MY LORD,

I INFORMED your Lordship, in my Dispatches of the 23rd and 30th October, of the Orders which I had given to Lieutenant-General Hill to move into Estremadura with the Troops under his Command, and with his Progress to the 26th October.

He marched on the 27th by Aldea del Cano to Alcuesca, and, on the 28th, in the Morning, surprised the Enemy's Troops under General Girard at Arroyo del Molino, and dispersed the Division of Infantry and the Cavalry which had been employed under the Command of that General, taking General Brune, the Duc d'Aremberg, and about One Thousand Three Hundred Prisoners, Three Pieces of Cannon, &c. &c. and having killed many in the Action with the Enemy, and in the subsequent Pursuit. General Girard escaped wounded; and, by all Accounts which I have received, General Dubrowski was killed.

I beg to refer your Lordship, for the Details of Lieutenant-General Hill's Operations to the 30th October, to his Dispatch to me of the Date from Merida, a Copy of which I enclose. I have frequently had the Pleasure to report to your Lordship the Zeal and Ability with which Lieutenant-General Hill had carried into Execution the Operations entrusted to his Charge; and I have great satisfaction in repeating my Commendations of him, and of the brave Troops under his Command, upon the present Occasion, in which the Ability of the General and the Gallantry and Discipline of the Officers and Troops have been conspicuous.

I send with General Hill's Dispatch a Plan of the Ground and of Operations on the 28th of October [*not present*], by Captain Hill, the General's Brother and Aid-de-Camp, who attended him in the Action, and who will be able to give your Lordship any further Details which you may require. I beg Leave to recommend him to your Protection.

———

Merida, 30th October, 1811.

MY LORD,

IN pursuance of the Instructions which I received from your Lordship, I put a Portion of the Troops under my Orders in Motion on the 22d Instant, from their Cantonments in the Neigh of Portalegre, and advanced with them towards the Spanish Frontier.

On the 23d the Head of the Column reached Alburquerque, where I learned that the Enemy, who had advanced to Aliseda, had fallen back to Arroyo del Puerco, and that the Spaniards were again in Possession of Aliseda.

On the 24th, I had a Brigade of British Infantry, and Half a Brigade of Portuguese Artillery (Six pounders), and some of my cavalry at Aliseda; and the Remainder of my Cavalry, another Brigade of British Infantry, and Half a Brigade of Portuguese Six pounders at Casa de Cantillana, about a League distant.

On the 25th, the Count de Penne Villamur made a Reconnaissance with his Cavalry, and drove the Enemy from Arroyo del Puerco. The Enemy retired to Malpartida, which Place he occupied as an Advanced Post with about Three Hundred cavalry and some Infantry, his Main Body being still at Caceres.

On the 26th, at Day-Break, the Troops arrived at Malpartida, and found that the Enemy had left that Place, retiring towards Caceres, followed by a small Party of the 2d Hussars, who skirmished with his Rear-Guard. I was shortly afterwards informed that the whole of the Enemy's Force had left Caceres; but the Want of Certainty as to the Direction he had taken, and the extreme Badness of the Weather, induced me to halt the Portuguese and British Troops at Malpartida for that Night. The Spaniards moved on to Caceres.

Having received certain Information that the Enemy had marched on Torre Mocha, I put the Troops at Malpartida in Motion on the Morning of the 27th, and advanced by the Road leading to Merida, through Aldea del Cano and Casas de Don Antonio, being a shorter Route than that followed by the Enemy, and which afforded a Hope of being able to intercept and bring him to Action; and I was here joined by the Spaniards from Caceres. On the March I received Information that the Enemy had only left Torre Mocha that Morning, and that he had again halted his Main Body at Arroyo del Molino, leaving a Rear-Guard at Albala, which was a satisfactory Proof that he was ignorant of the Movements of the Troops under my Command.

I therefore made a fored March to Alcuesca that Evening, where the Troops were so placed as to be out of Sight of the Enemy, and no Fires were allowed to be made. On my Arrival at Alcuesca, which is within a League of Arroyo del Molino, every Thing tended to confirm me in the Opinion that the Enemy was not only in total

Ignorance of my near Approach, but extremely off his Guard; and I determined upon attempting to surprise, or at least to bring him to Action, before he should march in the Morning, and the necessary Dispositions were made for that Purpose.

The town of Arroyo del Molino is situated at the Foot of one Extremity of the Sierra of Montanches; the Mountain running from it to the Rear in the Form of a Crescent, almost every where inaccessible, the Two Points being about Two Miles asunder. The Truxillo Road runs round that to the Eastward.

The road leading from the town to Merida runs at Right Angles with that from Alcuesca, and the Road to Medellin passes between those to Truxillo and Merida. The Grounds over which the Troops had to manoeuvre being a Plain, thinly scattered with Oak and Cork Trees, my Object of course was to place a Body of Troops so as to cut off the Retreat of the Enemy by these Roads.

The Troops moved from their Bivouack near Alcuesca about Two o'Clock in the Morning of the 28th, in one Column, Right in Front, direct on Arroyo del Molino, and in the following Order; Major-General Howard's Brigade of Infantry (1st Battalion 50th, 71st, and 92d Regiments, and one Company of the 60th); Colonel Wilson's brigade (1st Battalion, 28th, 2d Battalion, 34th and 2d Battalion 39th, and one Company of the 60th,) 6th Portuguese Regiment of the Line, and 6th Caçadores, under Colonel Ashworth; the Spanish Infantry under Brigadier-General Morillo, Major General Long's Brigade of Cavalry (2d Hussars, 9th and 13th Light Dragoons,) and the Spanish Cavalry, under the Count de Penne Villamur. They moved in this Order until within Half a Mile of the Town of Arroyo del Molino, when under Cover of a low Ridge the Column closed, and divided into Three Columns. Major General Howard's Brigade and Three Six-Pounders under Lieutenant-Colonel Stewart, supported by Brigadier-General Morillo's Infantry, the Left; Colonel Wilson's Brigade, the Portuguese Infantry under Colonel Ashworth, Two Six-Pounders and a Howitzer, the Right, under Major-General Howard; and the Cavalry the centre.

As the Day dawned, a violent Storm of Rain and thick Mist came on, under Cover of which the Columns advanced in the Direction and in the Order which had been pointed out to them. The Left Column, under Lieutenant-Colonel Stewart, marched direct upon the Town. The 71st, one Company of the 60th, and 92d Regiment at Quarter Distance, and the 50th in close Column somewhat in the Rear with the Guns as a Reserve.

The Right Column, under Major-General Howard, having the 39th Regiment as a Reserve, broke off to the Right so as to turn the Enemy's Left, and having gained about the Distance of a Cannon-Shot to that Flank, it marched in a circular Direction upon the further Point of the Crescent, on the Mountain above-mentioned.

The Cavalry under Lieueutenat-General Sir William Erskine moved between the Two Columns of Infantry ready to act in Front, or move round either of them, as Occasion might require.

The Advance of our Columns was unperceived by the Enemy until they approached very near, at which Moment he was filing out of the Town upon the Merida road; the Rear of his Column, some of his Cavalry and part of his Baggage being still in it; one Brigade of his infantry had marched for Medellin an Hour before Day-light.

The 71st and 92d Regiments charged into the Town with Cheers, and drove the Enemy everywhere at the Point of the Bayonet, having a few Men cut down by the Enemy's Cavalry.

The Enemy's Infantry, which had got out of the Town, had, by the Time these Regiments arrived at the Extremity of it, formed into Two Squares, with the Cavalry on their Left; the whole were posted between the Merida and Medellin Roads, fronting Alcuesca. The Right Square being formed within Half Musket-Shot of the Town, the Garden Walls of which were promptly lined by the 71st Light Infantry, while the 92d Regiment filed out and formed Line on their Right, perpendicular to the Enemy's Right Flank, which was much annoyed by the well directed Fire of the 71st. In the meantime one Wing of the 50th Regiment occupied the Town and secured the Prisoners, and the other Wing along with the Three Six-Pounders skirted the outside of it, the Artillery as soon as within range firing with great Effect upon the Squares.

Whilst the Enemy was thus occupied on his Right, Major-General Howard's Column continued moving round his Left; and our Cavalry advancing and crossing the Head of the Column, cut off the Enemy's Cavalry from his Infantry, charging it repeatedly, and putting it to the Route [*sic*]. The 13th Light Dragoons, at the same Time, took Possession of the Enemy's Artillery. One of the Charges made by Two Squadrons of the 2d Hussars, and one of the 9th Light Dragoons was particularly gallant; the latter commanded by Captain Gore, and the whole under Major Bussche of the Hussars. I ought previously to have mentioned, that the British Cavalry having, through the Darkness of the Night and the Badness of the Road, been somewhat delayed, the Spanish Cavalry under the Count de Penne Villemur was on this Occasion the first to form upon the Plain and engage the Enemy, until the British were enabled to come up.

The Enemy was now in full Retreat, but Major-General Howard's Column having gained the Point to which it was directed, and the Left Column gaining fast upon him, he had no Resource but to surrender, or to disperse and ascend the Mountain. He preferred the latter, and ascending near the Eastern Extremity of the Ascent, and which might have been deemed inaccessible, was followed closely by the 28th and 34th Regiments, whilst the 39th regiment and Colonel Ashworth's Brigade of Portuguese Infantry, followed round the Foot of the Mountain by the Truxillo Road, to take him again in Flank. At the same time Brigadier-General Morillo's Infantry ascended at some Distance to the Left with the same View.

As may be imagined, the Enemy's Troops were by this Time in the utmost Panic; his Cavalry was flying in every Direction, the Infantry threw away their Arms, and the only Effort of either was to escape. The troops under Major-General Howard's Command, as well as those he had sent round the Point of the Mountain, pursued them over the Rocks, making Prisoners at every Step, until his own Men became so exhausted and few in Number, that it was necessary for him to halt and secure the Prisoners, and leave the further Pursuit to the Spanish Infantry under Brigadier-General Morillo; who, from Direction in which they had ascended had now become the most advanced. The Force General Girard had with him at the commencement, which consisted of 2500 Infantry and 600 Cavalry, being at this Time totally dispersed. In the course of these operations Brigadier-General Campbell's Brigade of Portuguese Infantry (the 4th and 10th regiments), and the 18th Portuguese Infantry, joined from Casas de Don Antonio, where they had halted for the Preceding Night; and as soon as I judged they could no longer be required at the Scene of Action, I detached them with the Brigade consisting of the 50th, 71st, and 92d Regiments, and Major-General Long's Brigade of Cavalry towards Merida. They reached St Pedro that Night, and entered Merida this Morning; the Enemy having in the Course of the Night retreated from hence in great Alarm to Almendralego. The Count de Penne Villimur formed the Advanced Guard with his Cavalry, and had entered the Town previous to the Arrival of the British.

The ultimate Consequences of these Operations I need not point out to your Lordship; their immediate Result is the Capture of One General of Cavalry (Brune,) one Colonel of Cavalry (the Prince D'Aremberg), One Lieutenant-Colonel (Chef of the Etat Major,) One Aid-de-Camp of General Girard, Two Lieutenant-Colonels, One commissaire de guerre, Thirty Captains and Inferior Officers, and Upwards of One Thousand Non-Commissioned Officers and Soldiers, already sent off under an Escort to Portalegre; the whole of the Enemy's Artillery, Baggage, and Commissariat, some Magazines of Corn, which he had collected at Caceres and Merida; and the Contribution of Money which he had levied on the former Town, besides the total Dispersion of General Girard's Corps. The Loss of the Enemy in killed must also have been severe, while that on our Side was comparatively trifling, as appears by the accompanying Return, in which your Lordship will lament to see the name of Lieutenant Strenuwitz, Aid-de-Camp to Lieutenant-General Sir William Erskine, whose extreme Gallantry led him into the Midst of the Enemy's Cavalry, and occasioned his being taken Prisoner.

Thus has ended an Expedition which, although not bringing into Play to the full Extent the Gallantry and Spirit of those engaged, will, I trust, give them a Claim to your Lordship's Approbation. No Praise of mine can do Justice to their admirable Conduct; the Patience and good Will shown by all Ranks during forced Marches in the worst Weather; their strict Attention to the Orders they received, the Precision with which they moved to the Attack, and their Obedience to Command during the Action; in short, the Manner in which every one has performed his Duty, from the first Commencement of the Operations, merits my warmest Thanks, and will not, I am sure, pass unobserved by your Lordship.

To Lieutenant-General Sir W. Erskine, I must express my Obligations for his Assistance and advice upon all Occasions; to Major-General Howard, who dismounted and headed his Troops up the difficult Ascent of the Sierra, and throughout most ably conducted his Column, and to Major-General Long, for his Exertions at the Head of his Brigade, I feel myself particularly indebted. I must also Express my Obligations to Colonel Wilson, Colonel Ashworth, and Lieutenant-Colonel Stewart, commanding Brigades, for the able Manner in which they led them, Lieutenant-Colonel Cameron, the Hon. Lieutenant-Colonel Cadogan, the Honourable Lieutenant-Colonel Abercromby, and Lieutenant-Colonels Fenwick, Muter, and

Lindsay, Majors Harrison and Bussche, Major Parke commanding the Light Companies, and Captain Gore, commanding the 9th Light Dragoons, Major Hartmann, commanding the Artillery, Lieutenant-Colonel Grant and Major Birmingham of the Portuguese Service, Captain Arresaga of the Portuguese Artillery, whose Guns did so much Execution, severally merit my warmest Approbation by their Conduct; and I must not omit to mention the Exertions made by Brigadier-General Campbell and his Troops, to arrive in Time to give their Assistance.

General Giron, the Chief of General Castanos' Staff, and Second in Command of the 5th Spanish Army, has done me the Honour to accompany me during these Operations; and I feel much indebted to him for his Assistance and valuable advice.

Brigadier-General the Count De Penne Villemur, Brigadier-General Morillo, Colonel Downie, and the Spanish Officers and Soldiers in general have conducted themselves in a Manner to excite my warmest Approbation.

To Lieutenant-Colonel Rooke, Assistant-Adjutant-General, and Lieutenant-Colonel Offeney, Assistant-Quarter-Master-General, for the able Manner in which they have conducted their Departments, and also for the valuable Assistance and Advice which I have at all Times received from them; to the Officers of the Adjutant and Quarter-Master-General's Departments; to Captain Squire, Royal Engineers, for his Intelligence and indefatigable Exertions during the whole Operation, and to Captain Currie and my personal Staff, my warmest Thanks are due.

This Dispatch will be delivered to your Lordship by Captain Hill, my First Aid-de-Camp, to whom I beg to refer your Lordship for all further Particulars

I have the Honour to be, &c.
R. HILL, Lieut. Gen.

To General Viscount Wellington, K.B.

P.S.   Since writing the above Report a good many more Prisoners have been made, and I doubt not but the whole will amount to Thirteen or Fourteen Hundred.

Brigadier-General Morillo has just returned from the Pursuit of the dispersed, whom he followed for Eight Leagues. He reports that besides those killed in the plains, upwards of Six Hundred dead were found in the Woods and Mountains.

General Girard escaped in the Direction of Serena with Two or Three Hundred Men, mostly without Arms, and is stated by his own Aid-de-Camp to be wounded.

20

STORMING OF CIUDAD RODRIGO

Downing-Street, February 4, 1812.

MAJOR the Honourable A. Gordon, has arrived this evening at Lord Liverpool's Office with a dispatch, addressed to his Lordship by General Viscount Wellington, dated Gallegos, 20th January 1812.

MY LORD,

I INFORMED your Lordship, in my dispatch of the 9th, that I had attacked Ciudad Rodrigo, and in that of the 15th, of the progress of the operations to that period, and I have now the pleasure to acquaint your Lordship that we took the place by storm yesterday evening after dark.

We continued, from the 15th to the 19th, to complete the second parellel, and the communications with that work and we had made some progress by sap towards the crest of the glacis. On the night of the 15th we likewise advanced, from the left of the first parallel down the slope of the hill towards the Convent of St. Francisco, to a situation from which the walls of the Fausse Brayeand of the town were seen, on which a battery for seven guns was constructed, and these commenced their fire on the morning of the 18th.

In the mean time, the batteries in the first parallel continued their fire; and, yesterday evening, their fire had not only considerably injured the defences of the place, but had made breaches in the Fausse Brayewall, and in the body of the place, which were considered practicable; while the battery on the slope of the hill, which had been commenced on the night of the 15th, and had opened on the 18th, had been equally efficient still farther to the left, and opposite to the suburb of St. Francisco.

I therefore determined to storm the place, notwithstanding that the approaches had not been brought to the crest of the glacis, and the counterscarp of the ditch was still entire. The attack was accordingly made yesterday evening, in five separate columns, consisting of the troops of the 3d and light divisions, and of Brigadier-General Pack's brigade. The two right columns, conducted by Lieutenant-Colonel O'Toole of the 2d caçadores, and Major Ridge of the 5th regiment, were destined to protect the advance of Major General MacKinnon's brigade, forming the 3d, to the top of the breach in the Fausse Brayewall, and all these, being composed of troops of the 3d division, were under the direction of Lieutenant-General Picton.

The fourth column, consisting of the 43d and 52d regiments, and part of the 95th regiment, being of the light division, under the direction of Major-General Craufurd, attacked the breaches on the left in front of the suburb of St. Francisco, and covered the left of the attack of the principal breach by the troops of the 3d division; and Brigadier-General Pack was destined, with his brigade, forming the fifth column, to make a false attack upon the southern face of the fort. Besides these five columns, the 94th regiment, belonging to the 3d division, descended into the ditch in two columns, on the right of Major General Mackinnon's brigade, with a view to protect the descent of that body into the ditch and its attack of the breach in the Fausse Braye against the obstacles which it was supposed the enemy would construe to oppose their progress.

All these attacks succeeded; and Brig. General Pack even surpassed my expectations, having converted his false attack into a real one; and his advanced guard, under the command of Major Lynch, having followed the enemy's troops from the advanced works into the Fausse Braye,where they made prisoners all opposed to them.

Major Ridge, of the 2d battalion 5th regiment, having escaladed the Fausse Brayewall, stormed the principal breach in the body of the place, together with the 94th regiment, commanded by Lieutenant-Colonel Campbell, which had moved along the ditch at the same time, and had stormed the breach in the Fausse Braye both in front of Major-General MacKinnon's brigade. Thus, these regiments not only effectually covered the advance from the trenches of Major General MacKinnon's brigade by their first movements and operations, but they preceded them in the attack.

Major-General Craufurd, and Major-General Vandeleur, and the troops of the Light division, on the left, were likewise very forward on that side; and, in less than half an hour from the time the attack commenced, our troops were in possession, and formed on the ramparts, of the place, each body contiguous to the other. The enemy then submitted, having sustained a considerable loss in the contest.

Our loss was also, I am concerned to add, severe, particularly in officers of high rank and estimation in this army. Major-General Mackinnon was unfortunately blown up by the accidental explosion of one of the enemy's expense magazines, close to the breach, after he had gallantly and successfully led the troops under his command to the attack. Major-General Craufurd likewise received a severe wound while he was leading on the Light Division to the storm, and I am apprehensive that I shall be deprived for some time of his assistance. Major General Vandeleur was likewise wounded in the same manner, but not so severely, and he was able to continue in the field. I have to add to this list Lieutenant-Colonel Colborne of the 52d regiment, and Major George Napier, who led the storming party of the Light Division, and was wounded on the top of the breach.

I have great pleasure in reporting to your Lordship the uniform good conduct, and spirit of enterprise, and patience and perseverance in the performance of great labour, by which the general officers, officers, and troops of the 1st, 3d, 4th, and Light Divisions, and Brigadier-General Pack's brigade, by whom the siege was carried on, have been distinguished during the late operations. Lieutenant-General Graham assisted me in superintending the conduct of the details of the siege, besides performing the duties of the general officer commanding the 1st division; and I am much indebted to the suggestions and assistance I received from him for the success of this enterprise.

The conduct of all parts of the 3d division, in the operations which they performed with so much gallantry and exactness on the evening of the 19th in the dark, afford the strongest proof of the abilities of Lieut. General Picton and Major General MacKinnon, by whom they were directed and led; but I beg particularly to draw your Lordship's attention to the conduct of Lieutenant-Colonel O'Toole, of the 2d caçadores, of Major Ridge of the 2d battalion 5th foot, of Lieutenant-Colonel Campbell of the 94th regiment, of Major Manners of the 74th, and of Major Grey of the 2d battalion 5th foot, who has been twice wounded during this siege.

It is but justice also to the 3d division to report that the men who performed the sap belonged to the 45th, 74th, and 88th regiments, under the command of Captain McLeod of the Royal Engineers, and Captain Thompson of the 74th, Lieut. Beresford of the 88th, and Lieutenant Metcalfe of the 45th, and they distinguished themselves not less in the storm of the place than they had in the performance of their laborious duty during the siege.

I have already reported, in my letter of the 9th instant my sense of the conduct of Major-General Craufurd, and of Lieutenant-Colonel Colborne, and of the troops of the light division, in the storm of the redoubt of St. Francisco, on the evening of the 8th instant. The conduct of these troops was equally distinguished throughout the siege; and in the storm, nothing could exceed the gallantry with which these brave Officers and troops advanced and accomplished the difficult operation allotted to them, notwithstanding that all their leaders had fallen.

I particularly request your Lordship's attention to the conduct of Major-General Craufurd, Major-General Vandeleur, Lieutenant-Colonel Barnard of the 95th, Lieutenant-Colonel Colborne, Major Gibbs, and Major Napier of the 52d, and Lieutenant-Colonel McLeod of the 43d. The conduct of Captain Duffy of the 43d, and that of Lieutenant-Gurwood of the 52d regiment, who was wounded, have likewise been particularly reported to me; Lieutenant-Colonel Elder and the 3d Caçadores were likewise distinguished upon this occasion

The 1st Portuguese regiment, under Lieutenant-Colonel Hill, and the 16th, under Colonel Campbell, being Brigadier-General Pack's brigade, were likewise distinguished in the storm under the command of the Brigadier-General, who particularly mentions Major Lynch.

In my dispatch of the 15th, I reported to your Lordship the attack of the convent of Santa Cruz by the troops of the 1st division, under the direction of Lieutenant-General Graham, and that of the convent of Saint Francisco, on the 14th instant, under the direction of Major General the Honourable C. Colville. The first mentioned enterprise was performed by Captain Laroche de Starkerfels, of the 1st line batt.

King's German Legion, the last by Lieutenant-Colonel Harcourt, with the 40th regiment. This regiment remained from that time in the suburb of Saint Francisco, and materially assisted our attack on that side of the place.

Although it did not fall to the lot of the troops of the 1st and 4th divisions to bring these operations to a successful close, they distinguished themselves throughout their progress by the patience and perseverance with which they performed the labour of the siege. The Brigade of Guards under Major-General H. Campbell, were particularly distinguished in this respect.

I likewise request your Lordship's attention to the conduct of Lieutenant-Colonel Fletcher, the chief Engineer, and of Brigade Major Jones, and the officers and men of the Royal Engineers. The ability with which these operations were carried on exceeds all praise; and I beg leave to recommend these Officers to your Lordship most particularly.

Major Dickson of the royal artillery, attached to the Portuguese artillery, has for some time had the direction of the heavy train attached to this army, and has conducted the intricate details of the late operation, as he did that of the two sieges of Badajoz in the last summer, much to my satisfaction. The rapid execution produced by the well directed fire kept up from our batteries affords the best proof of the merits of the officers and men of the royal artillery, and of the Portuguese artillery, employed on this occasion. But I must particularly mention Brigade Major May, and Captains Holcombe, Power, Dynely, and Dundas, of the royal artillery, and Captains Da Cunha and Da Costa, and Lieutenant Silva, of the 1st regiment of Portuguese artillery.

I have likewise particularly to report to your Lordship the conduct of Major Sturgeon of the royal staff corps. He constructed and placed for us the bridge over the Agueda, without which the enterprise could not have been attempted, and he afterwards materially assisted Lieutenant-General Graham and myself in our reconnaissance of the place on which the plan of the attack was founded; and he finally conducted the 2d batt. 5th regiment, as well as the 2d Caçadores, to their points of attack.

The Adjutant-General, and the Deputy-Quarter-Master-General, and the officers of their several departments, gave me every assistance throughout this service, as well as those of my personal Staff; and I have great pleasure in adding notwithstanding the season of the year, and the increased difficulties of procuring supplies for the troops, the whole army have been well supplied, and every branch of the service provided for during the late operations, by the indefatigable exertions of Mr. Commissary-General Bissett, and the officers belonging to his department.

The Marshal del Campo, Don Carlos de Espana, and Don Julian Sanchez, observed the enemy's movements beyond the Tormes during the operations of the siege; and I am much obliged to them, and to the people of Castille in general, for the assistance I received from them. The latter have invariably shown their detestation of the French tyranny, and their desire to contribute, by every means in their power, to remove it.

I shall hereafter transmit to your Lordship a detailed account of what we have found in the place; but I believe that there are one hundred and fifty-three pieces of ordnance, including the heavy train belonging to the French army, and great quantities of ammunition and stores. We have the governor, General Banier, about seventy-eight officers, and one thousand seven hundred men, prisoners.

I transmit this dispatch by my Aide-de-Camp, the Honourable Major Gordon, who will give your Lordship any further details you may require; and I beg leave to recommend him to your protection.

I have the honor to be, &c.
WELLINGTON.

21

STORMING OF BADAJOZ

Downing-Street, April 24, 1812

CAPTAIN CANNING, Aid-de-Camp to General the Earl of Wellington, arrived last night at this Office, bringing dispatches, addressed by his Lordship to the Earl of Liverpool, of which the following are extracts or copies.

Extract of a Dispatch from the Earl of Wellington, dated Camp before Badajoz.
April 3,1812.

WE opened our fire on the 31st of March from twenty-six pieces of cannon, in the second parallel, to breach the face of the bastion at the south east angle of the fort called La Trinidad; and the flank of the bastion by which the face is defended called Santa Maria. The fire upon these has continued since with great effect.

The enemy made a sortie on the night of the 29th, upon the troops of General Hamilton's division, which invest the place on the right of the Guadiana, but were immediately driven in with loss. We lost no men on this occasion.

The movements of Lieutenant-General Sir Thomas Graham and of Lieutenant-General Sir Rowland Hill have obliged the enemy to retire by the different roads to Cordova, with the exception of a small body of infantry and cavalry, which remained at Zalmea de la Serena, in front of Belalcazar.

Marshal Soult broke up in from of Cadiz on the 23rd and 24th, and has marched upon Seville with all the troops which were there, with the exception of four thousand men.

I understand that he has to march from Seville again on the 30th or 31st.

I have not heard from Castille since the 30th ultimo. One division of the Army of Portugal, which had been in the province of Avila, had on that day arrived at Guadapero, within two leagues of Ciudad Rodrigo; and it was supposed that Marshal Marmont was on his march with other troops from the side of Salamanca.

The River Agueda was not fordable for troops on the 30th.

Copy of a Dispatch from the Earl of Wellington, dated Camp before Badajoz,
7th April, 1812.

MY LORD,

My dispatch of the 3rd instant will have apprized your Lordship of the state of the operations against Badajoz to that date, which were brought to a close on the night of the 6th, by the capture of the place by storm.

The fire continued during the 4th and 5th against the face of the bastion of La Trinidad; and the flank of the bastion of Santa Maria; and on the 4th, in the morning, we opened another battery of six guns in the second parallel against the shoulder of the ravelin of San Roque, and the wall in its gorge.

Practicable breaches were effected in the bastions above mentioned on the evening of the 5th; but as I had observed that the enemy had entrenched the bastion of La Trinidad, and the most formidable preparations were making for the defence, as well of the breach in that bastion, as of that in the bastion of Santa Maria, I determined to delay the attack for another day, and to turn all the guns in the batteries in the second parallel on the curtain of La Trinidad, in hopes, that by effecting a third breach, the troops would be enabled to turn the enemy's works for the defence of the other two, the attack of which would besides be connected by the troops destined to attack the breach in the curtain.

This breach was effected in the evening of the 6th, and the fire of the face of the bastion of Santa Maria, and of the flank of the bastion of La Trinidad being overcome, I determined to attack the place that night.

I had kept in reserve in the neighborhood of this camp, the 5th division under Lieutenant-General Leith, which had left Castile only in the middle of March, and had but lately arrived in this part of the country; and I brought them up on that evening.

The plan for the attack was, that Lieutenant-General Picton should attack the castle of Badajoz by escalade with the 3d division; and a detachment from the guard in the trenches furnished that evening by the 4th division, under Major Wilson of the 48th regiment, should attack the ravelin of St. Roque upon his left, while the 4th division under the Honourable Major-General Colville, and the light division under Lieutenant-Colonel Barnard, should attack the breaches in the bastions of La Trinidad and Santa Maria, and in the curtain by which they are connected. The 5th division were to occupy the ground which the 4th and light divisions had occupied during the siege; and Lieutenant-General Leith was to make a false attack upon the outwork called Pardaleras; and another on the works of the fort, towards the Guadiana, with the left brigade of the division under Major-General Walker, which he was to turn into a real attack, if circumstances should prove favourable; and Brigadier-General Power, who invested the place with his Portuguese brigade on the right of the Guadiana, was directed to make false attacks on the tête-du-pont, the fort St. Christoval, and the new redoubt called Mon-Coeur.

The attack was accordingly made at ten at night. Lieutenant-General Picton preceding by a few minutes, the attack by the remainder of the troops.

Major-General Kempt led this attack, which went out from the right of the first parallel; he was unfortunately wounded in crossing the river Rivellas below the inundation; but notwithstanding this circumstance, and the obstinate resistance of the enemy, the castle was carried by escalade; and the 3d division established in it at about half past eleven.

While this was going on, Major Wilson, of the 48th carried the ravelin of St. Roque by the gorge, with a detachment of two hundred men of the guard in the trenches; and with the assistance of Major Squire, of the engineers, established himself within that work.

The 4th and light divisions moved to the attack from the camp along the left of the river Rivellas, and of the inundation. They were not perceived by the enemy, till they reached the covered way; and the advanced guards of the two divisions descended, without difficulty, into the ditch protected by the fire of the parties stationed on the glacis for that purpose; and they advanced to the assault of the breaches led by their gallant officers, with the utmost intrepidity; but such was the nature of the obstacles prepared by the enemy at the top and behind the breaches, and so determined their resistance, that our troops could not establish themselves within the place. Many brave officers and soldiers were killed or wounded by explosions at the top of the breaches; others who succeeded to them were obliged to give way, having found it impossible to penetrate the obstacles which the enemy had prepared to impede their progress. These attempts were repeated till after twelve at night; when, finding that success was not to be attained, and that Lieutenant-General Picton was established in the castle, I ordered that the 4th and light divisions might retire to the ground on which they had been first assembled for the attack.

In the mean time, Lieututenat-General Leith had pushed forward Major-General Walker's brigade on the left, supported by the 38th regiment under Lieutenant-Colonel Nugent, and the 15th Portuguese regiment under Lieutenant-Colonel De Regoa; and he had made a false attack upon the Pardaleras with the 8th Caçadores under Major Hill. Major General Walker forced the barrier on the road of Olivença, and entered the covered way on the left of the bastion of St. Vicente, close to the Guadiana. He there descended into the ditch, and escaladed the face of the bastion of St. Vicente.

Lieutenant-General Leith supported this attack by the 38th regiment, and 15th Portuguese regiment; and our troops being thus established in the castle, which commands all the works of the town, and in the town; and the 4th and light divisions being formed again for the attack of the breaches, all resistance ceased; and at daylight in the morning, the Governor, General Philippon, who had retired to Fort St. Christoval, surrendered, together with General Vielande, and all the staff, and the whole garrison.

I have not got accurate returns of the strength of the garrison, or of the number of prisoners. But General Philippon has informed me that it consisted of five thousand men at the commencement of the siege, of which twelve hundred were killed or wounded during the operations; besides those lost in the assault of the place. There were five French battalions, besides two of the regiment of Hesse D'Armstadt, and the artillery, engineers, &c.; and I understand there are four thousand prisoners.

It is impossible that any expressions of mine can convey to your Lordship the sense which I entertain of the gallantry of the officers and troops upon this occasion.

The list of killed and wounded will show that the General officers, the staff attached to them, the commanding, and other officers of the regiments, put themselves at the head of the attacks which they severally directed, and set the example of gallantry which was so well followed by their men.

Marshal Sir William Beresford assisted me in conducting the details of this siege; and I am much indebted to him for the cordial assistance which I received from him, as well during its progress, as in the last operation which brought it to a termination.

The duties in the trenches were conducted successively by the Honourable Major-General Colville, Major-General Bowes, and Major-General Kempt, under the superintendence of Lieutenant-General Picton. I have had occasion to mention all these officers during the course of the operations; and they all distinguished themselves, and were all wounded in the assault. I am particularly obliged to Lieutenant-General Picton for the manner in which he arranged the attack of the castle; for that in which he supported the attack, and established his troops in that important post.

Lieutenant-General Leith's arrangements for the false attack upon the Pardaleras, and that under Major-General Walker, were likewise most judicious; and he availed himself of the circumstances of the moment, to push forward and support the attack under Major-General Walker, in a manner highly creditable to him. The gallantry and conduct of Major-General Walker, who was also wounded, and that of the officers and troops under his command, were conspicuous.

The arrangements made by Major-General Colville for the attack by the 4th division, were very judicious; and he led them to the attack in the most gallant manner.

In consequence of the absence, on account of sickness, of Major-General Vandeleur, and Colonel Beckwith, Lieutenant-Colonel Barnard commanded the light division in the assault, and distinguished himself not less by the manner in which he made the arrangements for that operation, than by his personal gallantry in its execution.

I have also to mention Brigadier-General Harvey of the Portuguese service, commanding a brigade in the 4th division, and Brigadier-General Champelmond, commanding the Portuguese brigade in the 3d division, as highly distinguished; Brigadier-General Harvey was wounded in the storm.

Your Lordship will see in the list of killed and wounded, a list of the commanding officers of regiments. In Lieutenant-Colonel McLeod, of the 43d regiment who was killed in the breach, His Majesty has sustained the loss of an officer who was an ornament to his profession, and was capable of rendering the most important services to the country. I must likewise mention Lieutenant-Colonel Gibbs of the 52d regiment who was wounded, and Major O'Hare of the 95th, unfortunately killed in the breach; Lieutenant-Colonel Elder of the 3d, and Major Algeo of the 1st Caçadores.

Lieutenant-Colonel Harcourt of the 40th, likewise wounded, was highly distinguished; and Lieutenant-Colonels Blakeney of the royal fusiliers, Knight of the 27th, Erskine of the 48th, and Captain Leaky, who commanded the 23d Fusiliers, Lieutenant-Colonel Ellis having been wounded during the previous operation of the siege.

In the 5th division I must mention Major Hill of the 8th Caçadores, who directed the false attack upon the fort Pardaleras. It was impossible for any men to behave better than these did.

I must likewise mention Lieutenant-Colonel Brooke of the 4th regiment, the Honourable Lieutenant-Colonel Carleton of the 44th, and Lieutenant-Colonel Gray of the 30th, who was unfortunately killed. The 2d battalion of the 38th regiment under Lieutenant-Colonel Nugent, and the 15th Portuguese regiment under Colonel De Regoa, likewise performed their part in a very exemplary manner.

The officers and troops in the 3d division have distinguished themselves as usual in these operations. Lieutenant-General Picton has reported to me particularly the conduct of Lieutenant-Colonel Williams of the 60th, Lieutenant-Colonel Ridge of the 5th, who was unfortunately killed in the assault of the castle; Lieutenant-Colonel Forbes of the 45th, Lieutenant-Colonel Fitzgerald of the 60th, Lieutenant-Colonels Trench and Manners of the 74th; Major Carr of the 83d, and the Honourable Major Pakenham, Assistant Adjutant-General to the 3d division.

He has likewise particularly reported the good conduct of Colonel Campbell of the 94th, commanding the Honourable Major-General Colville's brigade, during his absence in command of the 4th division, whose conduct I have so repeatedly had occasion to report to your Lordship. The officers and men of the corps of engineers and artillery were equally distinguished during the operations of the siege and in its close. Lieutenant-Colonel Fletcher continued to direct the works, (notwithstanding that he was wounded in the sortie made by the enemy on the 19th March,) which were carried on by Major Squire and Major Burgoyne, under his directions. The former established the detachments under Major Wilson, in the ravelin of St. Roque, on the night of the storm; the latter attended the attack of the 3d division on the castle. I have likewise to report the good conduct of Major Jones, Captain Nicholas, and Captain Williams, of the royal engineers.

Major Dickson conducted the details of the artillery service during the siege, as well as upon former occasions, under the general superintendence of Lieuteanr-Colonel Framingham, who, since the absence of Major General Borthwick, has commanded the artillery with the army. I cannot sufficiently applaud the officers and soldiers of the British and Portuguese artillery during the siege, particularly that of Lieutenant-Colonel Robe, who opened the breaching batteries; Majors May and Holcombe, Captain Gardiner and and Lieutenant Bourchier of the royal artillery; Captain De Rettberg of the King's German artillery, and Major Tulloh, of the Portuguese.

Adverting to the extent of the details of the ordnance department during this siege, to the difficulties of the weather, &c., with which Major Dickson had to contend, I must mention him most particularly to your Lordship.

The officers of the Adjutant and Quarter-Master-General's department rendered me every assistance on this occasion, as well as those of my personal staff; and I have to add that I have received reports from the general officers commanding divisions, of the assistance they received from the officers of those departments attached to them, the greatest number of whom, and of their personal staff, are wounded.

In a former dispatch I reported to your Lordship the difficulties with which I had to contend, in consequence of the failure of the civil authorities of the province of Alentejo to perform their duty and supply the army with means of transport; these difficulties have continued to exist; but I must do Major General Victoria, the Governor of Elvas, the justice to report that he, and the troops under his command, have made every exertion, and have done everything in their power to contribute to our success.

Marshal Soult left Seville on the 1st instant, with all the troops which he could collect in Andalusia; and he was in communication with the troops which had retired from Estremadura, under General Drouét, on the 3rd, and he arrived at Llerena on the 4th. I had intended to collect the army in proportion as Marshal Soult should advance; and I requested Lieutenant-General Sir Thomas Graham to retire gradually, while Lieutenant-General Sir Rowland Hill should do the same from Don Benito, and the upper parts of the Guadiana. I do not think it certain that Marshal Soult has made any decided movement from Llerena since the 4th, alhough he has patrolled forward with small detachments of cavalry, and the advanced guard of his infantry have been at Usagre.

None of the army of Portugal have moved to join him.

According to the last reports which I have received of the 4th instant, from the frontier of Castille, it appears that Marshal Marmont had established a body of troops between the Agueda and the Coa, and he had reconnoitred Almeida on the 3rd. Brigadier-General Trant's division of militia had arrived upon the Coa, and Brigadier-General Wilson's division was following with the cavalry, and Lieutenant-General the Conde d'Amarante was on his march, with a part of the corps under his command, towards the Douro.

This dispatch will be delivered to your Lordship by my aide de camp Captain Canning, whom I beg leave to recommend to your protection. He has likewise the colors of the garrison, and the colors of the Hesse D'Armstadt's regiment, to be laid at the feet of His Royal Highness the Prince Regent. The French battalions in the garrison had no eagles.

I have the honor to be, &c.
WELLINGTON.

22

BATTLE OF SALAMANCA

Downing-Street, August 16, 1812.

LORD CLINTON, Aid de Camp to the Earl of Wellington, arrived this morning at the War Department with Dispatches addressed by his Lordship to Earl Bathurst, dated the 24th ultimo, of which the following are extracts.

Flores de Amla, July 24, 1812.

MY Aide-de-Camp, Captain Lord Clinton, will present to your Lordship this account of a victory which the allied troops under my command gained in a general action fought near Salamanca on the evening of the 22 instant, which I have been under the necessity of delaying to send till now, having been engaged ever since the Action in the pursuit of the enemy's flying troops.

In my letter of the 21st I informed your Lordship, that both armies were near the Tormes; and the enemy crossed that river with the greatest part of his troops in the afternoon by the fords between Alba de Tormes and Huerta, and moved by their left towards the roads leading to Ciudad Rodrigo.

The allied army, with the exception of the 3d division and General Durban's cavalry, likewise crossed the Tormes in the evening by the bridge at Salamanca, and the fords in the neighbourhood; and I placed the troops in a position of which the right was upon one of the two heights called Dos Arapiles, and the left on the Tonnes below the ford of Santa Martha.

The 3d division and Brigadier-General D'Urban's cavalry were left at Cabrerizos, on the right of the Tormes, as the enemy had still a large corps on the heights above Babilafuente, on the same side of the river; and I, considered it not improbable, that, finding our army prepared for them in the morning on the left of the Tormes, they would alter their plan, and manoeuvre by the other bank.

In the course of the night of the 21st I received intelligence, of the truth of which I could not doubt, that General Clausel had arrived at Pollos on the 20th, with the cavalry and horse artillery of the army of the north, to join Marshal Marmont; and I was quite certain that these troops would join him on the 22d or 23d at the latest.

During the night of the 21st the enemy had taken possession of the village of Calvarasa de Ariba, and of the height near it called Nuestra Senora de la Pena, our cavalry being in possession of Calvarosa de Abaxo; and shortly after daylight detachments from both armies attempted to obtain possession of the more distant from our right of the two hills called Dos Arapiles.

The enemy however succeeded, their detachment being the strongest, and having been concealed in the woods nearer the hill than we were, by which success, they strengthened materially their own position, and had in their power increased means of annoying ours.

In the morning, the light troops of the 7th division, and the 4th Cacadores belonging to General Pack's brigade, were engaged with the enemy on the height called Nuestra Senora de la Pena, on which height they maintained themselves with the enemy throughout the day. The possession, by the enemy, however, of the more distant of the Arapiles, rendered it necessary for me to extend the right of the army in Potenceon the heights behind the village of Arapiles, and to occupy that village with light infantry; and here I placed the 4th division, under the command of the Honourable Lieutenant-General Cole; and although, from the variety of the enemy's movements, it was difficult to form a satisfactory judgment of his intentions. I considered that, upon the whole, his objects were upon the left of the Tonnes, I therefore ordered the Honourable Major-General Pakenham, who commanded the 3d division, in the absence of Lieutenant-General Picton, on account of ill health, to move across the Torme's with the troops under his command, including Brigadier-General D'Urban's cavalry, and to place himself behind Aldea Tejada, Brigadier-General Bradford's brigade of Portuguese infantry and Don Carlos D'Espana's infantry, having been moved up likewise to the neighbourhood of Las Torres, between the 3d and 4th division.

After a variety of evolutions and movements, the enemy appears to have determined upon his plan about two in the afternoon; and under cover of a very heavy cannonade, which however did us but very little damage, he extended his left and moved forward his troops, apparently with an intention to embrace, by the position of his troops, and his fire, our post on that of the two Arapiles which we possessed, and from thence to attack and break our line; or at all events to render difficult any movement of ours to our right.

The extension of his line to his left however, and its advance upon our right, notwithstanding that his troops still occupied very strong ground, and his position was well defended by cannon, gave me an opportunity of attacking him, for which I had long been anxious. I reinforced our right with the 5th division, under Lieutenant-General Leith, which I placed behind the village of Arapiles, on the right of the 4th division; and with the 5th and 7th divisions in reserve; and as soon as these troops had taken their stations, I ordered Major-General Pakenham to move forward with the 3d division, and General D'Urban cavalry, and two squadrons of the 14th light dragoons, under Lieutenant-Colonel Hervey, in four columns, to turn the enemy's left on the heights, while Brigadier-General Bradford's brigade, the 5th division, under Lieutenant-General Leith, the 4th division, under the Hon. Lieutenant-General Cole, and the cavalry, under Lieutenant-General Sir Stapleton Cotton, should attack them in front, supported in reserve by the 6th division, under Major-General Clinton, the 7th division, under Major-General Hope, and Don Carlos D'Espana's Spanish division, and Brigadier-General Pack should support the left of the 4th division, by attacking that of the Dos Arapiles, which the enemy held. The 1st and light divisions occupied the ground on the left, and were in reserve.

The attack upon the enemy's left was made in the manner above described, and completely succeeded. Major-General the Hon. Edward Pakenham formed the third division across the enemy's flank, and overthrew every thing opposed to him. These troops were supported in the most gallant style by the Portuguese cavalry under Brigadier-General D'Urban, and Lieutenant-Col. Hervey's squadrons of the 14th, who successfully defeated every attempt made by the enemy on the flank of the third division.

Brigadier-General Bradford's brigade, the 5th and 4th divisions and the cavalry under Lieutenant-General Sir Stapleton Cotton, attacked the enemy in front, and drove his troops before them, from one height to another, bringing forward their right, so as to acquire strength upon the enemy's flank, in proportion to the advance. Brigadier-General Pack made a very gallant attack upon the Arapiles, in which, however, he did not succeed, excepting in diverting the attention of the enemy's corps placed upon it, from the troops under the command of Lieutenant-General Cole, in his advance.

The cavalry under Lieutenant-General Sir Stapleton Cotton made a most gallant and successful charge against a body of the enemy's infantry, which they overthrew and cut to pieces. In this charge Major-General Le Merchant was killed at the head of his brigade; and I have to regret the loss of a most able officer.

After the crest of the height was carried, one division of the enemy's infantry made a stand against the 4th division, which, after a severe contest, was obliged to give way, in consequence of the enemy having thrown some troops on the left of the 4th division, after the failure of Brigadier-General Pack's attack upon the Arapiles, and the Honourable Lieutenant-General Cole having been wounded.

Marshal Sir William Beresford, who happened to be on the spot, directed Brigadier-General Spry's brigade of the fifth division, which was in the second line, to change its front, and to bring its fire on the flank of the enemy's division; and, I am sorry to add, that while engaged in this service, he received a wound, which, I am apprehensive will deprive me of the benefit of his counsel and assistance for some time. Nearly about the same Lieutenant-General Leith received a wound, which unfortunately obliged him to quit the field. I ordered up the 6th division under Major-General Clinton, to relieve the 4th, and the battle was soon restored to its former success.

The enemy's right, however, reinforced by the troops which had fled from his left, and by those which had now retired from the Arapiles, still continued to resist; and I ordered the 1st and light divisions, and Colonel Stubb's Portuguese brigade of the

4th division, which was reformed, and Major-General William Anson's brigade, likewise of the 4th division, to turn the right, while the 6th division, supported by the 3d and 5th, attacked the front. It was dark before this point was carried by the 6th division, and the enemy fled through the woods towards the Tormes. I pursued them with the 1st and light divisions, and Major-General William Anson's brigade of the 4th division, and some squadrons of cavalry under Lieut.-Gen. Sir Stapleton Cotton, as long as we could find any of them together, directing our march upon Huerta and the fords of the Tormes, by which the enemy had passed on their advance; but the darkness of the night was highly advantageous to the enemy, many of whom escaped under its cover, who must otherwise have been in our hands.

I am sorry to report that owing to this same cause, Lieutenant-General Sir Stapleton Cotton was unfortunately wounded by one of our own sentries after he had halted.

We renewed the pursuit at break of day in the morning with the same troops, and Major-General Bock's and Major-General Anson's brigades of cavalry, which joined during the night and having crossed the Tormes, we came up with the enemy's rear-guard of cavalry and infantry, near La Serna. They were immediately attacked by the two brigades of dragoons and the cavalry fled, leaving the infantry to their fate. I have never witnessed a more gallant charge than was made on the enemy's infantry by the heavy brigade of the King's German Legion, under Major-General Bock, which was completely successful, and the whole body of infantry, consisting of three battalions of the enemy's first division were made prisoners.

The pursuit was afterwards continued as far as Penaranda last night;and our troops are still following the flying enemy. Their head-quarters were in this town, not less than ten leagues from the field of battle, for a few hours last night; and they are now considerably advanced on the road towards Valladolid by Arevalo. They were joined yesterday on their retreat by the cavalry and artillery of the army of the North, which have arrived at too late a period, it is to be hoped, to be of much use to them.

It is impossible to form a conjecture of the amount of the enemy's loss in this action; but from all reports it is very considerable. We have taken from them eleven pieces of cannon*, several ammunition waggons, two eagles, and six colours; and one general, three colonels, three lieutenant-colonels, 130 officers of inferior rank, and between six and seven thousand soldiers are prisoners;† and our detachments are sending in more every moment. The number of dead on the field is very large.

I am informed that Marshal Marmont is badly wounded, and has lost one of his arms; and that four general officers have been killed, and several wounded.

Such an advantage could not have been acquired without material loss on our side; but it certainly has not been of a magnitude to distress the army, or to cripple its operations.

I have great pleasure in reporting to your Lordship that, throughout this trying day, of which I have related the events, I had every reason to be satisfied with the conduct of the general officers and troops.

The relation which I have written of its events will give a general idea of the share which each individual had in them; and I cannot say too much in praise of the conduct of every individual in his station.

I am much indebted to Marshal Sir William Beresford for his friendly counsel and assistance, both previous to, and during the action, to Lieutenant-Generals Sir Stapleton Cotton, Leith, and Cole, and Major-Generals Clinton, and the Honourable Edward Pakenham for the manner in which they led the divisions of cavalry and infantry under their command respectively; to Major-General Hulse, commanding, a brigade in the 6th division; Major-General G. Anson, commanding a brigade of cavalry; Colonel Hinde, Colonel the Honourable William Ponsonby, commanding Major-General Le Marchant's brigade, after the fall of that officer; to Major-General William Anson, commanding a brigade in the 4th division; Major-General Pringle, commanding a brigade in the 5th division, and the division after Lieutenant-General Leith was wounded; Brigadier-General Bradford; Brigadier-General Spry; Colonel Stubbs, and Brigadier-General Power of the Portuguese service; likewise to Lieutenant-Colonel Campbell, of the 94th, commanding a brigade in the 3d division; Lieutenant-Colonel Williams, of the 60th foot; Lieutenant-Colonel Wallace, of the 88th, commanding a brigade in the 3d division; Lieutenant-Colonel Ellis, of the 23d, commanding General the Hon. Edward Pakenham's brigade in the 4th division, during his absence in the command of the 3d division; the Hon. Lieutenant-Colonel Greville of the 38th regiment, commanding Major-General Hay's brigade in the 5th division, during his absence on leave; Brigadier-General Pack; Brigadier-General the Conde de Rezendi, of the Portuguese Service;Colonel Douglas, of the 8th Portuguese regiment; Lieutenant-Colonel the Conde de Ficalho, of the same regiment; and Lieutenant-Colonel Bingham, of the 53rd regiment; likewise to Brigadier-General d'Urban, and Lieutenant-Colonel Hervey, of the 14th Light Dragoons;Colonel Lord Edward Somerset, commanding the 4th Dragoons; and Lieutenant-Colonel the Honourable Frederick Ponsonby, commanding the 12th Light Dragoons.

I must also mention Lieutenant-Colonel Woodford, commanding the light battalion of the brigade of Guards, who, supported by two companies of the Fusileers, under the command of Captain Crowder, maintained the village of Arapiles against all the efforts of the enemy, previous to the attack upon their position by our troops.

In a case in which the conduct of all has been conspicuously good, I regret that the necessary limits of a dispatch, prevents me from drawing your Lordship's notice to the conduct of a larger number of individuals; but I can assure your Lordship that there was no Officers or Corps engaged in this action, who did not perform his duty by his Sovereign and his Country.

The royal and German artillery, under Lieutenant-Colonel Framingham, distinguished themselves by the accuracy of their fire, wherever it was possible to use them; and they advanced to the attack of the enemy's position with the same gallantry as the other troops.

I am particularly indebted to Lieutenant-Colonel De Lancy, the Deputy Quarter-Master-General, the head of the department present in the absence of the Quarter-Master-General, and to the officers of that department, and of the staff corps, for the assistance I received from them, particularly the Honourable Lieutenant-Colonel Dundas, and Lieutenant-Colonel Sturgeon of the latter, and Major Scovell of the former;and to. Lieut.-Col. Waters, at present at the head of the Adjutant

General's department at head-quarters, and to the officers of that department, as well at head-quarters, as with the several divisions of the army; and Lieutenant-Colonel Lord Fitzroy Somerset, and the officers of my personal staff. Among the latter I particularly request your Lordship to draw the attention of His Royal Highness the Prince Regent to His Serene Highness the Hereditary Prince of Orange, whose conduct in the field, as well as upon every other occasion, entitles him to him to my highest commendation, and has acquired for him the respect and regard of the whole army.

I have had every reason to be satisfied with the conduct of the Mariscal del Campo Don Carlos d'Espagna, and of Brigadier Don Julian Sanchez, and with that of the troops under their command respectively; and with that of the Mariscal del Campo Don Miguel Alava, and of Brigadier Don Joseph O'Lawlor, employed with this army by the Spanish government, from whom, and from the Spanish authorities, and people in general, I received every assistance I could expect.

It is but justice likewise to draw your Lordship's attention, upon this occasion, to the merits of the officers of the civil departments of the army. Notwithstanding the increased distance of our operations from our magazines, and that the country is completely exhausted, we have hitherto wanted nothing, owing to the diligence and attention of Commissary General, Mr. Bisset, and the officers of the department under his direction.

I have likewise to mention that by the attention and ability of Doctor Mac Gregor, and of the Officers of the department under his charge, our wounded as well as those of the enemy left in our hands have been well taken care of; and I hope that many of these valuable men will be saved to the service.

Captain Lord Clinton will have the honour of laying at the feet of His Royal Highness the Prince Regent, the Eagles and colours taken from the enemy in this action.

I have the honor to be, &c.
WELLINGTON.

*The official returns only account for eleven pieces of cannon; but it is believed that twenty have fallen into our hands.

†The prisoners are supposed to amount to seven thousand; but it has not been possible to ascertain their numbers exactly, from the advance of the army immediately the action was over.

23

ASSAULT OF BURGOS

Downing-Street, November 17, 1812.

DISPATCHES, of which the following are extracts, have been this day received at Earl Bathurst's office, addressed to his Lordship by General the Marquess of Wellington, dated Cabeçon 26th and 28th October, Rueda, 31st October and 3d November 1812.

Cabeçon, 26th October, 1812.

I have been so much occupied by the movements and operations of the army since the 18th instant, that I have not been able to write to your Lordship.

The operations of the siege of the Castle of Burgos continued nearly in the state in which they were when I addressed your Lordship on the 11th instant, until the 18th. Having at that time received a supply of musket ammunition from Santander, and having, while waiting for that necessary article, completed a mine under the church of St. Roman, which stood in an outwork of the second line, I determined that the breach which we had effected in the second line should be stormed that evening, at the moment this mine should explode; and that at the same time the line should be attacked by escalade.

The mine succeeded, and Lieutenant-Colonel Brown lodged a party of the 9th Caçadores and a detachment of Spanish troops of the regiment of Asturias in the outwork. A detachment of the King's German legion under Major Wurmb carried the breach, and a detachment of the Guards succeeded in escalading the line; but the enemy brought such a fire upon these two last detachments from the 3rd line and the body of the castle itself, and they were attacked by numbers so superior, before they could receive the support allotted to them, that they were obliged to retire, suffering considerable loss. Major Wurmb was unfortunately killed.

It is impossible to represent in adequate terms my sense of the conduct of the Guards and German Legion upon this occasion; and I am quite satisfied, that if it had been possible to maintain the posts which they had gained with so much gallantry, those troops would have maintained them. Some of the men stormed even the third line, and one was killed in one of the embrasures of that line; and I had the satisfaction of seeing, that if I could breach the wall of the castle, we should carry the place.

Another mine was commenced under the second line, from the Church of St. Roman, of which we remained in possession.

The enemy had on the 13th moved forward a considerable body of infantry and six squadrons of cavalry from Briviesca, to reconnoitre our outpost at Monasterio. They attacked the piquet at the bridge in front of the town, but were repulsed by the fire of a detachment of the infantry of the Brunswick Legion. In this affair Lieutenant-Colonel the Honourable Fredrick Ponsonby, who commanded at Monasterio, was wounded, but not severely; and I hope I shall soon again have the benefit of his assistance.

I had long had reports of the enemy's intention to advance for the relief of the castle of Burgos with the army of Portugal, reinforced by troops recently arrived from France, and with that part of the army of the north which was disposable; and they did advance in considerable force against the post of Monasterio, on the evening of the 18th. The subaltern of the Brunswick Legion, who commanded a piquet in St. Olalla, disobeyed his orders in remaining in that village upon the approach of the enemy; and he was taken with his piquet. The enemy consequently obtained possession of the heights which command the town of Monasterio, and our outpost was obliged to retire, on the morning of the 19th, to the Burgos side of the town.

I assembled the troops, excepting those necessary for carrying on the operations of the siege, as soon as it appeared, by the enemy's movement of the 18th, that they entertained serious intentions of endeavoring to raise it; and placed the allied army on the heights, having their right at Ibeas, on the Arlanzon, the centre at Riobena and Mijaradas, and the left at Soto Palacios. The enemy's army likewise assembled in the neighbourhood of Monasterio.

They moved forward on the evening of the 20th with about ten thousand men, to drive in our outposts from Quintana Palla and Olmos. The former withdrew by order; but the latter was maintained with great spirit by the Chasseurs Britanniques.

Seeing a fair opportunity of striking a blow upon the enemy, I requested Lieutenant-General Sir Edward Paget to move with the 1st and 5th divisions upon the enemy's right flank, which movement having been well executed, drove them back upon Monasterio; and our posts were replaced in Quintana Palla.

On the morning of the 21st, I received a letter from Sir Roland Hill of the 17th, in which he acquainted me with the enemy's intention to move towards the Tagus, which was already fordable by individuals in many places, and was likely to become so by an army.

The castle of Chinchilla had surrendered on the 9th instant.

The enemy's force in Valencia was supposed to amount to not less than seventy thousand men, a very large proportion of which, it was expected, would be disposable for service out of that kingdom.

I had desired Lieutenant-General Sir Rowland Hill to retire from his position on the Tagus, if he should find that he could not maintain himself in it with advantage, and it was necessary that I should be near him, in order that the corps under my command might not be insulated in consequence of the movements which he should find himself under the necessity of making; I therefore raised the siege of Burgos on the night of the 21st, and moved the whole army back towards the Duero.

I felt severely the sacrifice I was obliged to make. Your Lordship is well aware that I never was very sanguine in my expectations of success in the siege of Burgos, notwithstanding that I considered that success was attainable, even with the means in my power, within a reasonably limited period. If the attack on the first line, made on the 22nd or the 29th, had succeeded, I believe we should have taken the place, notwithstanding the ability with which the Governor conducted the defence, and the gallantry with which it was executed by the garrison. Our means were very limited; but it appeared to me that if we should succeed, the advantage to the cause would be great, and the final success of the campaign would have been certain.

I had every reason to be satisfied with the conduct of the officers and troops during the siege of Burgos, particularly with the brigade of Guards.

During the latter part of the siege, the weather was very unfavorable, and the troops suffered much from the rain. The officers at the head of the Artillery and Engineer departments, Lieutenant-Colonel Robe, and Lieutenant-Colonel Burgoyne, and Lieutenant-Colonel Dickson, who commands the reserve artillery, rendered me every assistance, and the failure of success is not to be attributed to them. By their activity we carried off every thing in the course of one night, excepting the three eighteen-pounders destroyed by the enemy's fire, and the eight pieces of cannon which we had taken from the enemy on the night of the 19th ultimo, in the storm of the horn-work, not having cattle to move them.

The enemy were not aware of our movements, and did not follow us till late on the 22nd, when ten thousand men encamped on this side of Burgos. The British army encamped at Celada del Camino and Hornillos, with the light cavalry at Estepan and Baniel. We continued our march the following day; the right of the army to Torquemada, the left to Cordevilla, at which places we crossed the Pisuerga.

The enemy followed our movement with their whole army. Our rear guard consisted of the two light battalions of the King's German Legion, under Colonel Halkett, and of Major-General Anson's brigade of cavalry; and Major General Bock's brigade was halted at the Venta del Pozo, to give them support. The whole under the command of Lieutenant General Sir Stapleton Cotton. Don Julian Sanchez marched on the left of the Arlanzon; and the party of Guerrillas heretofore commanded by the late Martinez, in the hills on the left of our rear guard.

Major General Anson's brigade charged twice, with great success, in front of Celada del Camino, and the enemy were detained above three hours by the troops under Lieutenant General Sir Stapleton Cotton, in the passage of the Hormaza, in front of that village.

The rear guard continued to fall back in the best order, till the Guerrillas on the left having been driven in, they rode towards the flank of the rear guard of Major General Anson's brigade, and four or five squadrons of the enemy mixed with them. These were mistaken for Spaniards, and they fell upon the flank and rear of our troops. We sustained some loss, and Lieutenant Colonel Pelly, of the 16th dragoons, having had his horse shot, was taken prisoner.

The delay occasioned by this misfortune enabled the enemy to bring up a very superior body of cavalry, which was charged by Maj. Gen. Bock's and Major-Gen Anson's brigades, near the Venta del Pozo, but unsuccessfully; and our rear guard was hard pressed. The enemy made three charges on the two light battalions of the King's German Legion, formed in squares, but were always repulsed with considerable loss by the steadiness of these two battalions. They suffered no loss, and I cannot sufficiently applaud their conduct, and that of Colonel Halkett, who commanded them.

The exertions and conduct of Lieutenant General Sir S. Cotton, and of the officers and Staff attached to him, throughout this day, were highly meritorious; and although the charge made by the cavalry was not successful, I had the satisfaction of observing great steadiness in their movements. Major Bull's troop of horse artillery, under Major Downman and Captain Ramsay, distinguished themselves.

The army continued its march on the 24th, and took up its ground on the Carrion, with its right at Duenas, and left at Villa Muriel, and the 1st battalion 1st Guards joined us from Coruna.

I halted there on the 25th, and the enemy attacked our left at Villa Muriel. They were repulsed, however, by the 5th division of infantry, under the command of Major General Oswald, in the absence of Lieutenant General Leith, on account of indisposition.

I had directed the 3rd battalion of the Royals to march to Palencia, to protect the destruction of the bridges over the Carrion at that place, but it appears that the enemy assembled in such force at that point, that Lieut. Colonel Campbell thought it necessary to retire upon Villa Muriel, and the enemy passed the Carrion at Palencia. This rendered it necessary to change our front, and I directed Major General Oswald to throw back our left, and the Spanish troops upon the heights, and to maintain the Carrion with the right of the 5th division. The bridge of Villa Muriel was destroyed, but the enemy discovered a ford and passed over a considerable body of cavalry and infantry. I made M. General Pringle and M. General Barnes attack these troops, under the orders of Major General Oswald; in which attack the Spanish troops co-operated, and they were driven across the river with considerable loss. The fire upon the left had been very severe throughout the day, from which we suffered a good deal; and M. General Don Miguel Alava was unfortunately wounded while carrying on the Spanish infantry in the pursuit of the enemy.

I broke up this morning from the Carrion, and marched upon Cabezon del Campo, where I have crossed the Pisuerga. The enemy appear to be moving in this direction from Duenas. I propose to halt here to-morrow.

I have the honor to be, &c.
WELLINGTON

24

BATTLE OF CASTALLA

Downing-Street, May 18, 1813.

A DISPATCH, of which the following is a Copy, was this morning received by Earl Bathurst, from Lieutenant-General Sir John Murray, Bart.

Head Quarters, Castalla, April 14th, 1813.

MY LORD,

I HAVE the satisfaction to inform your Lordship, that the allied army under my command defeated the enemy on the 13th instant, commanded by Marshal Suchet in person.

It appears that the French General had, for the purpose of attacking this army, for some time been employed in collecting his whole disposable force.

His arrangements were completed on the 10th, and in the morning of the 11th, he attacked and dislodged with some loss, a Spanish corps, posted by General Elio, at Yecla, which threatened his right, whilst it supported our left flank.

In the evening he advanced in considerable force to Villena, and I am sorry to say, that he captured, on the morning of the 12th, a Spanish garrison, which had been thrown into the castle by the Spanish General, for its defence.

On the 12th, about noon, Marshal Suchet began his attack on the advance of this army posted at Biar, under the command of Colonel Adam.

Colonel Adam's orders were to fall back upon Castalla, but to dispute the passage with the enemy; which he did with the utmost gallantry and skill, for five hours, though attacked by a force infinitely superior to that which he commanded.

The enemy's advance occupied the pass that evening, and Colonel Adam took up the ground in our position which had been allotted to him.

On the 13th at noon, the enemy's columns of attack were formed, composed of three divisions of infantry, a corps of cavalry of about sixteen hundred men, and a formidable train of artillery.

The position of the allied army was extensive. The left was posted on a strong range of hills, occupied by Major-General Whittingham's division of Spanish troops, and the advance of the allied army under Colonel Adam.

This range of hills terminates at Castalla, which, and the ground to the right, was occupied by Major-General Mackenzie's division, and the 58th regiment from that of Lieutenant-General Clinton.

The remainder of the position was covered by a strong ravine, behind which Lieutennt-General Clinton was stationed, supported by three battalions of General Roche's division, as a column of reserve.

A few batteries had been constructed in this part of the line, and in front of the castle of Castalla. The enemy necessarily advanced on the left of the position. The first movement he made, was to pass a strong body of cavalry along the line, threatening our right, which was refused. Of this movement no notice was taken; the ground to which he was pointing, is unfavorable to cavalry, and as this movement was foreseen, the necessary precautions had been taken; when this body of cavalry had passed nearly the half of our line of infantry, Marshal Suchet advanced his columns to the foot of the hills, and certainly his troops, with a degree of gallantry that entitles them to the highest praise, stormed the whole line, which is not less than two miles and a half in extent. But gallantly as the attack was made, the defence of the heights was no less brilliant: at every point the enemy was repulsed – at many with the bayonet.

He suffered a very severe loss; our gallant troops pursued him for some distance, and drove him, after a severe struggle, with precipitation on his battalions of reserve upon the plain. The cavalry which had slowly advanced along our right, gradually fell back to the infantry. At present his superiority in that arm enabled him to venture this movement, which otherwise he should have severely repented.

Having united his shattered battalions with those which he kept in reserve, Marshal Suchet took up a position in the valley; but which it would not have been creditable to allow him to retain. I therefore decided on quitting mine still, however, retaining the heights, and formed the allied army in his front covering my right flank with the cavalry, whilst the left rested on the hills. The army advanced in two lines to attack him a considerable distance, but unfortunately Marshal Suchet did not choose to risk a second action, with the defile in his rear.

The line of the allies was scarcely formed when he began his retreat, and we could effect nothing more than driving the French into the pass with defeat, which they had exultingly passed in the morning. The action terminated at dusk, with a distant but heavy cannonade.

I am sorry to say that I have no trophies to boast of. The enemy took no guns to the heights, and he retired too expeditiously to enable me to reach him. Those which he used in the latter part of the day, were posted, in the gorge of the defile, and it would have cost us the lives of many brave men to take them.

In the dusk, the allied army returned to its position at Castalla, after the enemy had retired to Biar. From thence he continued his retreat at midnight to Villena, which be quitted again this morning in great haste, directing his march upon Fuente de la Higuera and Onteniente.

But although I have taken no cannon from the enemy, in point of numbers his army is very considerably crippled, and the defeat of a French army, which boasted it had never known a check, cannot fail, I should hope, in producing a most favorable effect in this part of the Peninsula.

As I before mentioned to your Lordship, Marshal Suchet commanded in person.

The Generals Harispe, Habert, and Robert, commanded their respective divisions. I hear from all quarters that General Harispe is killed; and I believe, from every account that I can collect, that the loss of the enemy amounts fully to three thousand men; and he admits to two thousand five hundred. Upwards of eight hundred have already been buried in front of only one part of our line; and we know that he has carried off with him an immense number of wounded.

We had no opportunity of making prisoners, except such as were wounded; the numbers of which have not yet reached me.

I am sure your Lordship will hear with much satisfaction, that this action has not cost us the lives of many of our comrades.

Deeply must be felt the loss, however trifling, of such brave and gallant soldiers: but we know it is inevitable, and I can with truth affirm, that there not an officer or soldier engaged who did not court the glorious termination of an honorable life, in the discharge of his duty to his King and to his country.

The gallant and judicious conduct of those that were engaged, deprived much more than one half the army of sharing in the perils and glory of the day; but the steady countenance with which the divisions of Generals Clinton and Mackenzie remained for some hours under a cannonade, and the eagerness and alacrity with which the lines of attack were formed, sufficiently proved to me what I had to depend on from them, had Marshal Suchet awaited the attack.

I trust your Lordship will now permit me to perform the most pleasing part of my duty, that of humbly submitting for His Royal Highness the Prince Regent's approbation, the names of those officers and corps which have had the fortunate opportunity of distinguishing themselves, in as far at least as has yet come to my knowledge.

Colonel Adam, who commands the advance, claims the first place in this honorable list. I cannot sufficiently praise the judicious arrangements he made, and the ability with which he executed his orders on the 12th instant.

The advance consists only of the 2nd battalion 27th regiment, commanded by Lieutenant-Colonel Reeves; the 1st Italian regiment, commanded by Lieutenant-Colonel Burke; the Calabrian Free corps, commanded by Major Carey; one rifle company of the 3rd and 8th battalions King's German Legion, commanded by Captains Luedor and Brauns of those corps; and a troop of foreign hussars, under the orders of Captain Jacks, of the 20th dragoons, with four mountain guns, in charge of Captain Arabin, Royal artillery.

The enemy attacked this corps with from five to six thousand men, and for five hours (and then only in consequence of orders) succeeded in possessing himself of the pass.

This fact alone says more in favor of Colonel Adam, and in praise of those he commands, than any words of mine can express. I shall therefore confine myself to assuring your Lordship, that the conduct of all engaged in this brilliant affair merits, and has met with, my highest approbation.

Colonel Adam was wounded very early in the attack, but continued, and still continues in charge of his division.

On the 13th, the attack of the enemy on Colonel Adam's division was very severe, but the enemy was defeated at every point, and a most gallant charge of the 2nd, 27th, led by Colonel Adam and Lieutenant-Colonel Reeves, decided the fate of the day, at that part of the field of battle.

The skill, judgment, and gallantry displayed by Major-General Whittingham and his division of the Spanish army, rivals, though it cannot surpass, the conduct of Colonel Adam and the advance.

At every point the enemy was repulsed; at many at the point of the bayonet. At one point in particular I must mention, where a French grenadier battalion had gained the summit of the hill, but was charged and driven from the heights by a corps under the command of Colonel Casans.

Major-General Whittingham highly applauds, and I know it is not without reason the conduct of Colonel Casans, Colonel Romero, Colonel Campbell, Colonel Casteras, and Lieutenant-Colonel Ochoa, who commanded at various points of the hills. To the chief of his Staff, Colonel Serrano, he likewise expresses himself to be equally obliged on this, as well as many other occasions; – and he acknowledges with gratitude the services of Colonel Catinelli, of the Staff of the Italian Levy, who was attached to him during the day.

These my Lord, are the officers and corps that I am most anxious to recommend to His Royal Highness's notice and protection, and I earnestly entreat your Lordship will most respectfully, on my part report their merits to the Prince Regent, and to the Spanish Government.

It now only remains for me to acknowledge the cordial co-operation and support I have met with from the several General Officers and Brigadiers, as well as from the various officers in charge of departments attached to this army.

To Major General Donkin, Quarter-Master-General, I am particularly indebted, for the zeal and ability with which he conducts the duties of his extensive department, and the gallantry he displays on every occasion.

Major Kenah, who is at the head of the Adjutant-General's department affords me every satisfaction. Lieutenant-Colonel Holcombe, and under his orders Major Williamson, conduct the artillery branch of the service in a manner highly creditable. The different brigades of guns, under Captains Lacy, Thomson, and Gilmour, (and Garcia of the Sicilian army,) and Lieutenant Patton, of the flying artillery, were extremely useful, and most gallantly served; and the Portuguese artillery supported the reputation their countrymen have acquired.

The army is now in march. I proceed to Alcoy in the hope, but not the sanguine hope, that I may be enabled to force the Albayda Pass, and reach the entrenched position of the enemy of San Felippe, before he can arrive there.

I consider this movement as promising greater advantages than a direct pursuit, as the road which he has chosen being very favorable for cavalry, in which arm he is so much superior, I should probably be delayed too long to strike any blow of importance.

I have the honor to be, &c.

(Signed) J.MURRAY, Lieut. General.

P.S.   I have omitted to mention, that in retiring from Biar, two of the mountain guns fell into the hands of the enemy; they were disabled, and Colonel Adam very judiciously directed Captain Arabin, who then commanded the brigade, to fight them to the last, and then to leave them to their fate. Captain Arabia obeyed his orders, and fought them till it was quite impossible to get them off, had such been Colonel Adams's desire.

25

BATTLE OF VITORIA

Downing-Street, July 3, 1813.

DISPATCHES, of which the following are copies, have been this day received by Earl Bathurst, from the Marquess of Wellington, dated Salvatierra, June 22, 1813.

MY LORD,

THE enemy's army, commanded by Joseph Bonaparte, having Marshal Jourdan as the Major-General of the army, took up a position, on the night of the 19th instant, in front of Vitoria; the left of which rested upon the heights which end at La Puebla de Arlanzon, and extended from thence across the valley of the Zadora, in front of the village of Aruñez. They occupied with the right of the centre a height which commanded the valley to the Zadorra. The right of their army was stationed near Vittoria, and was destined to defend the passages of the river Zadora, in the neighbourhood of that city. They had a reserve in rear of their left, at the village of Gomecha.

The nature of the country through which the army had passed since it had reached the Ebro, had necessarily extended our columns, and we halted on the 20th, in order to close them up, and moved the left to Murguia, where it was most likely it would be required. I reconnoitred the enemy's position on that day, with a view to the attack to be made on the following morning, if they should still remain in it.

We accordingly attacked the enemy yesterday, and I am happy to inform your Lordship, that the allied army under my command gained a complete victory, having driven them from all their positions; having taken from them one hundred and fifty-one pieces of cannon, four hundred and fifteen waggons of ammunition, all their baggage, provisions, cattle, treasure, &c., and a considerable number of prisoners.

The operations of the day commenced by Lieutenant-General Sir Rowland Hill obtaining possession of the heights of La Puebla, on which the enemy's left rested, which heights they had not occupied in great strength.

He detached for this service one brigade of the Spanish division under General Morillo; the other brigade being employed in keeping the communication between his main body on the high road from Miranda to Vittoria, and the troops detached to the heights. The enemy, however, soon discovered the importance of these heights, and reinforced their troops there to such an extent, that Lieutenant-General Sir

Rowland Hill was obliged to detach, first, the 71st regiment and the light infantry battalion of Major-General Walker's brigade, under the command of the Hon. Lieut.-Colonel Cadogan, and successively other troops to the same point; and the Allies not only gained, but maintained possession of these important heights throughout their operations, notwithstanding all the efforts of the enemy to retake them.The contest here was, however, very severe, and the loss sustained considerable. General Morillo was wounded, but remained in the field; and I am concerned to have to report, that the Honourable Lieutenant-Colonel Cadogan has died of a wound which he received. In him His Majesty has lost an officer of great merit and tried gallantry, who had already acquired the respect and regard of the whole profession, and of whom it might have been expected that, if he had lived, he would have rendered the most important services to his country.

Under cover of the possession of these heights, Sir Rowland Hill successively passed the Zadora, at La Puebla, and the defile formed by the heights and the river Zadora, and attacked and gained possession of the village of Sabijana de Alava, in front of the enemy's line, which the enemy made repeated attempts to regain.

The difficult nature of the country prevented the communication between our different columns moving to the attack from their stations on the river Bayas at as early an hour as I had expected; and it was late before I knew that the column, composed of the 3rd and 7th divisions, under the command of the Earl of Dalhousie, had arrived at the station appointed for them.

The fourth and light divisions, however, passed the Zadora immediately after Sir Rowland Hill had possession of Sabijana de Alava; the former at the bridge of Nanclaus, and the latter at the bridge of Tres Puentes, and almost as soon as these had crossed, the column under the Earl of Dalhousie arrived at Mendouza, and the 3rd division, under Lieutenant-General Sir Thomas Picton, crossed at the bridge higher up, followed by the 7th division, under the Earl of Dalhousie.

These four divisions, forming the centre of the army, were destined to attack the height on which the right of the enemy's centre was placed, while Lieutenant-General Sir Rowland Hill should move forward from Sabijana de Alava to attack the left. The enemy, however, having weakened his line to strengthen his detachment on the hills, abandoned his position in the valley as soon as he saw our disposition to attack it, and commenced his retreat in good order towards Vittoria.

Our troops continued to advance in admirable order, notwithstanding the difficulty of the ground. In the mean time, Lieutenant-General Sir Thomas Graham, who commanded the left of the army, consisting of the 1st and 5th divisions, and General Pack's and Bradford's brigades of infantry, and General Bock's and Anson's of cavalry, and who had been moved on the 20th to Margina, moved forward from thence on Vittoria, by the high road from that town to Bilbao. He had, besides, with him the Spanish division under Colonel Longa; and General Giron, who had been detached to the left, under a different view of the state of affairs, and had afterwards been recalled, and had arrived on the 20th at Orduna, marched that morning from thence, so as to be in the field in readiness to support Lieutenant-General Sir Thomas Graham, if his support had been required.

The enemy had a division of infantry with some cavalry advanced on the great road from Vittoria to Bilbao, resting their right on some strong heights covering the village of Gamarro Maior. Both Gamarro and Abechuco were strongly occupied as têtes de pont and the bridges over the Zadora at these places. Brigadier General Pack with his Portuguese brigade, and Colonel Longa with his Spanish division, were directed to turn and gain the heights, supported by Major-General Anson's brigade of light dragoons, and the 5th division of infantry under the command of Major-General Oswald, who was desired to take the command of all troops.

Lieutenant-General Sir T. Graham reports, that in the execution of this service the Portuguese and Spanish troops behaved admirably. The 4th and 8th Caçadores, particularly distinguished themselves. Colonel Longa being on the left, took possession of Gamarra Menor.

As soon as the heights were in our possession, the village of Gamarra Maior was most gallantly stormed and carried by Brigadier-General Robinson's brigade of the 5th division, which advanced in columns of battalions, under a very heavy fire of artillery and musketry, without firing a shot, assisted by two guns of Major Lawson's brigade of artillery. The enemy suffered severely, and lost three pieces of cannon.

The Lieutenant-General then proceeded to attack the village of Abechuco with the 1st division, by forming a strong battery against it, consisting of Captain Dubourdieu's brigade, and Captain Ramsay's troop of horse artillery; and under cover of this fire, Colonel Halkett's brigade advanced to the attack of the village, which was carried; the light battalions having charged and taken three guns and a howitzer on the bridge. This attack was supported by General Bradford's brigade of Portuguese infantry.

During the operation at Abechuco the enemy made the greatest efforts to repossess themselves of the village of Gamarra Maior, which were gallantly repulsed by the 5th division, under the command of Major-General Oswald. The enemy had, however, on the heights on the left of the Zadora, two divisions of infantry in reserve; and it was impossible to cross by the bridges till the troops which had moved upon the enemy's centre and left had driven them through Vittoria.

The whole then co-operated in the pursuit, which was continued by all till after it was dark.

The movement of the troops under Lieutenant-General Sir Thomas Graham, and their possession of Gamarra and Abechuco, intercepted the enemy's retreat by the high road to France. They were then obliged to turn to the road towards Pamplona; but they were unable to hold any position for a sufficient length of time to allow their baggage and artillery to be drawn off. The whole, therefore, of the latter which had not already been taken by the troops in their attack of the successive positions taken up by the enemy in their retreat from their first position at Aruñey and on the Zadora, and all their ammunition and baggage, and ever thing they had were taken close to Vittoria. I have reason to believe that the enemy carried off with them one gun and one howitzer only.

The army under Joseph Buonaparte consisted of the whole of the armies of the South, and of the Centre, and of four divisions and all the cavalry of the army of

Portugal, and some troops of the army of the North. General Foy's division of the army of Portugal was in the neighbourhood of Bilbao; and General Clausel, who commanded the army of the North, was near Logrono with one division of the army of Portugal commanded by General Topin, and General Vandermaseu's division of the army of the North. The 6th division of the allied army under Major-General the Honourable Edward Pakenham was likewise absent, having been detained at Medina del Pomar for three days, to cover the march of our magazines and stores.

I cannot extol too highly the good conduct of all the general officers, officers, and soldiers of the army in this action. Lieutenant-General Sir Rowland Hill speaks highly of the conduct of General Morillo and the Spanish troops under his command, and of that of Lieutenant-General the Honourable W. Stewart, and the Conde d'Amarante, who commanded divisions of infantry under his directions. He likewise mentions the conduct of the Honourable Lieutenant-Colonel O'Callaghan, who maintained the village of Sabijana de Alava against all the efforts of the enemy to regain possession of it, and that of Lieutenant-Colonel Rooke of the Adjutant-General's department, and Lieutenant-Colonel the Honourable Alexander Abercromby of the Quarter-Master-General's department. It was impossible for the movements of any troops to be conducted with more spirit and regularity than those of their respective divisions, by Lieutenant-General the Earl of Dalhousie, Sir Thomas Picton, Sir Lowry Cole, and Major-General Charles Baron Alten. These troops advanced in echelons of regiments in two, and occasionally three lines; and the Portuguese troops in the 3rd and 4th divisions, under the command of Brigadier-General Power and Colonel Stubbs, led the march with steadiness and gallantry never surpassed on any occasion.

Major-General the Hon. C. Colville's brigade of the 3rd division was seriously attacked in its advance by a very superior force well formed, which it drove in, supported by General Inglis's brigade of the 7th division, commanded by Colonel Grant, of the 82nd. These officers and the troops under their command distinguished themselves.

Major-General Vandeleur's brigade of the light division was, during the advance upon Vittoria, detached to the support of the 7th division, and Lieutenant-General the Earl of Dalhousie has reported most favorably of its conduct.

Lieutenant-General Sir Thomas Graham particularly reports his sense of the assistance he received from Colonel Delancy, the Deputy Quarter-Master-General, and from Lieutenant-Colonel Bouverie, of the Adjutant-General's department, and from the officers of his personal staff; and from the Honourable Lieutenant-Colonel Upton, Assistant Quarter-Master General, and Major Hope, Assistant-Adjutant, with the 1st division; and Major-General Oswald reports the same of Lieutenant-Colonel Berkeley of the Adjutant-General's department, and Lieutenant-Colonel Gomm of the Quarter Master-General's department.

I am particularly indebted to Lieutenant-General Sir Thomas Graham, and to Lieutenant-General Sir Rowland Hill, for the manner in which they have respectively conducted the service entrusted to them since the commencement of the operations which have ended in the battle of the 21st, and for their conduct in that battle; as likewise to Marshal Sir William Beresford for the friendly advice and assistance which I have received from him upon all occasions during the late operations.

I must not omit to mention likewise the conduct of General Giron, who commands the Gallician army, who made a forced march from Orduña, and was actually on the ground in readiness to support Lieutenant-General Sir Thomas Graham.

I have frequently been indebted, and have had occasion to call the attention of your Lordship to the conduct of the Quarter-Master-General Major General Sir George Murray, who in the late operations, and in the battle of the 21st of June, has again given the greatest assistance. I am likewise much indebted to Lord Aylmer, the Deputy-Adjutant-General, and to the Officers of the Adjutant and Quarter-Master-General's Departments respectively, and also to Lieutenant-General Lord Fitzroy Somerset, Lieutenant-Colonel Campbell and the Officers of my personal Staff, and to Lieutenant-Colonel Sir Richard Fletcher, and the Officers of the Royal Engineers.

Colonel his Serene Highness the Hereditary Prince of Orange was in the field as my Aide-de-camp, and conducted himself with his usual gallantry and intelligence.

Mareschal del Campo Don Luis Wimpfen, and the Inspector-General Don Thomas O'Donoju, and the officers of the staff of the Spanish army have invariably rendered me every assistance in their power in the course of these operations; and I avail myself of this opportunity of expressing my satisfaction with their conduct; as likewise with that of Mareschal del Campo Don Miguel Alava; and of the Brigadier-General Don Joseph O'Lawlor, who have been so long and usefully employed with me.

The artillery was most judiciously placed by Lieutenant-Colonel Dickson, and was well served; and the army is particularly indebted to that corps.

The nature of the ground did not allow of the cavalry being generally engaged, but the General Officers commanding the several brigades kept the troops under their command respectively close to the infantry to support them, and they were most active in the pursuit of the enemy after they had been driven through Vittoria.

I send this dispatch by my Aide-de-camp Captain Fremantle, whom I beg leave to recommend to your Lordship's protection. He will have the honor of laying at the feet of His Royal Highness the colors of the 4th battalion of the 100th regiment and Marshal Jourdan's Bâton of a Marshal of France taken by the 87th regiment.

I have the honor to be, &c.
WELLINGTON.

26

BATTLE OF
THE PYRENEES

Downing-Street, August 16, 1813.

HIS Serene Highness the Hereditary Prince of Orange, has arrived at this office with dispatches addressed to Earl Bathurst, by Field-Marshal the Marquess of Wellington, of which the following are copies.

San Estevan, 1st August, 1813.

MY LORD,

TWO practicable breaches having been effected at San Sebastian on the 24th July, orders were given that they should be attacked on the morning of the 25th.

I am concerned to have to report that this attempt to obtain possession of the place failed, and that our loss was very considerable.

Marshal Soult had been appointed *Lieutenant de l'Empereur,* and Commander in Chief of the French armies in Spain and the southern provinces of France, by a *Decret Imperial* on the 1st of July; and he joined and took the command of the army on the 13th July, which having been joined nearly about the same time by the corps which had been in Spain under the command of General Clauzel, and by other reinforcements, was called the Army of Spain, and re-formed into nine divisions of infantry, forming the right, centre, and left, under the command of General Reille, the Comte d'Erlon, and General Clauzel, as Lieutenant-Generals, and a reserve under General Villatte; and two divisions of dragoons and one of light cavalry, the two former under the command of Generals Treillard and Tilly, and the latter under the command of General Pierre Soult. There was besides allotted to the army a large proportion of artillery, and a considerable number of guns had already joined.

The allied army was posted, as I have already informed your Lordship, in the passes of the mountains, with a view to cover the blockade of Pamplona and the siege of San Sebastian. Major-General Byng's brigade of British infantry, and General Morillo's division of Spanish infantry were on the right in the pass of Roncesvalles.

Lieutenant-General Sir Lowry Cole was posted at Viscarret to support those troops, and Lieutenant-General Sir Thomas Picton, with the third division, at Olaque in reserve.

Lieutenant-General Sir Rowland Hill occupied the valley of Bastan with the remainder of the second division, and the Portuguese division under the Conde de Amarante, detaching General Campbell's Portuguese brigade to Los Alduides, within the French territory. The light and seventh occupied the heights of Santa Barbara and the town of Vera, and the Puerto de Echalar, and kept the communication with the valley of Bastan; and the sixth division was in reserve at San Estevan. General Longa's division kept the communication between the troops at Vera and those under Lieutenant-General Sir Thomas Graham and Mariscal del Campo Giron on the great road. The Conde del Abisbal blockaded Pampeluna.

On the 24th, Marshal Soult collected the right and left wings of his army, with one division of the centre and two divisions of cavalry at St. Jean de Pied de Port, and on the 25th attacked with between thirty and forty thousand men, General Byng's post at Roncesvalles. Lieutenant-General Sir Lowry Cole moved up to his support with the 4th division, and these officers were enabled to maintain their post throughout the day. But the enemy turned it in the afternoon, and Lieutenant-General Sir Lowry Cole considered it to be necessary to withdraw in the night; and he marched to the neighbourhood of Zubiri.

In the actions which took place on this day the 20th regiment distinguished themselves.

Two divisions of the centre of the enemy's army attacked Sir R. Hill's position in the Puerto de Maya at the head of the valley of Bastan, in the afternoon of the same day. The brunt of the action fell upon Major-General Pringle's and Major-General Walker's brigades, in the second division, under the command of Lieutenant-General the Honourable William Stewart. These troops were at first obliged to give way, but having been supported by Major-General Barnes's brigade of the seventh division, they regained that part of their post which was the key of the whole, and which would have enabled them to reassume it if circumstances had permitted it. But Sir Rowland Hill having been apprized of the necessity that Sir Lowry Cole should retire, deemed it expedient to withdraw his troops likewise to Irurita, and the enemy did not advance on the following day beyond the Puerto de Maya.

Notwithstanding the enemy's superiority of numbers, they acquired but little advantage over these brave troops during the seven hours they were engaged - all the regiments charged with the bayonet. The conduct of the 82nd regiment, which moved up with Major-General Barnes's brigade, is particularly reported.

Lieutenant-General the Hon. William-Stewart was slightly wounded.

I was not apprized of these events till late in the night of the 25th and 26th; and I adopted immediate measures to concentrate the army to the right, still providing for the siege of San Sebastian, and for the blockade of Pamplona.

This would have been effected early on the 27th, only that Lieutenant-General Sir Lowry Cole and Lieutenant-General Sir Thomas Picton concurred in thinking their post at Zubiri not tenable for the time during which it would have been necessary for them to wait in it. They therefore retired early on the 27th, and took up a position to cover the blockade of Pamplona, having the right, consisting of the third division, in front of Huarte, and extending to the hills beyond Olaz; the left, consisting of the 4th division, Major-General Byng's brigade of the second division, and Brigadier-General Campbell's Portuguese brigade, on the heights in front of Villalba, having their left at a chapel behind Sorausen, on the high road from Ostiz to Pampeluna, and their right resting upon a height which defended the high road from Zubiri and Roncesvalles. General Morillo's division of Spanish infantry, and that part of the Condé del Abisbal's corps not engaged in the blockade, were in reserve. From the latter the regiment of Travia and that of El Principe were detached to occupy part of the hill on the right of the fourth division, by which the road from Zubiri was defended.

The British cavalry under Lieutenant-General Sir Stapleton Cotton were placed near Huarte on the right, being the only ground on which it was possible to use the cavalry.

The river Lanz runs in the valley which was on the left of the allied, and on the right of the French army along the road to Ostiz. Beyond this river there is another range of mountains connected with Ligasso and Marcalain, by which places it was now necessary to communicate with the rest of the army.

I joined the third and fourth divisions just as they were taking up their ground on the 27th, and shortly afterwards the enemy formed their army on a mountain, the front of which extends from the high road to Ostiz to the high road to Zubiri; and they placed one division on the left of that road on a height, and in some villages in front of the third division; they had here also a large body of cavalry.

In a short time after they had taken up their ground, the enemy attacked the hill on the right of the fourth division, which was then occupied by one battalion of the 4th Portuguese regiment, and by the Spanish regiment of Pravia.

These troops defended their ground, and drove the enemy from it with the bayonet. Seeing the importance of this hill to our position, I reinforced it with the 40th regiment, and this regiment, with the Spanish regiments, El Principe and Pravia, held it from this time, notwithstanding the repeated efforts of the enemy during the 27th and 28th to obtain possession of it.

Nearly at the same time that the enemy attacked this height on the 27th, they took possession of the village of Sorausen on the road to Ostiz, by which they acquired the communication by that road, and they kept up a fire of musketry along the line till it was dark.

We were joined on the morning of the 28th by the sixth division of infantry, and I directed that the heights should be occupied on the left of the valley of the Lanz, and that the sixth division should form across the valley in rear of the left of the fourth division, resting their right on Oricain, and their left on the heights above mentioned.

The sixth division had scarcely taken their position when they were attacked by a very large force of the enemy which had been assembled in the village of Sorausen.

Their front was however so well defended by the fire of their own light troops from the heights on their left, and by the fire from the heights occupied by the fourth division and Brigadier-General Campbell's Portuguese Brigade, that the enemy were soon driven back with immense loss from a fire on their front, both flanks, and rear.

In order to extricate their troops from the difficulty in which they found themselves in their situation in the valley of the Lanz, the enemy now attacked the height on which the left of the fourth division stood, which was occupied by the seventh Caçadores, of which they obtained a momentary possession. They were attacked, however, again by the seventh Caçadores, supported by Major-General Ross with his brigade of the 4th division, and were driven down with great loss.

The battle now became general along the whole front of the heights occupied by the 4th division, and in every part in our favor, excepting where one battalion of the 10th Portuguese regiment of Major-General Campbell's brigade was posted. This battalion having been overpowered, and having been obliged to give way immediately on the right of Major-General Ross's brigade, the enemy established themselves on our line, and Major-General Ross was obliged to withdraw from his post.

I however ordered the 27th and 48th regiments to charge, first, that body of the enemy which had first established themselves on the height, and next, those on the left. Both attacks succeeded, and the enemy were driven down with immense loss; and the 6th division, having moved forward at the same time to a situation in the valley nearer to the left of the 4th, the attack upon this front ceased entirely, and was continued but faintly on other points of our line.

In the course of this contest, the gallant fourth division, which had so frequently been distinguished in this army, surpassed their former good conduct. Every regiment charged with the bayonet, and the 40th, 7th, 20th, and 23rd, four different times. Their officers set them the example, and Major General Ross had two horses shot under him.

The Portuguese troops likewise behaved admirably; and I had every reason to be satisfied with the conduct of the Spanish regiments El Principe and Pravia.

I had ordered Lieutenant-General Sir Rowland Hill to march by Lanz upon Lizasso, as soon as I found that Lieutenant-Generals Sir Thomas Picton and Sir Lowry Cole had moved from Zubiri, and Lieutenant-General the Earl of Dalhousie from San Estevan to the same place, where both arrived on the 28th, and the seventh division came to Marcalain.

The enemy's force which had been in front of Sir Rowland Hill, followed his march, and arrived at Ostiz on the 29th. The enemy thus reinforced, and occupying a position on the mountains which appeared little liable to attack, and finding that they could make no impression on our front, determined to endeavor to turn our left by an attack on Sir Rowland Hill's corps.

They reinforced with one division the troops which had been already opposed to him, still occupying the same points in the mountain on which was formed their principal force; but they drew in to their left the troops which occupied the heights opposite the 3rd division; and they had, during the night of the 29th and 30th, occupied in strength the crest of the mountain on our left of the Lanz opposite to the sixth and seventh divisions; thus connecting their right in their position with the divisions detached to attack Lieutenant-General Sir Rowland Hill.

I, however, determined to attack their position, and ordered Lieutenant-General the Earl of Dalhousie to possess himself of the top of the mountain in his front, by which the enemy's right would be turned, and Lieutenant-General Sir Thomas Picton to cross the heights on which the enemy's left had stood, and to turn their left by the road to Roncesvalles. All the arrangements were made to attack the front of the enemy's position, as soon as the effect of these movements on their flanks should begin to appear. Major-General the Honourable Edward Pakenham, whom I had sent to take the command of the fourth division, Major-General Pack having been wounded, turned the village of Sorausen as soon as the Earl of Dalhousie had driven the enemy from the mountain by which that flank was defended; and the sixth division, and Major General Byng's brigade, which had relieved the 4th division on the left of our position on the road to Ostiz, instantly attacked and carried that village.

Lieutenant-General Sir Lowry Cole likewise attacked the front of the enemy's main position with the 7th caçadores, supported by the 11th Portuguese regiment, the 40th, and the battalion under Colonel Bingham, consisting of the 53rd and Queen's regiment. All these operations obliged the enemy to abandon a position which is one of the strongest and most difficult of access that I have yet seen occupied by troops.

In their retreat from this position, the enemy lost a great number of prisoners. I cannot sufficiently applaud the conduct of all the general officers, officers, and troops throughout these operations. The attack made by Lieutenant-General the Earl of Dalhousie was admirably conducted by his Lordship, and executed by Major-General Inglis and the troops composing his brigade; and that by Major General the Honourable Edward Pakenham, and Major-General Byng, and that by Lieutenant-General Sir Lowry Cole; and the movement made by Sir Thomas Picton merited my highest commendation.

The latter officer co-operated in the attack of the mountain, by detaching troops to his left, in which the Honourable Lieutenant-Colonel Trench was wounded, but I hope not seriously.

While these operations were going on, and in proportion as I observed their success, I detached troops to the support of Lieutenant-General Sir Rowland Hill.

The enemy appeared in his front late in the morning, and immediately commenced an extended manoeuvre upon his left flank, which obliged him to withdraw from the height which he occupied behind Lizasso to the next range. He there, however, maintained himself; and I enclose his report of the conduct of the troops. I continued the pursuit of the enemy after their retreat from the mountain to Olaque, where I was at sunset immediately in the rear of their attack upon Lieutenant-General Sir Rowland Hill. They withdrew from his front in the night, and yesterday took up a strong position with two divisions to cover their rear on the pass of Dona Maria.

Lieutenant-General Sir Rowland Hill and the Earl of Dalhousie attacked and carried the pass, notwithstanding the vigorous resistance of the enemy, and the strength of their position. I am concerned to add that Lieutenat-General the Honourable William Stewart was wounded upon this occasion.

I enclose Lieut. General Sir Rowland Hill's report.

In the mean time, I moved with Major-General Byng's brigade, and the 4th division, under Lieutenant-General Sir Lowry Cole, by the Pass of Velate, upon Irurita, in order to turn the enemy's position on Dona Maria. Major-General Byng took in Elizondo a large convoy going to the enemy, and made many prisoners.

We have this day continued the pursuit of the enemy in the valley of the Bidassoa, and many prisoners and much baggage have been taken. Major-General Byng has possessed himself of the valley of Bastan, and of the position on the Puerto de Maya, and the army will be this night nearly in the same positions which they occupied on the 25th July.

I trust that H. R. H. the Prince Regent will be satisfied with the conduct of the troops of His Majesty, and of his Allies on this occasion. The enemy having been considerably reinforced and re-equipped, after their late defeat, made a most formidable attempt to relieve the blockade of Pamplona, with the whole of their forces, excepting the reserve under General Villatte, which remained in front of our troops on the great road from Irun.

This attempt has been entirely frustrated by the operations of a part only of the allied army; and the enemy has sustained a defeat, and suffered a severe loss in officers and men.

The enemy's expectations of success beyond the point of raising the blockade of Pamplona, were certainly very sanguine. They brought into Spain a large body of cavalry, and a great number of guns; neither of which arms could be used to any great extent by either party in the battle which took place.

They sent off the guns to St. Jean Pied de Port, on the evening of the 28th, which have thus returned to France in safety.

The detail of the operations will shew your Lordship how much reason I have to be satisfied with the conduct of all the general officers, officers, and troops. It is impossible to describe the enthusiastic bravery of the 4th division; and I was much indebted to Lieutenant-General Sir Lowry Cole for the manner in which he directed their operations; to Major-General Ross, Major-General Anson, Major-General Byng, and Brigadier-General Campbell, of the Portuguese service. All the officers commanding, and the officers of the regiments, were remarkable for their gallantry; but I particularly observed Lieutenant-Colonel O'Toole, of the 7th caçadores, in the charge upon the enemy on our left on the 28th; and Captain Joaquim Telles Jurdao, of the 11th Portuguese regiment, in the attack of the mountain on the 30th.

I beg to draw your Lordship's attention likewise to the valuable assistance I received throughout these operations from Lieutenant-General Sir Rowland Hill; and from Lieutenant-General the Earl of Dalhousie, and Lieutenant-General Sir Thomas Picton, in those of the 30th and 31st of July. To the Conde del Abisbal also I am indebted for every assistance it was in his power to give consistently with his attention to the blockade. I have already mentioned the conduct of the regiments of Pravia and El Principe, belonging to the army of reserve of Andalusia, in a most trying situation; and the whole corps appeared animated by the same zealous spirit which pervaded all the troops in that position.

Marshal Sir William Beresford was with me throughout these operations, and I received from him all the assistance which his talents so well qualify him to afford me. The good conduct of the Portuguese officers and troops in all the operations of the present campaign, and the spirit which they show on every occasion, are not less honorable to that nation than they are to the military character of the officer, who, by his judicious measures, has re-established discipline, and renewed a military spirit in the army.

I have again to draw your Lordship's attention to the valuable assistance I received throughout these operations from the Quarter-Master-General, Major-General Murray, and Major-General Pakenham, the Adjutant-General, and the officers of those departments respectively; from Lord Fitzroy Somerset, Lieutenant-Colonel Campbell, and the officers of my personal staff.

Although our wounded are numerous, I am happy to say that the cases in general are slight; and I have great pleasure in reporting to your Lordship, that the utmost attention has been paid to them by the Inspector General, Dr. McGregor, and by the officers of the department under his direction.

Adverting to the extent and nature of our operations, and the difficulties of our communications at all times, I have reason to be extremely well satisfied with the zeal and exertions of Sir Robert Kennedy, the Commissary General, and the officers of his department, throughout the campaign; which, upon the whole, have been more successful in supplying the troops than could have been expected.

I transmit this dispatch to your Lordship by His Serene Highness the Hereditary Prince of Orange, who is perfectly acquainted with all that has passed, and with the situation of the army; and will be able to inform your Lordship of many details relating to this series of operations, for which a dispatch does not afford scope. His Highness had a horse shot under him in the battle near Sorauren on the 28th of July.

I have the honor to be &c.
WELLINGTON.

P.S.   I have omitted to inform your Lordship in the body of the dispatch, that the troops in the Puerto de Maya lost there four Portuguese guns on the 25th July. Major General Pringle, who commanded when the attack commenced, had ordered them to retire towards Maya; and when Lieut. General Stewart came up, he ordered that they might return, and retire by the mountain road to Elizondo. In the mean time, the enemy were in possession of the Pass, and the communication with that road was lost, and they could not reach it.

To Field Marshal the Marquis of Wellington, K.G.31st July, 1813.

MY LORD,

I HAVE the satisfaction to acquaint your Lordship that, although from the immense superiority of force which the enemy directed against the position entrusted to my charge yesterday, it became in my opinion imperiously necessary for me to retire from that ground; the conduct of the officers and troops, British and Portuguese, was such as to entitle them to my entire approbation, and I could not have wished it to be better.

Major-General Pringle, with Major-General Walker's brigade, under Lieutenant-Colonel Fitzgerald, of the 60th regiment, supported by the 34th regiment, and 14th Portuguese regiment, opposed the ascent of the enemy to the ridge on the left of the position, in a most gallant style; drove him repeatedly back, and although unable ultimately to prevent him from ascending the ridge, by a more distant movement, our troops kept their ground firmly, and when ordered to retire, performed it under Major-General Pringle with the greatest regularity, and with small loss, covered by a battalion of the 14th Portuguese regiment, under Lieutenant-Colonel McDonald, of the conduct of which officer, and the steadiness of his regiment, the Major-General speaks in terms of the greatest praise.

Colonel Ashworth's brigade, also attacked in his position by a superior force, met the attack with the greatest steadiness, and drove the enemy before him at the point of the bayonet, and held his ground as long as I thought it prudent for him to do so; and a battalion of Brigadier-General Costa's brigade held the ridge on the right of the position to the last, covering the formation of the troops on the ground they were directed to take up: the enemy attempted to force the point, but were repulsed by Brigadier-General Costa, and finally driven down the ridge at the point of the bayonet by that battalion, a part of Colonel Ashworth's brigade, and a small detachment of the 28th regiment. On the whole, I can assure your Lordship that the enemy had nothing to boast of, nor was our loss severe, considering the disparity of our forces.

I feel particularly indebted to Major-General Pringle for his conduct on this occasion, as well as to Colonel Ashworth, Colonel O'Callaghan, and Lieutenant-Colonel Fitzgerald, 60th foot, commanding brigades under him, and also to Lieutenant-General the Conde de Amarante, and Brigadier-General Costa, who was wounded.

I have the honor to be, &c.
ROWLAND HILL.

P.S. I must not omit to mention the services of Colonel Pampluna and Lieutenant-Colonel Pyn, 18th regiment, Lieutenant-Colonel Grant and Major Mitchell, commanding the 6th of the line and 6th Portuguese in Colonel Ashworth's brigade.

To Field Marshal the Marquis of Wellington, K.G.Elizondo, 1st August, 1813.

MY LORD,

I HAVE the honor to acquaint your Lordship, that, in compliance with the instructions I received through Major-General Murray, I proceeded yesterday with the column under my orders, on the road to Donna Maria. On our arrival at the foot of the pass, we found the enemy ascending the hill in great haste, and closely pressed by the 7th division, moving by a road parallel and to the right of that which my column was on. The rear of the enemy's column having begun to ascend the hills before our arrival, it was impossible to 'cut off' any part of it. It was, however, considerably annoyed on its march by one nine-pounder and a howitzer. I immediately ordered the 2d division, under Lieutenat-General Stewart, to ascend the hill by the road we were on, whilst the Earl of Dalhousie's column ascended by one more to the right. The enemy took up a strong position at the top of the pass, with a cloud of skirmishers in the front.

The attack on our side was led by Lieutenant-General Stewart, with Major-General Walker's brigade, under Lieutenant-Colonel Fitzgerald of the 60th, who forced back the enemy's skirmishers to the summit of the hill; but coming upon their main body, found them so numerous and so strongly posted, that Lieutenant-General Stewart was induced to withdraw them until the seventh division should be in closer co-operation with him. About this time the Lieutenant-General was wounded, and the command of the division devolved upon Major-General Pringle, who, with his own brigade, commanded by Colonel O'Callaghan, renewed the attack on our side, whilst the seventh division pressed them on the other, and both divisions gained the height about the same time, the enemy retiring, after sustaining a very considerable loss. The conduct of Lieutenant-General Stewart, Major-General Pringle, and of the officers and troops in general, was conspicuously good, and I regret that the very thick fog prevented our taking that advantage of the situation of the enemy which we might otherwise have done. A part of each division pursued them some distance down the hill, and occasioned them a considerable loss. Having thus far performed your Lordship's instructions, I withdrew my column from the pass, and moved it upon Almandoz.

Major-General Pringle praises the conduct of Captain Heise and Captain Thorn, on this occasion; and I believe it is the intention of Lieutenant-General Stewart to report the good conduct of some other officers, but his wound has probably delayed it.

I have the honor to be, &c.
ROWLAND HILL, Lieut.-Gen.

Lezaca, 4th August, 1813.

MY LORD,

The Prince of Orange having been detained till this day for the returns, I have to inform your Lordship that the enemy still continued posted in the morning of the 2d with a force of two divisions on the Puerto de Echalar, and nearly the whole army behind the Puerto, when the 4th, 7th, and light divisions advanced by the valley of the Bidassoa to the frontier, and I had determined to dislodge them by a combined attack and movement of the three divisions.

The seventh division, however, having crossed the mountains from Sumbilla, and having necessarily preceded the arrival of the fourth, Major-General Barnes' brigade was formed for the attack, and advanced, before the fourth and light divisions could co-operate, with a regularity and gallantly which I have seldom seen equalled, and actually drove the two divisions of the enemy, notwithstanding the resistance opposed to them, from those formidable heights. It is impossible that I can extol too highly the conduct of Major-General Barnes, and these brave troops, which was the admiration of all who were witnesses of it.

Major-General Kempt's brigade of the Light Division likewise drove a very considerable force from the rock which forms the left of the Puerto.

There is now no enemy, in the field, within this part of the Spanish frontier.

I have the honor to be, &c.
WELLINGTON

27

STORMING OF SAN SEBASTIAN

Downing-Street, Sept., 14, 1813.

MAJOR Hare has arrived at this Office with dispatches, addressed to Earl Bathurst, by Field-Marshal the Marquess of Wellington, of which the following are copies.

Lezaca, September 2, 1813.

MY LORD,

THE fire against the fort of San Sebastian was opened on the 26th of August, and directed against the towers which flanked the curtain on the eastern face, against the demy bastion on the south eastern angle, and the termination of the curtain of the southern face; Lieutenant-General Sir Thomas Graham had directed, that an establishment should be formed on the island of Santa Clara, which was effected on the night of the 26th and the enemy's detachment on that island were made prisoners. Captain Cameron, of the 9th, had the command of the detachment which effected this operation, and Sir Thomas Graham particularly applauds his conduct, and that of Captain Henderson, of the royal engineers.

The conduct of Lieutenant the Honourable James Arbuthnot, of the royal navy, who commanded the boats, was highly meritorious, as likewise that of Lieutenant Bell, of the royal marines.

All that it was deemed practicable to carry into execution, in order to facilitate the approach to the breaches before made in the wall of the town, having been effected on the 30th of August, and another breach having been made at the termination of the curtain, the place was stormed at eleven o'clock in the day on the 31st, and carried. The loss on our side has been severe. Lieutcnant-General Sir James Leith, who had joined the army only two days before, and Major-Generals Oswald and Robinson were unfortunately wounded in the breach; and Colonel Sir Richard Fletcher, of the Royal Engineers, was killed by a musket-ball at the mouth of the trenches. In this officer, and in Lieutenant-Colonel Crawford, of the 9th regiment, His Majesty's service has sustained a serious loss.

I have the honour to enclose Lieutenant-General Sir Thomas Graham's report of this operation, in which your Lordship will observe, with pleasure, another distinguished instance of the gallantry and perseverance of His Majesty's officers and troops, under the most trying difficulties...

Oyarzun, Sept. 1, 1813.

MY LORD,

IN obedience to your Lordship's orders of the preceding day, to attack and form a lodgement on the breach of St. Sebastian, which now extended to the left, so as to embrace the outermost tower, the end and front of the curtain immediately over the left bastion as well as the faces of the bastion itself, the assault took place at eleven o'clock, a.m. yesterday; and I have the honour to report to your Lordship, that the heroic perseverance of all the troops concerned was at last crowned with success.

The column of attack was formed of the second brigade of the fifth division, commanded by Major-General Robinson, with an immediate support of detachments as per margin,* and having in reserve the remainder of the fifth division, consisting of Major-General Sprye's Portuguese brigade, and the first brigade under Major-General Hay, as also the fifth battalion of Caçadores of General Bradford's brigade, under Major Hill; the whole under the direction of Lieutenant-General Sir James Leith, commanding the fifth division.

Having arranged every thing with Sir J. Leith, I crossed the Urumia to the batteries of the right attack, where every thing could be most distinctly seen, and from whence the orders for the fire of the batteries, according to circumstances, could be immediately given.

The column in filing out of the right of the trenches, was as before exposed to a heavy fire of shells and grape shot, and a mine was exploded in the left angle of the Counterscarp of the Hornwork, which did great damage, but did not check the ardour of the troops in advancing to the attack. There never was any thing so fallacious as the external appearance of the breach without some descriptior, the almost insuperable difficulties of the breach cannot be estimated. Notwithstanding its great extent, there was but one point where it was possible to enter, and there by single files. All the inside of the wall to the right of the Curtain formed a perpendicular scarp of at least 20 feet to the level of the streets.—So that the narrow ridge of the Curtain itself, formed by the breaching of its end and front, was the only accessible point. During the suspension of the operations of the siege, from want of amunition, the enemy had prepared every means of defence which art could devise, so that great numbers of men were covered by intrenchments and traverses, in the horn-work, on the ramparts of the curtain, and inside of the town opposite for the breach, and ready to pour a most destructive fire of musquetry on both flanks of the approach to the top of the narrow ridge of the curtain.

Every thing that the most determined bravery could attempt was repeatedly tried in vain by the troops, who were brought forward from the trenches in succession.— No man outlived the attempt to gain the ridge; and though the slope of the breach afforded shelter from the enemy's musquetry, yet still the nature of the stone-rubbish prevented the great exertions of the Engineers and working parties from being able to form a lodgment for the troops, exposed to the shells and grape from the batteries of the Castle, as was particularly directed, in obedience to your Lordship's instructions;and, at all events, a secure lodgment could never have been obtained without occupying a part of the curtain.

In this almost desperate state of the attack, after consulting with Colonel Dickson, commanding the Royal Artillery, I ventured to order the guns, to be turned against the curtain. A heavy fire of artillery was directed against it; passing a few feet only over the heads of our troops on the breach, and was kept up with a precision of practice beyond all example. Meanwhile I accepted the offer of a part of Major-General Bradford's Portuguese Brigade to ford the river near its mouth. The advance of the 1st battalion, 13th regiment, under Major Snodgrass, over the open beach, and across the river; and of a detachment of the 24th regiment, under Lieutenant-Colonel McBean, in support, was made in the handsomest style, under a very severe fire of grape. Major Snodgrass attacked, and finally carried the small breach on the right of the great one, and Lieutenant-Colonel McBean's detachment occupied the right of the great breach. I ought not to omit to mention, that a similar offer was made by the 1st Portuguese regiment of Brigadier-General Wilson's brigade, under Lieutenant-Colonel Fearon; and that both Major-General Bradford, and Brigadier-General Wilson, had, from the beginning, urged most anxiously the employment of their respective brigades in the attack, as they had had so large a share in the labour, and fatigues of the right attack.

Observing now the effect of the admirable fire of the batteries against the curtain, though the enemy was so much covered, a great effort was ordered to be made to gain the high ridge at all hazards, at the same time that an attempt should be made to storm the horn-work.

It fell to the lot of the 2d brigade of the fifth divisions, under the command of Colonel the Honourable Charles Greville, to move out of the trenches for this purpose, and the 3d battalion of the Royal Scots, under Lieutenant-Colonel Barnes, supported by the 38th, under Lieutenant.Colonel Miles, fortunately arrived to assault the breach, of the curtain, about the time when an explosion on the rampart of the curtain, (occasioned by the fire of the artillery), created some confusion among the enemy. The narrow pass was gained, and was maintained, after a severe conflict, and the troops on the right of the breach, having about this time succeeded in forcing the barricades on the top of the narrow line wall, found their way into the houses that joined it. Thus, after an assault which lasted above two hours, under the most trying circumustances, a firm footing was obtained.

It was impossible to restrain the impetuosity of the troops, and in an hour more the enemy were driven from all the complication of defences prepared in the streets, suffering a severe loss on their retreat to the castle, and leaving the whole town in our possession.

Though it must be evident to your Lordship, that the troops were all animated with the most enthusiastic and devoted gallantry, and that all are entitled to the highest commendation; yet, I am sure; your Lordship will wish to be informed more particularly concerning those, who, from their situations, had opportunities of gaining peculiar distinction; and, as the distance I was at myself, does not enable me to perform this act of justice from personal observation, I have taken every pains to collect information from the superior officers.

Lieuteant-General Sir James Leith justified, in the fullest manner, the confidence reposed in his tried judgment and distiuguished gallantry, conducting, and directing the attack, till obliged to be reluctantly carried off, after receiving a most severe contusion on the breast, and having his left arm broken.

Major-General Hay succeeded to the command, and ably conducted the attack to the last. Lieutenant-General Sir J. Leith expresses his great obligations to Major-Generals Hay and Robinson, (the latter was obliged to leave the field from a severe wound in the face), and to Lieutenant-Colonels Berkeley and Gomm, Assistant-Adjutant-General, and Assistant-Quarter-Master-Geueral of the 5th division, for their zealous services, during this arduous contest. He warmly recommends to your Lordship's notice, his Aid-de-Camp, Captain Belches, of the 59th foot; and, in conjunction with Major-General Hay, he bears testimony to the highly-meritorious conduct of Captain James Stewart, of the 3d battalion Royal Scots, Aid-de-Camp to Major-General Kay; and he recommends to your Lordship's notice, Major-General Robinson's Aid-de-Camp, Captain Wood, 4th foot, as also Captains Williamson and James of that regiment; the former was severely wounded in the command of the 4th, following the forlorn hope in the best style, and remaining long after his wound.

Captain Jones succeeded to the command of the brigade, and conducted it with great ability.

Sir James Leith likewise particularizes Captain Taylor, 48th regiment, Brigade Major to the 1st brigade, and Lieutenant Le Blanc, of the 4th foot, who led the light infantry company of the regiment, immediately after the forlorn hope, and is the only surviving officer of the advance.

Major-General Robinson unites his testimony of praise of Captains Williamson and Jones and Lieutenant Le Blanc, above mentioned. He likewise commends highly Captain Livesay, who succeeded to the command of the 47th foot, on Major Kelly's being killed, and kept it till wounded, when the command devolved on Lieutenant Power, who ably performed the duty, as also Captain Pilkington, who succeeded to the command of the 59th on Captain Scott's being killed, and retained it till wounded, when, the command of that battalion fell to Captain Halford, who led it with great credit, and also Brevet-Major Anwyll, Brigade-Major of the 2d brigade.

Major-General Hay having now the command of the 5th division, mentions in terms of great praise the excellent conduct of Major-General Sprye, commanding the Portuguese brigade, and the very distinguished gallantry of Colonel de Regoa, and the 15th Portuguese regiment, under his command, and of Colonel McCrae, with the 3d Portuguese regiment; and Major-General Sprye mentions in terms of high praise, Lieutenant-Colonel Hill, commanding the 8th Caçadores, and Major Charles Stuart Campbell, commanding the 3d regiment in Colonel McCrae's absence on general duty; and he expresses his great obligations to Captain Brackenburg, of the 61th regiment, his Aid-de-Camp, and to Brigade-Major Fitzgerald. Major-General Hay speaks most highly of the services of Colonel, the Honourable C. Greville, of the 38th, in command of the 2d brigade, and of the conspicuous gallantry of Lieutenant-Colonel Barnes, in the successful assault of the Curtain, with the brave battalion of the Royal Scots, and also of the exemplary conduct of Lieutenant-Colonel Cameron, of the 9th foot, and Lieutenant-Colonels Miles and Dean of the 38th, and all the officers and troops engaged;and he expresses himself as most particularly indebted to the zeal, intelligence, and intrepidity of Brigade-Major Taylor, and Captain Stewart, of the Royal Scots, acting as his Aid-de-Camp, formerly mentioned.

Major-General Hay likewise, expresses his great satisfaction with the gallant and judicious conduct of Lieutenant-Colonel Cooke, commanding the detachment of Guards; of Lieutenant-Colonel Hunt, commanding the detachment of the left division, who was severely wounded; and of all the other Officers and troops of the detachments.

Major-General Hay conducted the division along the ramparts himself, with the judgment and gallantry that has so often marked his conduct.

I have now only to repeat the expressions of my highest satisfaction with the conduct of the Officers of the Royal Artillery and Enginers, as formerly particularized in the report of the first attack. Every branch of the Artillery service has been conducted by Colonel Dickson, with the greatest ability, as was that of the Engineer department by Lieutenant-Colonel Sir Richard Fletcher, till the moment of his much-lamented fall at the mouth of the trenches. Lieutenant-Colonel Burgoyne succeeded to the command, and is anxious that I should convey to your Lordship Sir R. Fletcher's sense of the great merit and gallantry of Captain Henderson, in the attack of the Island, on the morning of the 27th ultimo; and of the persevering exertions of Majors Ellicombe and Smith, in pushing forward the.operations of the two attacks - the latter Officer having had the merit of the first arrangements for the attack on the right.

Lieut.-Colonel Burgoyne was himself wounded, and only quitted the field from loss of blood; but I am happy to say he is able to carry on the duty of the department.

The conduct of the Navy has been continued on the same principle of zealous co-operation by Sir George Collier; and the services of Lieutenant O'Reilley, with the seamen employed in the batteries, has been equally conspicuous as before.

Your Lordship will now permit me to call your attention to the conduct of that distinguished officer, Major-General Oswald, who has had the temporary command of the fifth division in Lieutenant-General Sir James Leith's absence, during the whole of the campaign, and who resigned the command of the division on Sir James Leith's arrival on the 30th ultimo.

Having carried on with indefatigable attention all the laborious duties of the left attack, no person was more able to give Sir James Leith the best information and assistance. This Sir James Leith acknowledges he did with a liberality and zeal for the service in the highest degree praiseworthy, and he continued his valuable services to the last, by acting as a volunteer, and accompanying Lieutenant-General Sir James Leith to the trenches on the occasion of the assault. I have infinite satisfaction in assuring your Lordship of my perfect approbation of Major-General Oswald's conduct, ever since the 5th dvision formed a part of the left column of the army.

I beg to assure your Lordship that Colonel Delancy, Deputy-Quarter-Master-General, and Lieutenant-Colonel Bouverie, Assistant-Adjutant-General, attached to the left column, have continued to render me the most valuable assistance, and that the zeal of Captain Calvert, of the 29th Regiment, my First Aid-de-Camp, as well as that of the rest of the officers of my personal Staff, entitle them all to my wannest and perfect approbation.

Your Lordship has, with an attention extremely grateful to me, permitted me to name an officer to be the bearer of your Lordship's dispatches home; and I beg to recommend for that commission Major Hare, of the 12th foot, a gallant soldier of fortune, who has on many former occasions served on my staff, and is now attached to it as Assistant Adjutant-General.

I have the honour, &c.
(Signed)
T. GRAHAM.

* *One hundred and fifty volunteers of the light division, commanded by Lieutenant-Colonel Hunt; of the 52d regiment; four hundred of the first division (consisting of two hundred of the brigades of Guards, under Lieut.-Colonel Cooke; of one hundred of the light battalion, and one hundred of the line battalions of the King's German Legion, under Major Robertson; and two hundred volunteers of the fourth division, under Major Rose, of the 20th foot.*

28

BATTLE OF
THE BIDASSOA

Downing-Street, October 18, 1813.

CAPTAIN the Earl of March arrived this morning with a dispatch from Field-Marshal the Marquess of Wellington, addressed to Earl Bathurst, one of His Majesty's Principal Secretaries of State, of which the following is a copy.

Lezaca, October 9, 1813.

MY LORD,

HAVING deemed it expedient to cross the Bidassoa with the left of the array, I have the pleasure to inform your Lordship that that object was effected on the 7th instant.

Lieutenant-General Sir Thomas Graham directed the 1st and 5th divisions, and the 1st Portuguese brigade, under Brigadier-General Wilson, to cross that river in three columns below and in one above the site of the Bridge, under the command of Major-General Hay, the Honourable Colonel Greville, Major-General the Honourable Edward Stopford, and Major-General Howard, and Lieutehant-General Don Manuel Freyre directed that part of the 4th Spanish army under his immediate command, to cross in three columns at fords, above those at which the allied British and Portuguese troops passed. The former were destined to carry the enemy's entrenchments about and above Andaye, while the latter should carry those on the Montague-Verte, and on the height of Mandale, by which, they were to turn the enemy's left.

The operations of both bodies of troops succeeded in every point. The British and Portuguese troops took seven pieces of cannon, in the redoubts and batteries which they carried, and the Spanish troops one piece of cannon in those by them.

I had particular satisfaction in observing the steadiness and gallantry of all the troops. The 8th British regiment were very strongly opposed, charged with bayonets more than once, and have suffered; but I am happy to add, that in other parts of these corps our loss has not been severe.

The Spanish troops under Lieutenant-General Don Manuel Freyre behaved admirably, and turned and carried the enemy's entrenchments in the hill, with great dexterity and gallantry; and I am much indebted to the Lieutenant-General, and to Lieuteuant-General Sir Thomas Graham, and to the General and Staff Officers of both Corps, for the execution of the arrangements for this operation.

Lieutenant-General Sir Thomas Graham, having thus established, within the French territory, the troops of the Allied British and Portuguese army which had been so frequently distinguished under his command, resigned the command to Lieutenant-General Sir John Hope, who had arrived from Ireland the preceding day.

While this was going on upon the left, Major-General C. Baron Alten attacked, with the light divison, the enemy's intrenchments in the Puerto de Vera, supported by the Spanish division under Brigadier-General Longa; and the Marescal del Campo Don Pedro Giron attacked the enemy's intrenchments and posts on the mountain, called La Rhune, immediately on the right of the light division, with the army of reserve of Andalusia.

Colonel Colborne, of the 52d regiment, who commanded Major-General Skerrett's brigade, in the absence of the Major-General on account of his health, attacked the enemy's right in a camp which they had strongly intrenched; and the 52d regiment, under the command of Major Mein, charged in a most gallant style and carried the intrenchment with the bayonet. The 1st and 3d caçadores, and the 2d battalion 95th regiment, as well as the 52d, distinguished themselves in this attack.

Major-General Kempt's brigade attacked by the Puerto, where the opposition was not so severe; and Major-General Charles Alten has reporterl his sense of the judgment displayed both by the Major-General and by Colonel Collaorne, in these attacks; and I am particularly indebted to Major-General Charles Alten for the manner in which he executed this service; the light division took twenty-two officers and four hundred men prisoners, and three pieces of cannon.

These troops carried every thing before them in the most gallant stile, till they arrived at the foot of the rock on which the hermitage stands, and they made repeated attempts to take even that post by storm; but it was impossible to get up, and the enemy remained during the night in possession of the hermitage;and on a rock on the same range of the mountain, with the right of the Spanish troops.

Some time elapsed yesterday morning, before the fog cleared away sufficiently to enable me to reconnoitre the mountain, which I found to be least inaccessible by its right, and that the attack of it might be connected with advantage with the attack of the enemy's works in front of the camp of Surra. I accordingly ordered the Army of Reserve to concentrate to their right; and, as soon as the concentration, commenced Mariscal del Campo Don Pedro Giron ordered the Battalion de las Ordenes to attack the enemy's post on the rock on the right of the position occupied by his troops, which was instantly carried in the mast gallant stile. Those troops followed up their success, and carried an intrenchment on a hill which protected the right of the Camp of Sarre, and the enemy immediately evacuated all their works to defend the approaches to the camp, which were taken possession of by detachments sent from the 7th division by Lieutenant-General the Earl of Dalhousie, through the Puerto de Eschalar, for this purpose.

Don P. Giron then established a battalion on the enemy's left, on the rock of the Hermitage. It was too late to proceed further last night, and the enemy withdrew from their post at the Hermitage, and from the camp of Sarre during the night.

It gives me singular satisfaction to report the good conduct of the officers and troops of the army of reserve of Andalusia, as well in the operations of the 7th inst. as in those of yesterday. The attack made by the battalion of Las Ordenes, under the command of Colonel Hore, yesterday, was made in as good order, and with as much spirit, as any that I have seen made by any troops; and I was much satisfied with the spirit and discipline of the whole of this corps.

I cannot applaud too highly the execution of the arrangement for these attacks by the Mariscal de Campo Don Pedro Giron, and the General and Staff Officers, under his directions.

I omitted to report to your Lordship in my Dispatch of the 4th inst. that upon my way to Roncevalles, on the 1st Inst. I directed Brigadier-General Campbell to endeavour to carry off the enemy's piquets in his front, which he attacked on that night, and completely succeeded, with the Portuguese troops under his command, in carrying the whole of one piquet, consisting of 70 men—a fortified post on the mountain of Arolla was likewise stormed, and the whole garrison put to the sword.

Since I addressed your Lordship last, I have received dispatches from Lieut.-Gen. Clinton, in Catalonia, to the 3d inst. The General was still at Tarragona, and the enemy were in their old position on the Lobregat.

Lieut.-General Lord William Bentinck had embarked for Sicily on the 22d of September.

I send this dispatch by my Aid-de-Camp, Capt. the Earl of March, whom I beg to recommend to your Lordship's protection.

I have, &c.
(Signed) WELLINGTON.

29

BATTLE OF NIVELLE

Downing-Street, November 21, 1813.

THE Marquess of Worcester has arrived with a dispatch, of which the following is a copy, addressed to the Earl Bathurst by the Marquess of Wellington, dated

St. Pé, 13th Nov., 1813.

MY LORD,

The enemy had since the beginning of August occupied a position with their right upon the sea in front of St. Jean de Luz, and on the left of the Nivelle, their centre on La Petite La Rhune in Sarré, and on the heights behind the village, and their left consisting of two divisions of infantry under the Comte d'Erlon on the right of that river, on a strong height in rear of Anhoue, and on the mountain of Mondarin, which protected the approach to that village. They had had one division under General Foy at St. Jean Pied de Port, which was joined by one of the army of Aragon under General Paris, at the time the left of the allied army crossed the Bidasoa. General Foy's division joined those on the heights behind Anhoue, when Sir R. Hill moved into the valley of Bastan. The enemy, not satisfied with the natural strength of this position, had the whole of it fortified; and their right in particular had been made so strong that I did not deem it expedient to attack it in front.

Pamplona having surrendered on the 31st of October, and the right of the army having been disengaged from covering the blockade of that place, I moved Lieutenant General Sir Rowland Hill on the 6th and 7th into the valley of Bastan, as soon as the state of the roads, after the recent rains, would permit, intending to attack the enemy on the 8th; but the rain which fell on the 7th having again rendered the roads impracticable, I was obliged to defer the attack till the 10th, when we completely succeeded in carrying all the positions on the enemy's left and centre, in separating the former from the latter, and by these means turning the enemy's strong positions occupied by their right on the lower Nivelle, which they were obliged to evacuate during the night; having taken fifty-one pieces of cannon, and fourteen hundred prisoners.

The object of the attack being to force the enemy's centre, and to establish our army in rear of their right, the attack was made in columns of divisions, each led by the General officer commanding it, and each forming its own reserve. Lieutenant-General Sir Rowland Hill directed the movements of the right, consisting of the 2d division under Lieutenant-General the Honourable Sir William Stewart; the 6th division under Lieutenant-General Sir H. Clinton; a Portuguese division under Lieutenant-General Sir John Hamilton, and a Spanish division under General Morillo, and Colonel Grant's brigade of cavalry and a brigade of Portuguese artillery, under Lieutenn-Colonel Tulloh, and three mountain guns under Lieutenant Robe, which attacked the positions of the enemy behind Anhoue.

Marshal Sir William Beresford directed the movements of the right of the centre, consisting of the 3d division under Major-General the Honourable Charles Colville, the 7th division under Mariscal de Campo Le Cor, and the 4th division under Lieutenant-General the Honourable Sir Lowry Cole.

The latter attacked the redoubts in front of Sarré, that village, and the heights behind it, supported on their left by the Army of Reserve of Andalusia, under the command of Mariscal de Campo Don Pedro Girou, which attacked the enemy's positions on the right of Sarré, on the slopes of La Petite La Rhune, and the heights behind the village on the left of the 4th division.

Major General Charles Baron Alten attacked, with the light division and General Longa's Spanish division, the enemy's positions on La Petite La Rhune; and, having carried them, co-operated with the right of the centre in the attack of the heights behind Sarré.

General Alten's brigade of cavalry, under the direction of Lieutenant-General Sir Stapleton Cotton, followed the movements of the centre, and there were three brigades of British artillery with this part of the army, and three mountain guns with General Giron, and three with Major-General Charles Alten.

Lieutenn-General Don Manuel Freyre moved in two columns from the heights of Mandale towards Ascain, in order to take advantage of any movement the enemy might make from the right of their position towards their centre; and Lieutenant-General Sir John Hope with the left of the army drove in the enemy's outposts in front of their intrenchments on the Lower Nivelle, carried the redoubt above Orogne, and established himself on the heights immediately opposite Sibour, in readiness to take advantage of any movement made by the enemy's right.

The attack began at daylight, and Lieutenant-General Sir Lowry Cole having obliged the enemy to evacuate the redoubt on their right in front of Sarré by a cannonade, and that in front of the left of the village having been likewise evacuated on the approach of the 7th division under General Le Cor to attack it, Lieutenant-General Sir Lowry Cole attacked and possessed himself of the village, which was turned on its left by the 3d division, under Major-General the Honourable Charles Colville, and on its right, by the reserve of Andalusia under Don Pedro Girou, and Major General C. Baron Alten carried the positions on La Petite La Rhune. The whole then co-operated in the attack of the enemy's main position behind the village. The 3d and 7th divisions immediately carried the redoubts on the left of the enemy's centre, and the Light division those on the right, while the 4th division with the reserve of Andalusia on their left, attacked their positions in their centre. By these attacks the enemy were obliged to abandon their strong positions which they had fortified with much care and labor; and they left in the principal redoubt on the height the 1st batt. 88th regiment, which immediately surrendered.

While these operations were going on in the centre, I had the pleasure of seeing the 6th division, under Lieutenant-General Sir Henry Clinton, after having crossed the Nivelle and having driven in the enemy's piquets on both banks, and having covered the passage of the Portuguese division under Lieutenant-General Sir John Hamilton on its right, make a most handsome attack upon the right of the enemy's position behind Anhoue and on the right of the Nivelle, and carry all the intrenchments, and the redoubt on that flank. Lieutenant-General the Honourable Sir John Hamilton supported, with the Portuguese division, the 6th division on its right, and both co-operated in the attack of the second redoubt, which was immediately carried.

Major-General Pringle's brigade of the 2d division, under the command of Lieutenant-General the Honourable Sir William Stewart, drove in the enemy's piquets on the Nivelle and in front of Anhoue, and Major-General Byng's brigade of the 2d division carried the intrenchments and a redoubt further on the enemy's left; in which attack, the Major-General and these troops distinguished themselves. Major General Morillo covered the advance of the whole to the heights behind Anhoue, by attacking the enemy's posts on the slopes of Mondarain, and following them towards Itszatce. The troops on the heights behind Anhoue were, by these operations, under the direction of Lieutenant-General Sir Rowland Hill, forced to retire towards the bridge of Cambo, on the Nive, with the exception of the division on Mondarain, which, by the march of a part of the 2d division, under Lieutenant-General Sir William Stewart, was pushed into the mountains towards Baygory.

As soon as the heights were carried on both banks of the Nivelle, I directed the 3d and 7th divisions, being the right of our centre, to move by the left of that river upon St. Pé, and the 6th division by the right of the river on the same place, while the 4th and light divisions, and General Giron's reserve, held the heights above Ascain, and covered this movement on that side, and Lieutenant-General Sir Rowland Hill covered it on the other. A part of the enemy's troops had retired from their centre and had crossed the Nivelle at St. Pé; and as soon as the 6th division approached, the 3rd division, under Major General the Hon. C. Colville, and the 7th division, under General Le Cor, crossed that river, and attacked, and immediately gained possession of, the heights beyond it.

We were thus established in the rear of the enemy's right; but so much of the day was now spent, that it was impossible to make any further movement; and I was obliged to defer our further operations till the following morning.

The enemy evacuated Ascain in the afternoon, of which village Lieutenant-General Don Manuel Freyre took possession, and quitted all their works and positions in front of St. Jean de Luz during the night, and retired upon Bidart, destroying all the bridges on the lower Nivelle. Lieut. General Sir John Hope followed them with the left of the army as soon as he could cross the river; and Marshal Sir W. Beresford moved the centre of the army as far as the state of the roads, after a violent fall of rain, would allow; and the enemy retired again on the night of the 11th into an intrenched camp in front of Bayonne.

In the course of the operations, of which I have given your Lordship an outline, in which we have driven the enemy from positions which they had been fortifying with great labour and care for three months, in which we have taken fifty-one of cannon and six tumbrils of ammunition, and fourteen hundred prisoners, I have great satisfaction in reporting the good conduct of all the officers and troops. The report itself will show how much reason I had to be satisfied with the conduct of Marshal Sir William Beresford, and of Lieutenant-General Sir Rowland Hill, who directed the attack of the centre and right of the army; and with that of Lieutenant-Generals the Honourable Sir G. L. Cole, the Honourable Sir William Stewart, Sir John Hamilton, and Sir Henry Clinton; Major-General the Honourable C. Colville, Charles Baron Alten; Mariscal de Carnpo P. Le Cor, and Mariscal de Campo Don Pablo Morillo, commanding divisions of infantry; and with that of Don Pedro Giron, commanding the reserve of Andalusia.

Lieutenant-General Sir Rowland Hill, and Marshal Sir William Beresford, and these general officers, have reported their sense of the conduct of the generals and troops under their command respectively; and I particularly request your Lordship's attention to the conduct of Major-General Byng, and of Major-General Lambert, who conducted the attack of the 6th division. I likewise particularly observed the gallant conduct of the 51st and 68th regiments, under the command of Major Rice and Lieutenat-Colonel Hawkins, in Major-General Inglis's brigade, in the attack of the heights above St. Pé, in the afternoon of the 30th.The 8th Portuguese brigade, in the 3d division, under Major-General Power, likewise distinguished themselves in the attack of the left of the enemy's centre, and Major-General Anson's brigade of the 4th division, in the village of Sarré and the centre of the heights.

Although the most brilliant part of this service did not fall to the lot of Lieutenant-General Sir John Hope and Lieutenant-General Don M. Frere, I had every reason to be satisfied with the mode in which these general officers conducted the service of which they had the direction. Our loss, although severe, has not been so great as might have been expected, considering the strength of the positions attacked, and the length of time, from daylight in the morning till night, during which the troops were engaged; but I am concerned to add that Colonel Barnard, of the 95th, has been severely, though I hope not dangerously, wounded; and that we have lost in Lieutenant-Colonel Lloyd, of the 94th, an officer who had frequently distinguished himself, and was of great promise.

I received the greatest assistance in forming the plan for this attack, and throughout the operations, from the Quarter-Master General, Sir George Murray, and the Adjutant-General, the Hon. Sir Edward Pakenham, and from Lieutenant-Colonel Lord Fitzroy Somerset, Lieut.-Colonel Campbell, and all the officers of my personal staff, and His Serene Highness the Prince of Orange.

The artillery, which was in the field, was of great use to us; and I cannot sufficiently acknowlege the intelligence and activity with which it was brought to the point of attack under the directions of Colonel Dickson, over the bad roads through the mountains in this season of the year.

I send this dispatch by my Aide-de-Camp, Lieutenant Marquis of Worcester, whom I beg leave to recommend to your Lordship.

I have the honor to be, &c,
WELLINGTON.

30

BATTLE OF THE NIVE

Downing-Street, December 29, 1813.

MAJOR Hill, Aide-de-Camp to Lieutenant-General Sir Rowland Hill, has arrived with a dispatch, of which the following is a copy, addressed to Earl Bathurst by Field-Marshal the Marques of Wellington, K. G. dated

St. Jean de Luz, Dec. 14, 1813.

MY LORD,

SINCE the enemy's retreat from the Nivelle, they had occupied a position in front of Bayonne, which had been entrenched with great labour since the battle fought at Vittoria in June last. It appears to be under the fire of the works of place, the right rests upon the Adour, and the front in this part is covered by a morass, occasioned by a rivulet which falls into the Adour. The right of the centre rests upon this same morass, and its left upon the River Nive. The left is between the Nive and the Adour, on which river the left rests. They had their advanced posts from their right in front of Anglet and towards Biaritz. With their left they defended the River Nive, and communicated with General Paris's division of the army of Catalonia, which was at St. Jean Pied de Port, and they had a considerable corps cantoned in Ville Franche and Mouguerre.

It was impossible to attack the enemy in this position, as long as they remained in force in it. I had determined to pass the Nive immediately after the passage of the Nivelle, but was prevented by the bad state of the roads, and the swelling of all the rivulets occasioned by the fall of rain in the beginning of that month, but the state of the weather and roads, having at length, enabled me to collect the materials, and make the preparations for forming bridges for the passage of that river, I moved the troops out of their cantonments on the 8th, and ordered that the right of the army under Lieutenant-General Sir Rowland Hill should pass on the 9th, and in the neighbourhood of Cambo, while Marshal Sr William Beresford should favour and support his operation, by passing the 6th divison under Lieutenant-General Sir Henry Clinton at Ustaritz; both operations succeeded completely. The enemy were immediately driven from the right bank of the river, and retired towards Bayonne, by the great road of St. Jean Pied de Port. Those posted by Cambo were nearly intercepted by the 6th division, and one regiment was driven from the road, and obliged to march across the country.

The enemy assembled in considerable force on a range of heights running parallel with the Adour, and still keeping Ville Franche by their right. The 8th Portuguese Regiment under Colonel Douglas, and the 9th Caçadores, under Colone Brown, and the British light infantry battalions of the 6th division, carried this village and the heights in the neighbourhood. The rain which had fallen the preceding night and on the morning of the 8th, had so destroyed the road, that the day had nearly elapsed before the whole of Sir Rowland Hill's corps had come up, and I was therefore satisfied with the possession of the ground which we occupied.

On the same day, Lieutenant-General Sir John Hope, with the left of the army under his command, moved forward by the great road from St. Jean de Luz towards Bayonne, and reconnoitred the right of the intrenched camp under Bayonne, and the course of the Adour below the town, after driving in the enemy's posts from the neighbourhood of Biaritz and Anglet. The light division, under Major-General Alten, likewise moved forward from Bassusarry, and reconnoitred that part of the enemy's intrenchments.

Sir John Hope and Major-General Alten retired in the evening to the ground they had before occupied.

On the morning of the 10th Lieutenant-General Sir Rowland Hill found that the enemy had retired from the position which they had occupied the day before on the heights, into the entrenched camp on that side of the Nive; and he therefore occupied the position intended for him, with his right towards the Adour, and his left at Ville Franche, and communicating with the centre of the army under Marshal Sir William Beresford, by a bridge laid over the Nive; and the troops under the Marshal were again drawn to left of the Nive.

General Morillo's division of Spanish infantry, which had remained with Sir Rowland Hill when the other Spanish troops went into cantonments, was placed at Urcuray with Colonel Vivian's brigade of light dragoons at Hasparren, in order to observe the movements of the enemy's division under General Paris, which upon the passage of the Nive, had retired towards St. Palais.

On the 10th in the morning the enemy moved out of the intrenched camp with their whole army, with the exception only of what occupied the works opposite Sir Rowland Hill's position, and drove in the picquets of the light division, and of Sir John Hope's corps, and made a most desperate attack upon the post of the former at the chateau and church of Alcangnes, and upon the advanced posts of the latter, on the high road from Bayonne to St. Jean de Luz, near the Mayor's house of Biaritz. Both attacks were repulsed in the most gallant style by the troops, and Sir John Hope's corps took about five hundred prisoners.

The brunt of the action with Sir John Hope's advanced post fell upon the 1st Portuguese brigade, under Brigadier-General A. Campbell, which were on duty; and upon Major-General Robinson's brigade of the 5th division, which moved up to their support. Lieutenaut-General Sir John Hope reports most favourably of the conduct of those, and of all the other troops engaged, and I had great satisfaction in finding that this attempt made by the enemy upon our left, in order to oblige us to draw in our right, was completely defeated by a comparatively small part of our force.

I cannot sufficiently applaud the ability, coolness, and judgement of Lieutenant-General Sir John Hope, who, with the General and Staff Officers under his command, shewed the troops an example.of gallantry, which must have tended to produce the favourable result of the day.

Sir John Hope received a severe contusion, which, however, I am happy to say, has not deprived me for a moment of the benefit of his assistance.

After the action was over, the regiments of Nassau and Frankfort, under the command of Colonel Kruse came over to the posts of Major-General Ross's brigade of the 4th division, which were fomed for the support of the center.

When the night closed, the enemy were still in large force in front of our posts, on the ground from which they had driven the picquets. They retired, however, during the night, from Lieutenant-General Sir John Hope's front; leaving small posts, which were immediately driven in. They still occupied, in force, the ridge on which the picquets of the light division had stood;and it was obvious that the whole army was still in front of our left; and about three in the afternoon, they-again drove in Lieutenant-General Sir John Hope's picquets, and attacked his posts. They were again repulsed with considerable loss.The attack was recommenced on the morning of the 12th; with the same want of success; the first division, under Major-General Howard, having relieved the fifth division; and the enemy discontinued it in the afternoon, and retired entirely within the intrenched camp on that night. They never renewed the attack on the posts of the light division after the 10th.

Lieutenant-General Sir John Hope reports most favourably of the conduct of all the officers and troops, particularly of the 1st Portuguese brigade under Brigadier-General Archibald Campbell; and of Major-General Robinson's, and Major-General Hay's brigade of the 5th division under the command of the Honourable Colonel Greville. He mentions, particularly Major-General Hay, commanding the 5th division, Major-Generals Robinson and Bradford, Brigadier-General Campbell, Colonels De Regoa and Greville, commanding the several brigades, Lieut. Col. Lloyd, of the 84th, who was unfortunately killed, Lieutenant-Colonels, Barnes of the Royals, and Cameron of the 9th, Captain Ramsay of the Royal Horse Artillery, Colonel De Lancey, Deputy-Quarter-Master-General, and Lieutenant-Colonel McDonald, Assistant Adjutant-General, attached to Sir John Hope's corps, and the officers of his personal staff.

The 1st division, under Major-General Howard, were not engaged until the 12th, when the enemy's attack was more feeble; but the Guards conducted themselves with their usual spirit.

The enemy having thus failed in all their attacks, with their whole force, upon our left, withdrew into their intrenchments, on the night of the 12th, and passed a large force through Bayonne, with which, on the morning of the 13th, they made a most desperate attack upon Lieutenant-General Sir Rowland Hill.

In expectation of this attack, I had requested Marshal Sir W. Beresford to reinforce the Lieutenant-General, with the 6th division, which crossed the Nive at daylight on that morning; and I further reinforced him by the 4th division, and two brigades of the 3d division.

The expected arrival of the fifth division gave the Lieutenant-General great facility in making his movements; but the troops under his own immediate command, had defeated and repulsed the enemy with immense loss before their arrival. The principal attack having been made along the high road, from Bayoune to St. Jean Pied-de-Port.

Major-General Barne's brigade of British infantry, and the 5th Portuguese brigade, under Brig. Gen. Ashworth, were particularly engaged in the contest with the enemy on that point, and these troops conducted themselves admirably. The Portuguese division of infantry, under the command of Mariscal del Campo Don F. Le Cor, moved to their support on their left in a very gallant style, and regained an important position between, these troops and Major-General Pringle's brigade, engaged with the enemy in front of Ville Franche. I had great satisfaction also in observing the conduct of Major General Byng's brigade of British infantry, supported by the 4th Portuguese brigade, under the command of Brigadier-General Buchan, in carrying an important height from the enemy on the right of our position and maintaining it against all their efforts to regain it.

Two guns and some prisoners were taken from the enemy, who, being beaten at all points, and having suffered considerable loss, were obliged to retire from their intrenchment.

It gives me the greatest satisfaction to have another opportunity of reporting my sense of the merits and services of Lieutenant-General Sir Rowland Hill upon this occasion, as well as of those of Lieutenant-General Sir William Stewart, commanding the 2d division; Major-Generals Pringle, Barnes and Byng; Mariscal del Campo Don F. Le Cor, and Brigadier-Generals Da Costa, Ashworth, and Buchan. The British artillery, under Lieutenant-Colonel Ross, and Portuguese artillery, under Colonel Tulloch, distinguished themselves; and Lieuteuant-General Sir Rowland Hiil reports particularly the assistance he received from Lientenant-Colonels Bouverie and Jackson, the Assistant Adjutant and Assistant Quarter-Master General attached to his corps; Lieutenant-Colonel Goldfinch, of the Royal Engineers, and from the officers of his personal Staff.

The enemy marched a large body of cavalry across the bridge of the Adour yesterday evening, and retired their force opposite to Sir R. Hill this morning towards Bayonne.

Throughout these various operations I have received every assistance from the Quarter-Master-General Major-General Sir George Murray, and the Adjutant-General Major-General Sir Edward Pakenham, and Lieutenant-Colonel Lord Fitzroy Somerset, Lieutenant-Colonel Campbell, and the Officers of my personal Staff.

I send this dispatch by Major Hill Aide-de-Camp of Lieutenant-General Sir Rowland Hill, whom I beg leave to recommend to your Lordship's protection.

I have the honour to be, &c.
WELLINGTON.

31

BATTLE OF GARRIS

Downing-Street, March 11, 1814.

A dispatch, of which the following is an extract, has been this day received at Earl Bathurst's Office, addressed to his Lordship by Field-Marshal the Marquess of Wellington, dated

St Jean de Luz, February 20, 1814.

MY LORD,

IN conformity with the intention which I communicated to your Lordship in my last dispatch, I moved the right of the army, under Lieutenant-General Sir R. Hill, on the 14th, he drove in the enemy's picquets on the Joyeuse river, and attacked their position at Hellete, from which he obliged General Harispe to retire, with loss, towards St. Martin. I made the detachment of General Mina's troops, in the valley of Bastan, advance on the same day upon Baygorey and Bidarray; and the direct communication of the enemy with St. Jean Pied de Port being cut off by Lieutenant-General Sir Rowland Hill, that fort has been blockaded by the Spanish troops above-mentioned.

On the following morning, the 15th, the troops under Lieutenant-General Sir Rowland Hill continued the pursuit of the enemy, who had retired to a strong position in front of Garris, where General Harispe was joined by General Paris's division, which had been recalled from the march it had commenced for the interior of France, and by other troops from the enemy's centre.

General Murillo's Spanish division, after driving in the enemy's advanced posts, was ordered to move towards St. Palais, by a ridge parallel to that on which was the enemy's position, in order to turn their left and cut off their retreat by that road, while the 2d division, under Lieutenant-General Sir W. Stewart, should attack in front. Those troops made a most gallant attack upon the enemy's position, which was remarkably strong, but which was carried without very considerable loss. Much of the day had elapsed before the attack could be commenced, and the action lasted till after dark, the enemy having made repeated attempts to regain the position, particularly in two attacks, which were most gallantly received and repulsed by the 39th regiment, under the command of the Honourable Colonel O'Callaghan, in Major-General Pringle's brigade.

The Major-General, and Lieutenant-Colonel Bruce, of the 39th, were unfortunately wounded: we took ten officers, and about two hundred prisoners.

The right of the centre of the army made a corresponding movement with the right on these days, and our posts were on the Bidouze River on the evening of the 15th.

The enemy retired across the river at St. Palais in the night, destroying the bridges, which however were repaired, so that the troops under Lieutenant-General Sir Rowland Hill crossed on the 16th; and on the 17th the enemy were driven across the Gave de Mouleon. They attempted to destroy the bridge at Arriverete, but they had not time to compleat its destruction; and a ford having been discovered above the bridge, the 92d regiment, under the command of Lieutenant-Colonel Cameron, supported by the fire of Captain Beane's troop of horse artillery, crossed the ford, and made a most gallant attack upon two battalions of French Infantry posted in the village, from which the latter were driven with considerable loss. The enemy retired in the night across the Gave de'Oleron, and took up a strong position in the neighbourhood of Sauveterre, in which they were joined by other troops.

On the 18th, our posts were established on the Gave d'Oleron.

In all the actions which I have above detailed to your Lordship, the troops have conducted themselves remarkably well; and I had great satisfaction in observing the good conduct of those under General Murillo, in the attack of Hellete on the 14th, and in driving in the enemy's advanced posts in front of their position, at Garris, on the 15th.

Since the 14th, the enemy have considerably weakened, their force in Bayonne; and they have withdrawn from the right of the Adour, above the town.

I have received no intelligence from Catalonia since I addressed your Lordship last; but I have this day received a report from the Governor of Pamplona, stating that the fort of Jaca had surrendered to General Mina by capitulation, on the 17th instant. I am not acquainted with the particulars of this event, but I know that the place contained eighty-four pieces of brass cannon.

I have the honour to be, &c.

WELLINGTON.

32

BATTLE OF ORTHEZ

Downing-Street, March 20, 1814.

MAJOR Freemantle has arrived at this Office, bringing dispatches from the Marquess of Wellington, addressed to Earl Bathurst, of which the following are copies.

St. Sever, March 1, 1814.

MY LORD,

I returned to Garris on the 21st, and ordered the 6th and light divisions to break up from the blockade of Bayonne, and General Don Manuel Freyre to close up the cantonments of his corps towards Irun, and to be prepared to move when the left of the army should cross the Adour.

I found the pontoons collected at Garris, and they were moved forward on the following days to and across the Gave de Mouleon, and the troops of the centre of the army arrived.

On the 24th, Lieutenant-General Sir Rowland Hill passed the Gave d'Oleron at Villenave, with the light, 2d, and Portuguese divisions, under the command of Major-General Baron Charles Alten, Lieutenant-General Sir William Stewart, and Marischal de Campo Don Frederick Le Cor; while Lieutenant-General Sir Henry Clinton passed with the 6th division between Monfort and Laas, and Lieutenamt-General Sir Thomas Picton made demonstrations, with the 3rd division, of an intention to attack the enemy's position at the bridge of Sauveterre which induced the enemy to blow up the bridge.

Marischal de Campo Don Pablo Morillo drove in the enemy's posts near Navarrens, and blockaded that place.

Field-Marshal Sir William Beresford likewise, who, since the movement of Sir Rowland Hill on the 14th and 15th, had remained with the 4th and 7th divisions, and Colonel Vivian's brigade, in observation on the Lower Bidouze, attacked the enemy on the 23rd in their fortified posts at Hastingues and Oyregave, on the left of the Gave de Pau, and obliged them to retire within the tête de pont at Peyrehorade.

Immediately after the passage of the Gave d'Oleron was effected, Sir Rowland

Hill and Sir Henry Clinton moved towards Orthes and the great road leading from Sauveterre to that town; and the enemy retired in the night from Sauveterre across the Gave de Pau, and assembled their army near Orthes on the 25th, having destroyed all the bridges on the river.

The right and right of the centre of the army assembled opposite Orthes, Lieutenant-General Sir Stapleton Cotton, with Lord Edward Somerset's brigade of cavalry, and the 3rd division, under Lieutenant-General Sir Thomas Picton, were near the destroyed bridge of Bereus, and Field-Marshal Sir William Beresford, with the 4th and 7th divisions, under Lieutenant-General Sir Lowry Cole and Major General Walker, and Colonel Vivian's brigade, towards the junction of the Gave de Pau with the Gave d'Oleron.

The troops opposed to the Marshal having moved on the 25th, he crossed the Gave de Pau below the junction of the Gave d'Oleron on the morning of the 26th, and moved along the high road from Peyrehorade towards Orthes, on the enemy's right. As he approached, Lieutenant-General Sir Stapleton Cotton crossed with the cavalry, and Lieutenant-General Sir Thomas Picton with the 3d division, below the bridge of Bereus; and I moved the 6th and light divisions to the same point, and Lieutenant-General Sir Rowland Hill occupied the heights opposite Orthes and the high road leading to Sauveterre.

The 6th and light divisions crossed in the morning of the 27th at daylight, and we found the enemy in a strong position near Orthes, with his right on a height on the high road to Dax, and occupying the village of St. Boes, and his left on the heights above Orthes and that town, and opposing the passage of the river by Sir Rowland Hill.

The course of the heights on which the enemy had placed his army necessarily retired his centre, while the strength of the position gave extraordinary advantages to the flanks.

I ordered Marshal Sir William Beresford to turn and attack the enemy's right with the 4th division under Lieutenant-General Sir Lowry Cole, and the 7th division under Major-General Walker and Colonel Vivian's brigade of cavalry; while Lieutenant-General Sir Thomas Picton should move along the great road leading from Peyrehorade to Orthes, and attack the heights on which the enemy's centre and left stood, with the 3rd and 6th divisions supported by Sir Stapleton Cotton, with Lord Edward Somerset's brigade of cavalry. M-General Charles Baron Alten, with the light division, kept the communication, and was in reserve between these two attacks. I likewise desired Lieutenant-General Sir Rowland Hill to cross the Gave, and to turn and attack the enemy's left.

Marshal Sir W Beresford carried the village of St. Boes with the 4th division, under the command of Lieutenant-General Sir Lowry Cole, after an obstinate resistance by the enemy; but the ground was so narrow that the troops could not deploy to attack the heights, notwithstanding the repeated attempts of Major-General Ross and Brigadier-General Vasconcellos' Portuguese brigade; and it was impossible to turn them by the enemy's right without an excessive extension of our line.

I therefore so far altered the plan of the action as to order the immediate advance of the 3d and 6th divisions, and I moved forward Colonel Barnard's brigade of the light division to attack the left of the height on which the enemy's right stood.

This attack, led by the 52nd regiment under Lieutenant-Colonel Colborne, and supported on their right by Major-General Brisbane's and Colonel Keane's brigades of the 3d division, and by simultaneous attacks on the left by Major-General Anson's brigade of the 4th division, and on the right by Lieutenant-General Sir Thomas Picton, with the remainder of the 3d division and the 6th division, under Lieutenant-General Sir Henry Clinton, dislodged the enemy from the heights and gave us the victory.

In the mean time, Lieutenant-General Sir Rowland Hill had forced the passage of the Gave above Orthes, and seeing the state of the action he moved immediately, with the 2d division of infantry under Lieutenant-General Sir William Stewart and Major-General Fane's brigade of cavalry, direct for the great road from Orthes to St. Sever, thus keeping upon the enemy's left.

The enemy retired at first in admirable order, taking every advantage of the numerous good positions which the country afforded him. The losses, however, which he sustained in the continued attacks of our troops, and the danger with which he was threatened by Lieutenant-General Sir Rowland Hill's movement, soon accelerated his movements, and the retreat at last became a flight, and the troops were in the utmost confusion.

Lieutenant-General Sir Stapleton Cotton took advantage of the only opportunity which offered to charge with Major-General Lord Edward Somerset's brigade, in the neighbourhood of Sault de Navailles, where the enemy had been driven from the high road by Lieutenant-General Sir Rowland Hill. The 7th hussars distinguished themselves upon this occasion, and made many prisoners.

We continued the pursuit till it was dusk; and I halted the army in the neighbourhood of Sault de Navailles.

I cannot estimate the extent of the enemy's loss; we have taken six pieces of cannon and a great many prisoners, the numbers I cannot at present report. The whole country is covered by their dead. The army was in the utmost confusion when I last saw it passing the heights near Sault de Navailles, and many soldiers had thrown away their arms. The desertion has since been immense.

We followed the enemy on the following day to this place; and we this day passed the Adour; Marshal Sir William Beresford marched with the light division and General Vivian's brigade upon Mont de Marsan, where he has taken a very large magazine of provisions.

Lieutenant-General Sir Rowland Hill has moved upon Aire, and the advanced posts of the centre are at Casares.

The enemy are apparently retiring upon Agen, and have left open the direct road towards Bordeaux.

While the operations of which I have above given the report were carrying on on the right of the army, Lieutenant-General Sir John Hope, in concert with Rear-Admiral Penrose, availed himself of an opportunity which offered on the 23rd of February to cross the Adour below Bayonne, and to take possession of both banks of the river at its mouth. The vessels destined to form the bridge could not get in till the

24th, when the difficult, and at this season of the year dangerous, operation of bringing them in was effected with a degree of gallantry and skill seldom equalled. Lieutenant-General Sir John Hope particularly mentions Captain O'Reilly, Lieutenant Cheshire, Lieutenant Douglas, and Lieutenant Collins, of the royal navy, and also Lieutenant Debenham, agent of transports; and I am infinitely indebted to Rear-Admiral Penrose for the cordial assistance I received from him in preparing for this plan, and for that which he gave Lieutenant-General Sir John Hope in carrying it into execution.

The enemy, conceiving that the means of crossing the river which Lieutenant-General Sir John Hope had at his command, viz., rafts made of pontoons, had not enabled him to cross a large force in the course of the 23rd, attacked the corps which he had sent over on that evening. This corps consisted of six hundred men of the 2d brigade of Guards under the command of Major-General the Honourable Edward Stopford, who repulsed the enemy immediately. The rocket brigade was of great use upon this occasion.

Three of the enemy's gun boats were destroyed this day, and a frigate lying in the Adour received considerable damage from the fire of a battery of eighteen-pounders, and was obliged to go higher up the river to the neighbourhood of the bridge.

Lieutenant-General Sir John Hope invested the citadel of Bayonne on the 25th, and Lieutenant-General Don Manuel Freyre moved forward with the 4th Spanish army in consequence of directions which I had left for him. On the 27th, the bridge having been completed, Lieutenant-General Sir John Hope deemed it expedient to invest the citadel of Bayonne more closely than he had done before; and he attacked the village of St. Etienne, which he carried, having taken a gun and some prisoners from the enemy; and his posts are now within nine hundred yards of the outworks of the place.

The result of the operations which I have detailed to your Lordship is, that Bayonne, St. Jean Pied de Port, and Navarrens, are invested; and the army, having passed the Adour, are in possession of all the great communications across that river, after having beaten the enemy, and taken their magazines.

Your Lordship will have observed with satisfaction the able assistance which I have received in these operations from Marshal Sir W. Beresford, Lieutenant-General Sir Rowland Hill, Sir John Hope, and Sir Stapleton Cotton, and from all the general officers, officers, and troops acting under their orders respectively.

It is impossible for me sufficiently to express my sense of their merits, or of the degree in which the country is indebted to their zeal and ability for the situation in which the army now finds itself.

All the troops distinguished themselves; the 4th division, under Lieutenant-General Sir Lowry Cole, in the attack of St. Boes, and the subsequent endeavors to carry the right of the heights; the 3d, 6th, and Light divisions, under the command of Lieutenant-General Sir Thomas Picton, Sir H. Clinton, and Major-General Charles Baron Alten, in the attack of the enemy's position on the heights; and these, and the 7th division under Major-General Walker, in the various operations and attacks on the enemy's retreat.

The charge made by the 7th hussars under Lord Edward Somerset was highly meritorious.

The conduct of the artillery throughout the day deserved my highest approbation.

I am likewise much indebted to the Quarter-Master-General Sir George Murray, and the Adjutant-General Sir Edward Pakenham, for the assistance I have received from them, and to Lord Fitzroy Somerset, and the officers of my personal Staff, and to the Marishcal de Campo Don Miguel Alava.

The last accounts which I have received from Catalonia are of the 20th. The French Commanders of the garrisons of Llerida, Mequinenza, and Monzon, had been induced to evacuate those places by orders sent to them by the Baron de Eroles in Marshal Suchet's cipher, of which he had got possession.

The troops composing these garrisons, having joined, were afterwards surrounded in the pass Martorell, on their march towards the French frontier, by a detachment from the 1st Spanish army, and by a detachment from the Anglo-Sicilian corps. Lieutenant-General Copons allowed them to capitulate, but I have not yet received from him any report on this subject, nor do I yet know what is the result.

It was expected in Catalonia that Marshal Suchet would immediately evacuate that province; and I hear here that he is to join Marshal Soult.

I have not yet received the detailed report of the capitulation of Jaca.

I send this dispatch by my Aid-de-Camp Major Fremantle, whom I beg leave to recommend to your Lordship's protection.

I have the honor to be, &c,
WELLINGTON.

33

BATTLE OF TOULOUSE

Downing-Street April 26, 1814.

MAJOR Lord William Russell arrived last night at this Office, bringing a dispatch, from the Marquess of Wellington to Earl Bathurst, of which the following is a copy:

Toulouse, 12th April, 1814.

MY LORD,

I have the pleasure to inform your Lordship that I entered this town this morning, which the enemy evacuated during the night, retiring by the road of Carcassone.

The continued fall of rain and the state of the river prevented me from laying the bridge till the morning of the 8th, when the Spanish corps and the Portuguese artillery, under the immediate orders of Lieutenant-General Don Manuel Freyre, and the head quarters, crossed the Garonne.

We immediately moved forward to the neighbourhood of the town, and the 18th hussars, under the immediate command of Colonel Vivian, had an opportunity of making a most gallant attack upon a superior body of the enemy's cavalry, which they drove through the village of Croix d'Orade, and took about a hundred prisoners, and gave us possession of an important bridge over the river Ers, by which it was necessary to pass, in order to attack the enemy's position. Colonel Vivian was unfortunately wounded upon this occasion; and I am afraid that I shall lose the benefit of his assistance for some time.

The town of Toulouse is surrounded on three sides by the canal of Languedoc and the Garonne. On the left of that river, the suburb, which the enemy had fortified with strong field works in front of the ancient wall, formed a good tête-de-pont. They had likewise formed a tête-de-pont at each bridge of the canal, which was besides defended by the fire in some places of musketry, and in all of artillery from the ancient wall of the town. Beyond the canal to the eastward, and between that and the river Ers, is a height which extends as far as Montaudran, and over which pass all the approaches to the canal and town from the eastward, which it defends; and the enemy, in addition to the têtes-de-pont on the bridges of the canal, had fortified this height with five redoubts, connected by lines of entrenchments, and had, with extraordinary diligence, made every preparation for defence. They had likewise broken all the bridges over the Ers within our reach, by which the right of their position could be approached. The roads, however, from the Ariege to Toulouse being impracticable for cavalry or artillery, and nearly so for infantry, as reported in my dispatch to your Lordship of the 1st instant, I had no alternative, excepting to attack the enemy in this formidable position.

It was necessary to move the Pontoon Bridge higher up the Garonne, in order to shorten the communication with Lieutenant-General Sir Rowland Hill's corps, as soon as the Spanish corps had passed; and this operation was not effected till so late an hour on the 9th as to induce me to defer the attack till the following morning.

The plan, according to which I determined to attack the enemy, was for Marshal Sir William Beresford, who was on the right of the Ers with the 4th and 6th divisions, to cross that river at the bridge of Croix d'Orade, to gain possession of Montblanc, and to march up the left of the Ers to turn the enemy's right, while Lieutenant-General Don Manuel Freyre, with the Spanish corps under his command, supported by the British cavalry, should attack the front. Lieutenant-General Sir Stapleton Cotton was to follow the Marshal's movement with Major-General Lord Edward Somerset's brigade of hussars; and Colonel Vivian's brigade, under the command of Colonel Arentschildt, was to observe the movements of the enemy's cavalry on both banks of the Ers beyond our left.

The 3d and light divisions, under the command of Lieutenant-General Sir Thomas Picton and Major-General Charles Baron Alten, and the brigade of German cavalry, were to observe the enemy on the lower part of the canal, and to draw their attention to that quarter by threatening the têtes-de-pont, while Lieutenant-General Sir Rowland Hill was to do the same on the suburb on the left of the Garonne.

Marshal Sir William Beresford crossed the Ers, and formed his corps in three columns of lines in the village of Croix d'Orade, the 4th division leading, with which he immediately carried Montblanc. He then moved up the Ers in the same order, over most difficult ground, in a direction parallel to the enemy's fortified position; and as soon as he reached the point at which he turned it, he formed his lines and moved to the attack. During these operations, Lieutenant-General Don Manuel Freyre moved along the left of the Ers to the front of Croix d'Orade, where he formed his corps in two lines with a reserve on a height in front of the left of the enemy's position, on which height the Portuguese artillery was placed; and Major-General Ponsonby's brigade of cavalry in reserve in the rear.

As soon as formed, and that it was seen that Marshal Sir William Beresford was ready, Lieutenant-General Don Manuel Freyre moved forward to the attack. The troops marched in good order, under a very heavy fire of musketry and artillery, and showed great spirit, the General and all his staff being at their head; and the two lines were soon lodged under some banks immediately under the enemy's entrenchments; the reserve and Portuguese artillery, and British cavalry, continuing on the height on which the troops had first formed. The enemy, however, repulsed the movement of the right of General Freyre's line round their left flank; and having followed up their success, and turned our right by both sides of the high road leading from Toulouse to Croix d'Orade, they soon compelled the whole corps to retire. It gave me great satisfaction to see that, although they suffered considerably in retiring, the troops rallied again as soon as the light division, which was immediately on their right, moved up; and I cannot sufficiently applaud the exertions of Lieutenant-General Don Manuel Freyre, the officers of the Staff of the 4th Spanish army, and of the officers of the General Staff, to rally and form them again.

Lieutenant-General Mendizabal, who was in the field as a volunteer, General Ezpeleta, and several officers of the staff and chiefs of corps, were wounded upon this occasion; but General Mendizabal continued in the field. The regiment de Tirad. de Cantabria,under the command of Colonel Sicilio, kept its position, under the enemy's entrenchments, until I ordered it to retire.

In the mean time, Marshal Sir William Beresford, with the 4th division, under the command of Lieutenant-General Sir Lowry Cole, and the 6th division, under the command of Lieutenant-General Sir Henry Clinton, attacked and carried the heights on the enemy's right, and the redoubt which covered and protected that flank; and he lodged those troops on the same height with the enemy; who were, however, still in possession of four redoubts, and of the entrenchments and fortified houses.

The badness of the roads had induced the Marshal to leave his artillery in the village of Montblanc; and some time elapsed before it could be brought to him, and before Lieutenant-General Don Manuel Freyre's corps could be reformed and brought back to the attack. As soon as this was effected the Marshal continued his movement along the ridge, and carried, with General Pack's brigade of the 6th division, the two principal redoubts and fortified houses in the enemy's centre. The enemy made a desperate effort from the canal to regain these redoubts, but they were repulsed with considerable loss; and the 6th division continuing its movement along the ridge of the height, and the Spanish troops continuing a corresponding movement upon the front, the enemy were driven from the two redoubts and entrenchments on the left; and the whole range of heights were in our possession. We did not gain this advantage, however, without severe loss; particularly in the brave 6th division. Lieutenant-Colonel Coghlan of the 61st, an officer of great merit and promise, was unfortunately killed in the attack of the heights. Major General Pack was wounded, but was enabled to remain in the field; and Colonel Douglas, of the 8th Portuguese regiment, lost his leg; and I am afraid that I shall be deprived for a considerable time of his assistance.

The 36th, 42nd, 79th, and 61st, lost considerable numbers, and were highly distinguished throughout the day.

I cannot sufficiently applaud the ability and conduct of Marshal Sir William Beresford throughout the operations of the day; nor that of Lieutenant-Generals Sir Lowry Cole, Sir Henry Clinton; Major-Generals Pack and Lambert, and the troops under their command. Marshal Sir William Beresford particularly reports the good conduct of Brigadier-General D'Urban, the Quarter-Master-General, and General Brito Mozinho, the Adjutant-General to the Portuguese army.

The 4th division, although exposed on their march along the enemy's front to a galling fire, were not so much engaged as the 6th, and did not suffer so much; but they conducted themselves with their usual gallantry.

I had also every reason to be satisfied with the conduct of Lieutenant-General Don Manuel Freyre, Lieutenant-General Don Gabriel Mendizabal, Mariscal de Campo Don Pedro Barcena, Brigadier-General Don J. de Espelleta, Mariscal de Campo Don A. Garces de Marcilla, and the Chief of the Staff Don E.S. Salvador, and the Officers of the Staff of the fourth army. The officers and troops conducted themselves well in all the attacks which they made subsequent to their being re-formed.

The ground not having admitted of the operations of the cavalry, they had no opportunity of charging.

While the operations above detailed were going on, on the left of the army, Lieutenant-General Sir Rowland Hill drove the enemy from their exterior works in the suburb, on the left of the Garonne, within the ancient wall. Lieutenant-General Sir Thomas Picton likewise, with the 3d division, drove the enemy within the tête-de-ponton the bridge of the canal nearest to the Garonne, but the troops having made an effort to carry it they were repulsed, and some loss was sustained. Major-General Brisbane was wounded, but I hope not so as to deprive me for any length of time of his assistance; and Lieutenant-Colonel Forbes, of the 45th, an officer of great merit, was killed.

The army being thus established on three sides of Toulouse, I immediately detached our light cavalry to cut off the communication by the only road practicable for carriages which remained to the enemy, till I should be enabled to make arrangements to establish the troops between the canal and the Garonne.

The enemy, however, retired last night, leaving in our hands General Harispe, General Burrot, General St. Hilaire, and sixteen hundred prisoners. One piece of cannon was taken on the field of battle; and others, and large quantities of stores of all descriptions, in the town.

Since I sent my last report, I have received an account from Rear-Admiral Penrose of the successes in the Gironde of the boats of the squadron under his command.

Lieutenant-General the Earl of Dalhousie crossed the Garonne nearly about the time that Admiral Penrose entered the river, and pushed the enemy's parties under General L'Huillier beyond the Dordogne. He then crossed the Dordogne on the 4th, near St. Andre de Cubzac, with a detachment of the troops under his command, with a view to the attack of the fort of Blaye. His Lordship found General L'Huillier and General Des Barneaux posted near Etauliers, and made his disposition to attack them, when they retired, leaving about three hundred prisoners in his hands.

In the operations which I have now reported, I have had every reason to be satisfied with the assistance I received from the Quarter-Master and Adjutant-General, and the officers of those departments respectively; from Marescal de Campo Don Louis Wimpfen and the officers of the Spanish Staff, and from Major-General Alava; from Colonel Dickson, commanding the allied artillery; and from Lieutenant-Colonel Lord Fitzroy Somerset and the officers of my personal staff.

I send this dispatch by my Aid-de-camp, Major Lord William Russell, whom I beg leave to recommend to your Lordship's protection.

I have the honour to be, &c.
WELLINGTON.

34

BATTLE OF BAYONNE

Baucaut, April 14, 1814.

MY LORD,

IT is to my infinite regret that, owing to the unfortunate circumstance of the capture of Lieut.-General Sir John Hope, the duty devolves upon me of informing your Lordship of a sortie which the made this morning at three o'clock, from the entrenched camp in front, of the Citadel of Bayonne, with false attacks in front of the posts of the 5th division, &c. at Auglet and Bellevue.

I am happy to say, that the ground which had been lost on this side was all recovered, and the picuqets re-posted on their original points by seven o'clock.

The injury done to the defences is as little as could be well supposed, in an attack made in the

Force this one was, and will, I hope, be mostly repaired in the course of this night. The casualties are what we have to regret most; on a rough guess Lieutenant-Colonel Macdonald estimates them at four hundred men.

I much lament to have to mention the death of Major-General Hay, general officer of the night. His last words were (a minute before he was shot) an order to hold the Church of St. Etienne, and fortified house adjoining, to the last extremity.

Major-General Stopford is wounded, not, I hope, severely; among the killed are, I am sorry to say, Lieutenant-Colonel Sir H. Sullivan and Captain Crofton, of the Guards; Lieutenant-Colonel Townsend is prisoner, as are also Captain Herries, Deputy Assistant-Quarter-Master-General; and Lieutenant Moore, Aide-de-Camp, to Sir John Hope.

Not wishing, however, to lose any time in sending off this report, I have requested Major-General Howard will detail for you Lordship's further information the circumstances of the attack, and its repulse, having been myself at the time with the 5th division.

Sir John Hope's horse was shot and fell upon him, which prevented his extricating himself. We hear that he is wounded in the arm, and a French officer speaks also of a wound, in his thigh, but we trust this may have reference to his former injury. The boot of his left leg was found under his horse.

In a flag of truce, the proposal was rejected of Lieutenant-Colonel Macdonald's being admitted to see him; but we now expect that Captain Wedderburn, and what other assistance may be require, will be admitted to him, on condition of their not returning.

The arrival of the 62d and 84th regiments on the other side of the Vera, this day, will allow of my strengthening the force on this, by withdrawing from that in front of Auglet.

I have, &c.
(Signed)
C. COLVILLE

To Field-Marshal the Marquis of Wellington, K.G. &c. &c. &c.
Camp near Bayonne, April 15, 1814.

SIR,

IN consequence of Lieutenant General Sir John Hope having been wounded and taken prisoner it falls to my lot to have the honour to detail to you, for the information to His Exellency the Commander of the Forces, the result of an attack made by the enemy on our position in front of the Citadel of Bayonne on the14th instant.

Yesterday morning, a considerable time before daybreak, the enemy made a sortie and attack in great force, principally on the left and centre of our position of St. Etienne; in front of the citadel. The left of the position was occupied by picquets of Major General Hay's brigade; the brigade itself had been directed to form in case of alarm near the village Boneaut as it was merely serving provisionally this side of the Adour; the centre by piquets of the 2d brigade of guards, and the right by piqutes of the 1st brigade of guards. Major-General Hay was the General Officer of the day, in command of the line of outposts, and I regret much to say, was killed, shortly after the attack commenced, having just given directions that the church of St. Etienne should be defended to the last.

The enemy however by great superiority of numbers, succeeded in getting in towards the left of the village, and got momentary possession of it, with the exception of a house occupied by a picquet of the 38th regiment, under Captain Foster of that corps, and who maintained himself till the support coming up, Major-General Hinuber, with the 2d line battalion, King's German legion, under the command of Lieutenant-Colonel Bock, immediately attacked and retook the village.

The enemy attacked the centre of our position likewise in great numbers, and by bearing in great force on one point, after a sharp resistance, they succeeded in compelling one of our picquets to retire, and which enabled him to move up a road in the rear of the line of picquets of the centre of the position, and which compelled the other picquets of the 2d brigade of guards to fall back till the support arrived up to their assistance, when the enemy was immediately charged, and the line of posts reoccupied as before. Major-General Stopford, I regret to say, was wounded, when the command of the brigade devolved on Colonel Guise. In consequence of the enemy having gained temporary possession of some houses which had been occupied by the picquets of the centre of the position, Colonel Maitland found the enemy was in possession of ground, on the rear of his left, and immediately advanced against him rapidly with the 3d battalion 1st guards, commanded by Lieutenant-Colonel the Honourable W. Stewart, on a ridge of ground which runs parallel with the roads, and Lieutenant-Colonel Woodford, of the Coldstream, ascending the hill at the same time by a simultaneous charge, these two corps immediately dislodged the enemy, and re-occupied all the posts which we had before possessed, and from the time the enemy was dislodged, he did not shew the least disposition to renew the attack. Colonel Maitland expressed his satisfaction at the conduct of both his officers and men, and also his obligation to Lieutenant-Colonel Woodford, for his prompt concurrence in the movements above mentioned.

It was towards the right that Lieutenant-General Sir John Hope was taken. In endeavouring to bring up some troops to the support of the picquets, he came unexpectedly in the dark on a party of the enemy; his horse was shot dead and fell upon him, and not being able to disengage himself from under it, he was unfortunately made prisoner. I regret to say that from a letter I have received from him, I find he was wounded in two places, but in neither of them dangerously; you will easily conceive, Sir, that only one feelling, that of the greatest regret, pervades all the troops at the Lieutenant-General's misfortune.

The enemy having commenced their attack between two and three o'clock in the morning, a considerable part of the operations took place before daylight, which gave them a great advantage from their numbers, but whatever end they might propose to themselves by their attack, I am happy to say it has been completely frustrated as they effected no one object by it, except setting fire to one house in the centre of our position, which from being within three hundred yards of their guns, they had rendered perfectly untenable before, whenever they chose to cannonade it. From the quantity of fire of every description which the enemy brought upon us, you will easily conceive our loss could not be inconsiderable. In Major-General Hay, who was well known to you, His Majesty's service has lost a most zealous and able officer, who has served a considerable time in this army with great distinction. The loss of the enemy must however have been severe, as he left many dead behind him, and he was afterwards observed burying a good number of men. In regard to prisoners, we had no opportunity of making many, from the facility the enemy possessed of immediately retiring under the guns of their works.

To Major-Generals Hinuber and Stopford, and Colonel Maitland, commanding brigades, as well as to Colonel Guise, who took the command of the 2d brigade of guards after Major-General Stopford was wounded, I beg to express my best thanks for their exertions and promptitude during the affair, as well as to Lieutenant-Colonel-the Honourable A. Upton, Assistant-Quarter-Master-General, and to Lieutenant-Colonel Dashwood, Assistant- Adjutant-General of the Division, from both of whom I received every assistance, and also from Captain Battersby, my Aide-de-Camp, till he was wounded.

I must also express my thanks to Lieutenant-Colonel McDonald, the Assistant-

Adjutant-General of the left Column for his assistance, he having joined me after Lieutenant-General Sir John Hope as wounded. Indeed, all the troops throughout the whole business behaved with the greaest galantry.

I am, &c.

K.A. HOWARD

Commanding 1st Division

35

BATTLE OF BERGEN-OP-ZOOM

Downing- Street, March 14, 1814.

DISPATCHES, of which the following are copies, were received last night from General Sir Thomas Graham, K. B.

Head-Quarters, Calmhout,
March 10, 1814

MY LORD,

IT becomes my painful task to report to your Lordship, that an attack on Bergen-op-Zoom, which seemed at first to promise complete success, ended in failure, and occasioned a severe loss to the 1st division, and to Brigadier-General Gore's brigade.

It is unnecessary for me to state the reasons which determined me to make the attempt to carry such a place by storm, since the success of two of the columns, in establishing themselves on the ramparts, with very trifling loss, must justify the having incurred the risk for the attainment of so important an object, as the capture of such a fortress.

The troops employed were formed in four columns, as per margin*. No.1, the left column, attacked between the Antwerp and Water Port Gates. No.2 attacked to the right of the New Gate. No.3 was destined only to draw attention by a false attack near the Steenbergen Gate, and to be afterwards applicable according to circumstances. No.4, right column, attacked at the entrance of the harbour, which could be forded at low water, and the hour was fixed accordingly at half past ten P.M. of the 8th instant.

Major-General Cooke accompanied the left column. Major-General Skerrett and Brigadier-General Gore both accompanied the right column; this was the first which forced its way into the body of the place. These two columns were directed to move along the rampart so as to form a junction as soon as possible, and then to proceed to clear the rampart and assist the centre column, or to force open the Antwerp Gate.

An unexpected difficulty about passing the ditch on the ice, having obliged Major-General Cooke to change the point of attack, a considerable delay ensued, and that column did not gain the rampart till half past eleven.

Meanwhile the lamented fall of Brigadier-General Gore, and Lieutenant-Colonel the Honourable George Carleton, and the dangerous wound of Major-General Skerrett, depriving the right column of their able direction, it fell into disorder and suffered great loss in killed, wounded and prisoners. The centre column having been forced back with considerable loss by the heavy fire of the place (Lieutenant-Colonel Morrice its commander, and Lieutenant-Colonel Elphinstone commanding the 33d regiment, being both wounded), was reformed under Major Muttlebury, marched round and joined Major-General Cooke, leaving the, left wing of the 55th, to remove the wounded from the glacis. However, the guards too had suffered very severely during the night, by the galling fire from, the houses on their position, and by the loss of the detachment of the 1st guards, which, having been sent to endeavour to assist Lieutenant-Colonel Carleton, and to secure the Antwerp Gate, was cut off, after the most gallant resistance, which cost the lives of many most valuable officers.

At day break the enemy having turned the guns of the place, opened their fire against the troops on the unprotected rampart, and the reserve of the 4th column (the Royal Scotch) retired from the Water Port Gate, followed by the 33d. The former regiment getting under a cross fire from the place and Water Port redoubt, soon afterwards laid down their arms.

Major-General Cooke then despairing of success, directed the retreat of the guards, which was conducted in the most orderly manner, protected by the remains of the 69th regiment, and of the right wing of the 55th (which corps repeatedly drove the enemy back with the bayonet) under the Major-General's immediate direction. The General afterwards found it impossible to withdraw these weak battalions, and having thus, with the genuine feelings of a true soldier, devoted himself, he surrendered, to save the lives of the gallant men remaining with him.

I should wish to do justice to the great exertions and conspicuous gallantry of all these officers who had the opportunities of distinguishing themselves. I have not as yet been able to collect sufficient information.

Major-General Cooke reports to me his highest approbation generally of all the officers and men employed near him, particularly mentioning Colonel Lord Proby, Lieutenant-Colonels Rooke, commanding the Coldstream Guards, Mercer, of the 3d Guards, commanding the light companies ofthe Brigade, (the latter unfortunately among the killed) Majors Muttlebury and Hog, of tbe 69th and 55th, as deserving of his warm praise. He laments, in common with the whole corps, the severe loss to the service of these distinguished officers, Lieutenant-Colonel Clifton., commanding the 1st Guards, and Lieutenant-Colonel the Honourable James Macdonald, of that regiment. These officers fell, with many others, at the Antwerp Gate, all behaving with the greatest intrepidity; and Lieutenant-Colonel Jones, with the remainder of the detachment, was forced to surrender.

The service of conducting the columns was ably provided for by Lieutenant-Colonel Carmichael Smyth, of the Royal Engineers, (he himself accompanied

Major-General Cooke as did also Lieutenant-Colonel Sir George Wood, commanding royal artillery) who attached officers to lead each column, viz. Captain Sir George Hoste, and Lieutenant Abbey, to the left;and Lieutenant Sparling to the right, and Captain Edward Michell, royal artillery, who volunteered his services, to the centre column, each having a party of sappers and miners under his command.

Lieutenant Abbey was dangerously wounded, and Captain Michell was covered with wounds, in the act of escalading the scarp wall of the place, but I trust there are good hopes, of his not being lost to the service.

Your Lordship will readily believe, that though it is impossible not to feel the disappointment of our ultimate failure in this attack, I can only think at present with the deepest regret of the loss of so many of my gallant comrades.

I have the honour to be, &c
THOMAS GRAHAM.

Bergen-op-Zoom, March 10, 1814.

SIR,

I HAVE now the honour of reporting to your Excellency, that the column which made the attack on the Antwerp side got into the place about eleven o'clock on the night of the 8th, by the clock of this town; but at about half-past eleven, by the time we were regulated by, a delay having occurred at Bourgbliet, occasioned by my finding it necessary to change the point of attack, on account of the state of the ice at the first intended spot. Every exertion was made by Lieutenant-Colonel Smyth and Captain Sir G. Hoste, of the royal engineers, in getting on the ladders and planks requisite for effecting the enterprize, and in directing the placing them for the descent into the ditch, the passing the feet in the ice, and ascending the ramparts of the body of the place; during which operation several men were lost by a fire from the rampart. After we were established on the rampart, and had occupied some houses, from whence we might have been much annoyed, and had sent a strong patrole towards the point at which Major-General Skerrett and Lieutenant-Colonel Carleton had entered, I detached Lieutenant-Colonel Clifton with part of the 1st guards, to secure the Antwerp Gate, and to see if he could get any information of the column under Lieutenant-Colonel Morrice. Lieutenant-Colonel Clifton reached the gate, but found that it could not be opened by his men, the enemy throwing a very heavy fire up a street leading to it. It was also found that they occupied an outwork, commanding the bridge, which would effectually render that outlet useless to us. I heard nothing more of this detachment, but considered it as lost, the communication having been interrupted by the enemy.

Lieutenant-Colonel Rooke, with part of the 3d guards, was afterwards sent in that direction, drove the enemy from the intermediate rampart, and reached the gate, when he found it useless to attempt anything, and ascertained that the outwork was still occupied. We were joined in the course of the night by the 33d, 55th, and 2d battalion of 69th regiment, but the state of uncertainty as to what had passed at other points, determined me not to weaken the force now collected, by attempting to carry points which we could not maintain, or penetrate through the streets with the certain loss of a great number of men, particularly as I heard that the troops at the Water Port Gate, under Lieutenant-Colonel Muller, were very seriously opposed. I sent the 33d to reinforce him.

The enemy continued a galling fire upon us, and at one time held the adjoining bastion, from the angle of which they completely commanded our communication with the exterior, and brought their guns at that angle to bear against us. They were charged and driven away by Majors Muttlebury and Hog, with the 69th and 55th, in a very spirited and gallant style.

Finding that matters were becoming more serious, and being still without any information from other points, excepting that of the failure of Lieutenant-Colonel Morrice's column near the Nourd Gate, I determined, at the suggestion of Colonel Lord Proby, to let part of the troops withdraw, which was done at the ladders where they entered.

About day-light the enemy having again possessed themselves of the before-mentioned bastion, they were again driven from it by Majors Muttlebury and Hog, with their weak battalions, in the same gallant manner. I soon afterwards began sending off some more men when, Lieutenant-Colonel Jones, who had been taken prisoner in the night, came to me, (accompanied by a French officer, who summoned me to surrender), and informed me that Lieutenant-Colonel Muller, and the troops at the Water Port Gate had been obliged to surrender, and were marched prisoners into the town, when I also learnt the fate of Lieutenant-Colonel Clifton's detachment, and of Major-General Skerrett, Major-General Gore, and Lieut. Colonel Carleton, and that the troops which had followed them had suffered very much, and had been repulsed from the advanced points along the rampart where they had penetrated to. I was convinced that a longer continuance of the contest would be an useless loss of lives, and without a prospect of relief as we were situated. I therefore consented to adopt the mortifying alternative of laying down our arms.

I have now to perform the just and satisfactory duty, of conveying to your Excellency, my sense of the merits and good conduct of the officers and soldiers in this bold and arduous enterprise: I have only a knowledge of what passed under my own observation, and I lament that the loss of Major-General Skerrett, from his dangerous wounds, and of the other superior officers employed at the other points of attack, prevents me from giving such detailed praise of the merits of the officers and soldiers, as I have no doubt they deserve.

I beg to repeat my sense of the distinguished conduct of Colonel Lord Proby; Lieutenant-Colonels Rooke and Mercer, commanding the 3d guards, and light infantry, distinguished themselves by their activity and bravery; and Majors Muttlebury and Hog, of the 69th and 55th regiments, deserve my warm praise for the conduct displayed by those corps in the charges I have before mentioned. I have every reason to know that Lieutenant-Colonel Clifton conducted his detachment in the most gallant and officer-like manner, and I have to lament that his death deprives me of receiving his report of the conduct of Lieutenant-Colonels McDonald and Jones, and the officers and soldiers of the 1st guards, under his command.

I am not yet enabled to transmit an exact return of the prisoners taken at different times by the enemy, nor of the numbers taken from them.

I have the honour to be, &c.
(Signed) G. COOKE, Major-Gen

36

BATTLE OF WATERLOO

Downing-Street, June 22, 1815

MAJOR the Honourable H. Percy arrived here last night with a dispatch from Field Marshal the Duke of Wellington, K.G. to Earl Bathurst, His Majeisty's Principal Secretary of State for the War Department, of which the following is a copy:

Waterloo, June 19, 1815.

MY LORD,

BUONAPARTE, having collected the 1st, 2d, 3d, 4th, and 6th corps of the French army, and the Imperial Guards, and nearly all the cavalry, on the Sambre, and between that river and the Meuse, between the 10th and 14th of the month, advanced on the 15th and attacked the Prussian posts at Thuin and Lobes, on the Sambre, at daylight in the morning.

I did not hear of these events till in the evening of the 15th, and I immediately ordered the troops to prepare to march; and afterwards to march to their left, as soon as I had intelligence from other quarters to prove that the enemy's movement upon Charleroy was the real attack.

The enemy drove the Prussian posts from the Sambre on that day; and General Zieten, who commanded the corps which had been at Charleroy, retired upon Fleurus; and Marshal Prince Blucher concentrated the Prussian army upon Sombref, holding the villages in front of his position of St. Amand and Ligny.

The enemy continued his march along the road from Charleroy towards Bruxelles; and, on the same evening, the 15th, attacked a brigade of the army of the Netherlands, under the Prince de Weimar, posted at Frasne, and forced it back to the farm house, on the same road, called Les Quatre Bras.

The Prince of Orange immediately reinforced this brigade with another of the same division, under General Perponcher, and, in the morning early, regained part of the ground which had been lost, so as to have the command of the communication leading from Nivelles and Bruxelles with Marshal Blucher's position.

In the mean time, I had directed the whole army to march upon Les Quatre Bras, and the 5th division, under Lieutenant-General Sir Thomas Picton, arrived at about half past two in the day, followed by the corps of troops under the Duke of Brunswick, and afterwards by the contingent of Nassau.

At this time the enemy commenced an attack upon Prince Blucher with his whole force, excepting the 1st and 2d corps, and a corps of cavalry under General Kellermann, with which he attacked our post at Les Quatre Bras.

The Prussian army maintained their position with their usual gallantry and perseverance against a great disparity of numbers, as the 4th corps of their army, under General Bülow, had not joined; and I was not able to assist them as I wished, as I was attacked myself, and the troops, the cavalry in particular, which had a long distance to march, had not arrived.

We maintained our position also, and completely defeated and repulsed all the enemy's attempts to get possession of it. The enemy repeatedly attacked us with a large body of infantry and cavalry, supported by a numerous and powerful artillery. He made several charges with the cavalry upon our infantry, but all were repulsed in the steadiest manner. In this affair, His Royal Highness the Prince of Orange, the Duke of Brunswick, and Lieutenant-General Sir Thomas Picton, and Major-General Sir James Kempt, and Sir Denis Pack, who were engaged from the commencement of the enemy's attack, highly distinguished themselves, as well as Lieutenant-General Charles Baron Alten, Major-General Sir C. Halkett, Lieutenant-General Cooke, and Major-Generals Maitland and Byng, as they successively arrived. The troops of the 5th division, and those of the Brunswick corps, were long and severely engaged, and conducted themselves with the utmost gallantry. I must particularly mention the 28th, 42d, 79th, and 92nd regiments, and the battalion of Hanoverians.

Our loss was great, as your Lordship will perceive by the enclosed return; and I have particularly to regret His Serene Highness the Duke of Brunswick, who fell fighting gallantly at the head of his troops.

Although Marshal Blucher had maintained his position at Sombref, he still found himself much weakened by the severity of the contest in which he had been engaged, and, as the 4th corps had not arrived, he determined to fall back and to concentrate his army upon Wavre; and he marched in the night, after the action was over.

This movement of the Marshal's rendered necessary a corresponding one upon my part; and I retired from the farm of Quatre Bras upon Genappe, and thence upon Waterloo, the next morning, the 17th, at ten o'clock.

The enemy made no effort to pursue Marshal Blucher. On the contrary, a patrole which I sent to Sombref in the morning found all quiet, and the enemy's videttes fell back as the patrole advanced. Neither did he attempt to molest our march to the rear, although made in the middle of the day, excepting by following, with a large body of cavalry brought from his right, the cavalry under the Earl of Uxbridge.

This gave Lord Uxbridge an opportunity of charging them with the 1st Life Guards, upon their debouché from the village of Genappe, upon which occasion his Lordship has declared himself to be well satisfied with that regiment.

The position which I took up in front of Waterloo crossed the high roads from Charleroi and Nivelles, and had its right thrown back to a ravine near Merke Braine, which was occupied, and its left extended to a height above the hamlet Ter la Haye, which was likewise occupied. In front of the right centre, and near the Nivelles road, we occupied the house and gardens of Hougoumont, which covered the return of that flank; and in front of the left centre we occupied the farm of La Haye Sainte. By our left we communicated with Marshal Prince Blucher at Wavre, through Ohain; and the Marshal had promised me that, in case we should be attacked, he would support me with one or more corps, as might be necessary.

The enemy collected his army, with the exception of the third corps, which had been sent to observe Marshal Blucher, on a range of heights in our front, in the course of the night of the 17th and yesterday morning, and at about ten o'clock he commenced a furious attack upon our post at Hougoumont. I had occupied that post with a detachment from General Byng's brigade of Guards, which was in position in its rear; and it was for some time under the command of Lieutenant-Colonel Macdonell, and afterwards of Colonel Home; and I am happy to add that it was maintained throughout the day with the utmost gallantry by these brave troops, notwithstanding the repeated efforts of large bodies of the enemy to obtain possession of it.

This attack upon the right of our centre was accompanied by a very heavy cannonade upon our whole line, which was destined to support the repeated attacks of cavalry and infantry, occasionally mixed, but sometimes separate, which were made upon it. In one of these the enemy earned the farm house of La Haye Sainte, as the detachment of the light battalion of the legion, which occupied it, had expended all its ammunition; and the enemy occupied the only communication there was with them.

The enemy repeatedly charged our infantry with his cavalry, but these attacks were uniformly unsuccessful; and they afforded opportunities to our cavalry to charge, in one of which Lord E. Somerset's brigade, consisting of the life guards, the royal horse guards, and 1st dragoon guards, highly distinguished themselves, as did that of Major-General Sir William Ponsonby, having taken many prisoners and an eagle.

These attacks were repeated till about seven in the evening, when the enemy made a desperate effort with cavalry and infantry, supported by the fire of artillery, to force our left centre, near the farm of La Haye Sainte, which, after a severe contest, was defeated, and, having observed that the troops retired from this attack in great confusion, and that the march of General Bulow's corps, by Euschermont, upon Planchenorte and La Belle Alliance, had begun to take effect, and as I could perceive the fire of his cannon, and as Marshal Prince Blucher had joined in person with a corps of his army to the left of our line by Ohain, I determined to attack the enemy, and immediately advanced the whole line of infantry, supported by the cavalry and artillery. - The attack succeeded in every point; the enemy was forced from his positions on the heights, and fled in the utmost confusion, leaving behind him, as far as I could judge, one hundred and fifty pieces of cannon, with their ammunition, which fell into our hands.

I continued the pursuit till long after dark, and then discontinued it only on account of the fatigue of our troops, who had been engaged during twelve hours, and because

I found myself on the same road with Marshal Blucher, who assured me of his intention to follow the enemy throughout the night. He has sent me word this morning that he had taken sixty pieces of cannon belonging to the Imperial Guard, and several carriages, baggage, &c., belonging to Buonaparte, in Genappe.

I propose to move this morning upon Nivelles, and not to discontinue my operations.

Your Lordship will observe that such a desperate action could not be fought, and such advantages could not be gained, without great loss; and I am sorry to add that ours has been immense. In Lieutenant-General Sir Thomas Picton His Majesty has sustained the loss of an officer who has frequently distinguished himself in his service, and he fell gloriously leading his division to a charge with bayonets, by which one of the most serious attacks made by the enemy on our position was repulsed. The Earl of Uxbridge, after having successfully got through this arduous day, received a wound by almost the last shot fired, which will, I am afraid, deprive His Majesty for some time of his services.

His Royal Highness the Prince of Orange distinguished himself by his gallantry and conduct, till he received a wound from a musket ball through the shoulder, which obliged him to quit the field.

It gives me the greatest satisfaction to assure your Lordship that the army never, upon any occasion, conducted itself better. The division of guards, under Lieutenant-General Cooke, who is severely wounded, Major-General Maitland, and Major-General Byng, set an example which was followed by all; and there is no officer nor description of troops that did not behave well.

I must, however, particularly mention, for His Royal Highness's approbation, Lieutenant-General Sir H. Clinton, Major-General Adam, Lieutenant-General Charles Baron Alten, severely wounded, Major-General Sir Colin Halkett, severely wounded, Colonel Ompteda, Colonel Mitchell, commanding a brigade of the 4th division, Major Generals Sir James Kempt and Sir Denis Pack, Major-General Lambert, Major-General Lord E. Somerset, Major-General Sir W. Ponsonby, Major-General Sir C. Grant, and Major-General Sir H. Vivian, Major-General Sir O. Vandeleur; Major General Count Dornberg. I am also particularly indebted to General Lord Hill for his assistance and conduct upon this, as upon all former occasions.

The artillery and engineer departments were conducted much to my satisfaction by Colonel Sir George Wood and Colonel Smyth; and I had every reason to be satisfied with the conduct of the Adjutant-General, Major-General Barnes, who was wounded, and of the Quarter-Master-General, Colonel Delancey, who was killed by a cannon shot in the middle of the action. This officer is a serious loss to His Majesty's service, and to me at this moment. I was likewise much indebted to the assistance of Lieutenant-Colonel Lord Fitzroy Somerset, who was severely wounded and of the officers composing my personal staff, who have suffered severely in this action. Lieutenant-Colonel the Honourable Sir Alexander Gordon, who has died of his wounds, was a most promising officer, and is a serious loss to His Majesty's service.

General Kruse, of the Nassau service, likewise conducted himself much to my satisfaction; as did General Trip, commanding the heavy brigade of cavalry, and

General Vanhope, commanding a brigade of infantry in the service of the King of the Netherlands.

General Pozzo di Borgo, General Baron Vincent, General Muffling, and General Alava, were in the field during the action, and rendered me every assistance in their power. Baron Vincent is wounded, but I hope not severely; and General Pozzo di Borgo received a contusion.

I should not do justice to my own feelings, or to Marshal Blucher and the Prussian army, if I did not attribute the successful result of this arduous day to the cordial and timely assistance I received from them. The operation of General Bülow upon the enemy's flank was a most decisive one; and, even if I had not found myself in a situation to make the attack which produced the final result, it would have forced the enemy to retire if his attacks should have failed, and would have prevented him from taking advantage of them if they should unfortunately have succeeded.

I send with this dispatch two eagles, taken by the troops in this action, which Major Percy will have the honor of laying at the feet of His Royal Highness.

I beg leave to recommend him to your Lordship's protection.

I have the honor to be, &c.
WELLINGTON.

P.S.   Since writing the above, I have received a report that Major-General Sir William Ponsonby is killed; and, in announcing this intelligence to your Lordship, I have to add the expression of my grief for the fate of an officer who had already rendered very brilliant and important services, and was an ornament to his profession.

INDEX OF PERSONS

INDEX OF MILITARY AND NAVAL UNITS